DAGGERS SWORDS AND BAYONETS OF THE THIRD REICH

DAGGERS SWORDS AND BAYONETS OF THE THIRD REICH

Frederick J. Stephens

PSL

Patrick Stephens Limited

First published in 1989

British Library Cataloguing in Publication Data

Stephens, Frederick J. (Frederick John), *1945–*
Daggers, swords and bayonets of the Third Reich.
1. German edged weapons, 1933–1945
I. Title
739.7′2′0943

ISBN 1-85260-145-0

Patrick Stephens is part of the Thorsons Publishing Group

Typeset by Avocet-Robinson, Buckingham
Printed in Great Britain by Butler & Tanner Ltd, Frome, Somerset

10 9 8 7 6 5 4 3 2 1

Contents

Dedicated to the memory of W. H. 'Bill' Yeo of Belfast, Northern Ireland: A gentleman, a collector, and a true friend.

Introduction and Acknowledgements

It has been some 44 years since the Allied Powers finally, after momentous efforts, brought the Second World War to a close. Forty-four years in which Europe has experienced, more or less, a continual period of peace. Aggressive trends and provocative conflicts, such as those which have occurred in Czechoslovakia and elsewhere in what is known as the Eastern Bloc have been allowed to defuse themselves politically. Generally speaking, the peoples of Europe have enjoyed a longer period of peace than at any other time in modern history. This peace, which we all benefit from, probably contributes in some way to our historical fascination with the stark contrast of war, with the events which lead up to war, and the colourful pageantry which masks the less acceptable faces of war. The pageantry of war is one of the spectacles of military history.

This then is a book about one aspect of the articles of war—weapons, yet not weapons which were designed for fighting. The dress weapons carried by soldiers and militarists, and all from a specifically identifiable period of history, the Third Reich. However one views the advent of the National Socialist State, the circumstances which it engendered, and the price it inflicted upon itself as well as the rest of Europe, it is impossible not to be fascinated to some degree by the pageantry with which the Third Reich adorned itself. A singular aspect of that pageantry is the subject of the bladed weapon; and in perpetuating the culture of the bladed weapon, the Third Reich not only continued a tradition which had existed in Germany since medieval times, but successfully showed that the lure of a fine blade on a smart uniform was as instinctively appealing in the twentieth century as it had been 500 years previously.

This book, therefore, is not so much a book about war, or politics, or National Socialism, but a book about the art of the armourer. In an age when the traditional skills of the armourer were thought to be forgotten, Germany revived those traditions and skills, and recreated them in a new and modern form. The appeal of those weapons is self-evident; for once they were worn as items of authority and dress; today they are avidly collected as fascinating relics of a momentous period of history.

In the past 20 years a number of

well-researched books have been written by authorities all over the world, fascinated with the edged weapons of the Third Reich. The majority of these have concerned themselves primarily with the status of daggers, swords, and bayonets of Nazi Germany, and the events and organizations which promoted them. Such perspective of these items is not without merit, it is true, and we cannot rewrite history just to make the overall subject more palatable.

Instead, I have chosen in this study to endeavour to show how the blades of the Third Reich were a continuation of an ancestral line, twentieth century developments which owed their concept to skills formulated in a distant time. The skills which allowed the bladesmiths of Solingen to create fine swords and daggers for nobles and warriors in the Middle Ages were carried forward into the present century; and the daggers, swords, and bayonets shown in this work are a testament to that fact.

Every work of research has its limitations, and this book is no different. A diligent attempt to document every known pattern of bladed weapon produced during the Third Reich would have necessitated hundreds, if not thousands, of pages of text and photographs. The selection illustrated, therefore, is merely a representative sample, intended to give the reader, collector, or historian, a basic concept of what the total subject really amounts to. More importantly, from the author's point of view at least, was the need to show how historical events and developments had an impact on the creation of these weapons. With that in mind, it becomes progressively easier to see why the skills of the bladesmith were revered not only in the past, but retained respect in the modern age. Both aspects contribute greatly to the appreciation felt by the interested collector—the daggers, swords, and bayonets of the Third Reich are not merely surviving relics from a modern dark age, but in fact the continued products of skilled artisans who originally discovered their arts and developed their talents at a time when much of the world about us lay undiscovered. These relics are fascinating pieces of history; and this work is merely a primer—a foundation stone from which to observe the general subject, and consider it in its terms of historical perspective.

That numerous obscure, and diverse variations of the general subject have been omitted from this work is not an oversight—it has been done for the sake of brevity. The arrangement detailed within is my own preferred choice, selected to illustrate the general principles of this discipline to form the basis of appreciation without swamping with repetitive photographs of minute variations. If at the end of the day, the lay reader has learned enough to whet the appetite and to seek further information, then this book will have done its job. For the more advanced collector, I will accept that observations can be made that some items are not fully represented and some perhaps not at all, but it is no loss; there is new information in this work which cannot be found elsewhere—the objective is not to show you what you already know, but to tell you something that you never knew before. That objective, too, I believe is achieved in this work.

In accumulating data and photographs for this work, I acknowledge the debt of gratitude I owe to a great many interested collectors and researchers. Their fascination and enthusiasm for the subject at large was a continual source of encouragement. All have contributed valuable material for inclusion, and all—I hope—will find something extra in this work which they had not anticipated. This book is really *their* book, the product of a sharing of knowledge. I am pleased to express my appreciative thanks to all the following: Barry Brown; Mike Bassett; Skipper Greenwade; Gordon Williamson; Chris Ailsby; Ted Daly; Dave Blackman; Dr Julian Milestone; Graham Boddy; Lt. Col. (retd.) T. M. Johnson; Lt. Col. (retd.) J. R. Angolia; Mr Roy Butler and staff, Wallis and Wallis; Doug Nie; Weller & Dufty Ltd.; Brian L. Davis; Gailen David; Thomas J. Gorman jr; Gordon White; Gailen David; Robert McCarthy; Malcolm Bowers; Mst. Sgt. John G. Schaeffer; John Hewitt; Tony McCall; the late Bill Yeo; the estate of the late A. S. Walker; Dr H.-U. Haedeke and staff of the Deutsche Klingemuseum; the Criminal History Museum, Rotenburg; Mr Frederick Wilkinson; Chuck Scaglione; Chris Farlowe; Thomas W. Pooler; Stewart Wilson of the Old Brigade, Northampton; Mike Long; J. Jeffrey Roth and Associates; Eric Campion; Thomas T. Wittman; Fiona Petrou.

In addition I also wish to thank numerous other acquaintances, who have passed on information and tidbits of interest over the years, and who accommodated my persistence to gain photographs or information—which was willingly given—but who declined to receive recognition. My appreciation remains, and I thank you all.

In concluding, a final vote of thanks must go to my wife and daughter, who have tolerated my interest in this subject over many years, sometimes with misgivings, but invariably with patience. Without their self-sufficiency (and ability to cut the lawn when it needed doing) this book would never have been completed.

Frederick J. Stephens
Milton Keynes
January, 1989

1 Fire and Wind

ME FECIT SOLINGEN—'Solingen Created Me'—the words which tell the story of a legend, and which at one time, were invariably engraved or etched upon the blades of swords and daggers. The proof and testimony that proclaimed that the blade bearing this legend was not only made by the most gifted bladesmith, but that he served in the very heart of the blade-making centre of Europe. Solingen: a small town in the Wupper Valley of the Ruhr region of Germany; the epicentre of European blade-smithing for over 500 years, and a name uttered with pride by those who worked there, and with awe by those who competed with the craftsmen of this industrial German heartland.

The area of the Wupper Valley, around the cathedral city of Cologne, is rich in iron ore. In medieval times it became the premier site of mining, steel production, and arms fabrication, and it was largely controlled by the merchants of Cologne—a city which in itself in medieval times had promoted a certain reputation for commercial enterprise backed up by artisan skills. Cologne was the foremost centre of commercial production in the old German states; it was the name of Cologne which had been spread far and wide by merchants anxious to promote their wares, and it was Solingen which had done so much to provide the goods upon which Cologne's reputation was so tenuously based.

In the 1920s, Albert Weyersberg in writing his essay *The Solingen Sword Manufacture down through the Ages* had this to say about Solingen:

> The art of forging blades is, as is well known, very old in Solingen and arose permanently out of natural conditions. Above all will the inhabitants of the thinly-sprinkled settlements have been led to seek out the iron stones which in the earliest days came to light during the clearing and tilling of the land at Solingen and other parts of the Bergisch Land, and to melt them in *wind and smelting ovens* [author's italics] and to fashion them into axes, spades and weapons. It is possible that experienced smiths and skilled sword cutlers from Cologne attached themselves later to the existing settlers.

The 1920s translation of Weyersberg's

original essay is literal, in every sense of the word. The reference to 'wind and smelting ovens' highlights one of the great breakthroughs which enabled European bladesmiths to achieve the technology of higher steel refinement which had for centuries previously been practised in Asia. It was during the latter part of the thirteenth century that the bellows was first introduced into Europe, by which means of air injection into a furnace, smelting could be effected at higher temperatures, resulting in finer purity of metal. 'Wind and smelting ovens' first became widely used in the smithies of Solingen; and the reputation and quality of all their products was, thereafter, directly related to the adoption of the bellows innovation.

Archbishop Bruno I of Cologne was, at the time of his death in the year 925, known also as the Lord of Solagon—a reference generally believed to mean the city now known as Solingen. In the declining years of the Holy Roman Empire, it was the Church which had survived the warring times to remain as an international empire, and it was the Church which maintained influence over the Christian royal families who ruled the European peoples. Through the royal households over which it held sway, the Church governed vast territories, and the establishment of cathedral cities reinforced the power of the papal domains. It was not, however, a purely theological situation. The Church represented a real power in those times, both politically and commercially. Cologne was a centre which gained a far-reaching reputation for the products which the city could produce, amongst which was the trade in 'Cologne Swords'—reputed (though this was unstated) to have been produced by artisans in that city.

The small township of Solagon, nestling in the foothills of the Wupper Valley, relied upon its larger neighbour of Cologne as an outlet for its wares. As the influence of the growing cathedral centres expanded, other communities were brought under more direct influence of the papal states. Solagon, once ruled under the county palatine of Aix-la-Chapelle (now the city of Aachen) became increasingly reliant upon Cologne as the capital city to which the producers of Solagon had to turn.

From the tenth to thirteenth centuries, Solingen was very closely connected with Cologne, and it would seem that bladesmiths and cutlers trading out of the city of Cologne most probably existed purely as merchanting concerns; no blades existing from that period of history have been discovered which bear markings to show that they were actually created in Cologne. It is more probable that the merchanting houses of Cologne purchased their swords, or possibly just the blades, from the producers of Solingen. Whence afterwards they were refurbished, finished, and decorated, and ultimately marketed as 'Cologne swords'.

The skills of the bladesmith, just like the skills of the stonemason, or the goldsmith, were jealously guarded arts. The ability to produce an artisan product in defiance of another's knowledge was the foundation stone upon which almost all the craft guilds came into existence—closed societies which taught only their own, and some other chosen few, the skills and secrets of their craft, thus ensuring for perpetuity their labour, market, and wealth from their own skilled hands.

An edict of the Cologne Council during the year 1492 gave permission to the guild of swordsmiths and cutlers to have their polishing done at three mills which lay in the Bergisch Land. The reason for this requirement lay in the fact that the Cologne area did not possess a sufficient source of water power to continually drive the heavy grinding and milling stones necessary for polishing metal. A rapidly-flowing river was the motive force which made the grinding wheel turn, and these sources of natural power were only readily available in the hillsides and valleys of the mountains—and from which the Bergisch Land (i.e. mountainous land) took its name.

The edict of 1492 serves to demonstrate just how tightly-knit was the closed community of sword and blade-makers. It was an act of protectionism that contained the skills of their craft within their own community, and it additionally demonstrated the recognition of protected, specialized artisans.

The introduction of the bellows, and knowledge of other skills involved in the working of steel ware, followed in the wake of returning Crusaders, who between the eleventh and thirteenth centuries had undertaken several military campaigns to regain the Holy Land from the Muslims. Royal armies and mercenary soldiers from all over the European mainland, and from England, had banded together to wage a religious war on behalf of Christianity. For almost two hundred years countless numbers of armed troops had trudged their way back and forth across Europe, all hopeful of returning home with the laurels of victory and the spoils of war. Amongst the prizes looted from the Islamic world were not only swords and weapons, but also some knowledge regarding how they had been made and the existence of specialized craftsmen who produced such work. It was knowledge which was to effect influence and change amongst the merchants and artisans of northern Germany.

Until the thirteenth century, the production of weapons and armour had been mostly the work of blacksmiths. The same hands which had wrought steel armour and chain mail also produced the metal plough and tools of agriculture. It was a situation which had existed without change for centuries, until the knowledge of specialist skills in the making of weapons was brought back by returning Crusaders. The new knowledge opened the doorway to a new, and specialized era in the production of weapons.

The creative work in sword and cutlery making—deploying new skills and knowledge brought back from the Crusades—became the province of the families who worked in the Solingen area. The techniques of their skills became jealously guarded 'family' secrets, to which outsiders were excluded. Family groups producing like work formed 'brotherhoods'—the beginning of the Craft Guilds which were to flourish in later years. There were three such types of 'brotherhood', and each was con-

Two metalsmiths working on armour: a German woodcut from the year 1479.

In the background can be seen the furnace in which the iron plates were heated until almost white hot. Pulled from the furnace with tongs, the glowing billet was pounded into shape. The plates for armour were formed from thick billets and hammered to spread the shape, producing the characteristic feature of the armour, remaining thickest in the centre area and tapering towards the edges.

Portions of partially completed armour are shown hanging on the rack at the right of the woodcut. A feature of particular interest in this illustration – mounted on the wall behind the smith on the right – is the bellows, the introduction of which after the time of the Crusades dramatically advanced the manufacturing techniques of metal products. (Die Klinge, 1933).

cerned with a specific area of the cutler's trade; combined together, they held all the artisan skills required to create and produce the finished product. Commercial tactics were drawn up and agreed between the producing families of Solingen and the merchanting families of Cologne, to protect the exclusivity of their products, the ability to create them, the price that could be demanded, and the assurance of a continued living.

Some time after the establishment of the three brotherhoods, legal ratification of their status was granted which afforded them certain privileges. Probably the first edict confirming the protection of their commercial endeavours was one issued on 25 November 1401, for the Grinders and Temperers. Another such edict dated 9 March 1412, gave recognition to the Furbishers—those who made and applied the fittings to blades; and yet another dated 25 November 1472, gave recognition and protection to the Swordsmiths.

The essence of these edicts confirmed the right of the families concerned to exclusively work in their respective trades, and that only the legitimate sons of the families could follow their fathers into the craft. The merchants of Cologne would guarantee to exclusively market all the products of Solingen; but that the Solingen families must bind themselves on oath to their craft and their town, and not to leave the area to set up competitive trade elsewhere. The brotherhoods were to bind themselves to each other, and to supply or obtain services only within their select grouping. This was protectionism; the artisan skills of Solingen would stay within the town and for the benefit of the town. Artisans from competing towns, such as Passau, Nuremberg, Milan, Brescia and other noted sword and cutlery centres were to be excluded from discovering any of the skills and techniques that the families of Solingen were carefully developing.

It is of some interest to discover that the protectionism inherent in containing the artisan skills of Solingen, also included protection and limitation regarding the quantity of product that each swordsmith was permitted to complete. At one time this was defined as being limited to not more than four broad-swords, and six small swords and daggers (or eight stilettos) in any one day. The limitation on quantity was devised to ensure that the quality of the products did not diminish due to over-production; as well as to guarantee for the merchants that the highest prices could be charged for goods which were not commonly available.

The family connection in the Solingen trades became an established and enduring bond. A tithe document (record of payments to the clergy in recognition of their support) of the Altenburg Abbey for 1483, recording many names, details 20 family names from the Solingen area who were part

A cutler at work, finishing knives. German, circa *1500. The craftsman is depicted using a file to clean up the scales (grip plates on the hilt) of the assembled knives. Note the appearance of the anvil in this illustration. Cast metal anvils were unknown until the advent of the bellows made it possible for European smiths to smelt sufficient quantities of iron to produce the heavy, one-piece anvil.* (Die Klinge, 1933).

Above *A trade advertisement published by the Paul Weyersberg concern in 1938, and highlighting the family name as one of the famed Solingen producers of quality weapons in olden times as well as in the then present Third Reich. The text of the advertisement itemizes numerous weapon patterns that were being purchased by organizations in the National Socialist state.*

of the sword-making brotherhood. These were not simply individual families, but whole groups of families—invariably related to each other at some point and sharing the same family name—whose 20 names were recorded in that 1488 document. Descendent families bearing the same names were still working in the Solingen trades almost 500 years later.

Of the families detailed in the original list of known names, about 70 families were practising as swordsmiths; a further 100 or so as temperers and grinders; some 12 families working as furbishers; and

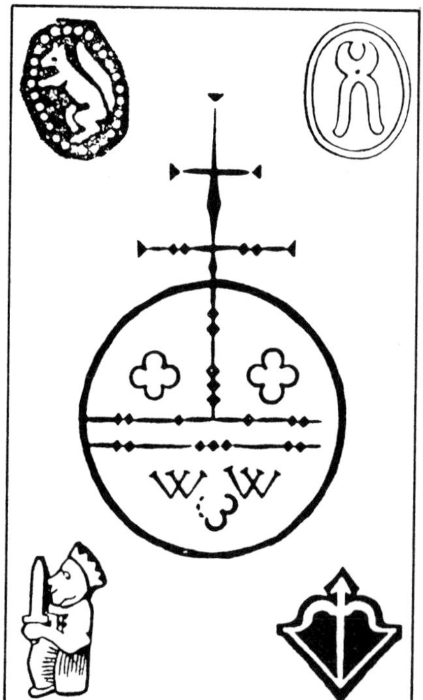

Right *A selection of ancient armourers' marks, as observed on sword blades. The squirrel emblem, at the top left, was originally used by the smith Peter Lobach. The emblem was revived in the late nineteenth century by the Eickhorn concern, whose family name means 'squirrel'. Other marks too survived their origin in the Middle Ages to appear later in the twentieth century. The pincer emblem was subsequently used by the Friedrich Plücker concern, and the seated king with sword became the trademark of the Solingen Metal Fabrik (SMF) company, which produced some very fine quality Luftwaffe daggers amongst their many edged weapons products.* (Leisten und Dienen, 1940).

over 80 families classified as knife makers. Most of the family names were local to the area, and about ten of the family names appear to have been exclusive to the Solingen cutlers, these names being unknown as artisans in other trades.

The classification 'knife makers' provides an interesting insight on how restrictive the brotherhoods were within their own sphere. Knife making (i.e. cutlery and tool-type knives, as opposed to weapons) was not accepted into the privileged closed society of the 'brotherhood' until so specified by an edict dated 14 January, 1571. Hitherto, knife makers had remained outside the exclusive group of sword and dagger makers, meaning that any craftsmen who wanted to engage in knife-making work was free to do so. The 1571

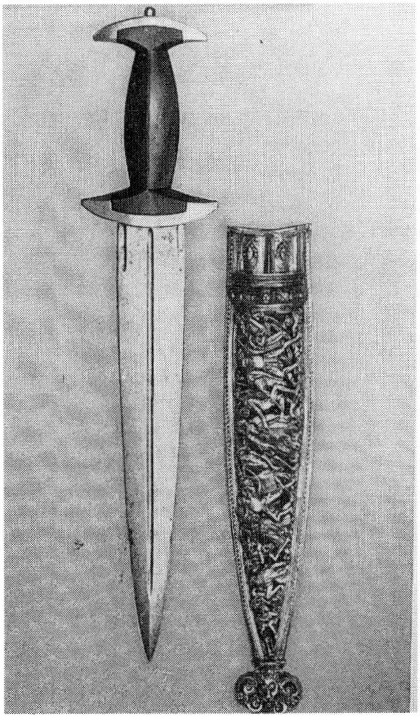

The 'Holbein' dagger, a classic pattern knife produced in Germany in the fifteenth and sixteenth centuries. The clean and symmetrical style of this weapon was revived again in the 1930s, when it emerged as the dress dagger pattern of the SA and SS organizations, as well as that of the NSKK and NAPOLA (see relevant sections in this book). (The Wallace Collection).

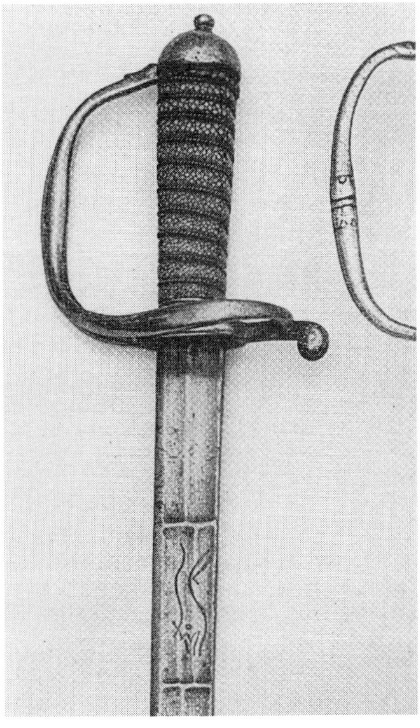

The quality of a good sword blade could outlast the rest of the weapon. This example shows a late sixteenth or early seventeenth century sword blade, with the Wolfsmarke of Solingen clearly visible. The original hilt and fittings have long since vanished, having been replaced with mid-eighteenth century sword furniture. (Frederick Wilkinson).

decree altered that situation, and knife making was declared a protected craft, to be pursued only by those already engaged in it, and their subsequent descendants. Thus swordsmiths were denied the right to make cutlery knives; and knife makers could make only knives, and nothing else.

Another small group of artisans who had worked as a select brotherhood, and finally received recognition of their privileged status, was that of the Cross and Pommel makers. The cross (or 'crossguard' as it is now called) was the portion beneath the grip of the sword, which in combat was designed to protect the bearer's hand from the blade of his opponent. The pommel was a bulbous portion at the top of the hilt, the fitment of which had a dual purpose—to hold together all the components of the sword; and to act as a counter-balance to the weight of the blade. The skill in producing these final portions which completed the sword assembly had never been in doubt, yet it was not until the edict of 10 October 1682, that the protection of the brotherhood was bestowed upon these craftsmen. The exclusivity of the protectionism was short lived, however. Other arms-manufacturing centres, envious of the reputation and the quality of Solingen products, had been endeavouring to lure craftsmen away, and they had found some response amongst the less-privileged members of the Solingen working classes.

2 The Golden Age

The period known as the Middle Ages, and the Reformation, had given birth to the beginnings of some of the great armies and sea powers that would commence to reshape Europe; and indeed, ultimately, much of the rest of the known world.

Technology was beginning to play a part in weapons and warfare. Gunpowder (probably first invented in China, but brought to Europe by—yet again—Crusaders returning with their spoils) had made an early appearance in the arsenals of war; Stone cannon, which fired a projectile not dissimilar to a spear, had been tried out, albeit with limited success. Cast iron cannon, however had been developed by the English, and are believed to have been first used with military success against the French at the Battle of Crécy in 1302.

Such innovations, however, were still crude and unreliable. Wars were still being won with the bow and arrow, and of course, the sword. Armies moved around by foot, and sometimes on horse. The decisive moments of all battles were settled with the clash of steel, and the thrust and parry of blades. Upon such needs was the future fortune of Solingen to be based.

So valuable were the skills of the swordsmith, and so increasingly powerful were the brotherhoods into which these craftsmen were bonded, that little could be done to increase their volume of production or reduce their level of prices. It was an enviable situation for Solingen to be in—the finest craftsmen of their type in Europe, with a reputation that was almost holy; and a seemingly limitless supply of customers clamouring for their wares. The cartels that controlled the production and sale of Solingen wares had brought continuing prosperity—a veritable Golden Age that glistened from polished blades.

The restrictions of practice enforced by the agreements of the Solingen brotherhood and the royal court together with the merchants of Cologne did, inevitably, interfere with the needs of other artisans to find meaningful employment and an outlet for their wares. The skilled hands of Solingen had earned an enviable reputation throughout the rest of Europe, and a continuing increase in demand for their products—offset by a deliberately restricted cartel of supply. This situation unwittingly left open opportunities that were soon to be seized upon by others anxious to exploit the potential for business.

A family of skilled halberd- and gunsmiths (halberd—a type of lance or pike) had been denied entrance to the closed brotherhoods of Solingen. Their family name was Kaitoff, and having worked in the Solingen region for centuries they had amassed at least some of the skills of their more famous contemporaries. Eventually their exclusion from the closed Solingen brotherhoods, and invitations from outside competitors, had the inevitable effect. The Kaitoffs abandoned their connections with Solingen and emigrated; part of the family went to Paris, and others went to Copenhagen and Moscow. There they individually set up arms manufacturing concerns, and achieved some notable successes.

In England, too, a lack of success in the home-production of good quality arms, allied to excessive taxation applied to imported weapons, engendered circumstances which made it imperative that skilled craftsmen from the Continent be brought in and established in England. More artisans from Solingen, every bit as skilled as their brothers in the protected guild yet denied the privileges of protection, were lured to

The shop of a Sword Merchant, circa *1700. The original caption to this illustration suggested that the potential customer was examining the sword to determine if it featured the Wolfsmarke.* (Die Klinge).

A Landsknecht pattern sword, German, circa 1500–10. One of the classic styles of German sword, with its distinctive dome-shaped pommel with concaved recesses, leather and wood grip, and the S-shaped crossguard. (Frederick Wilkinson).

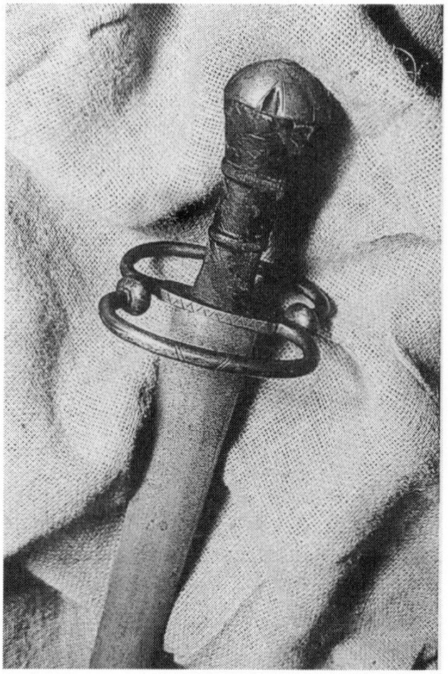

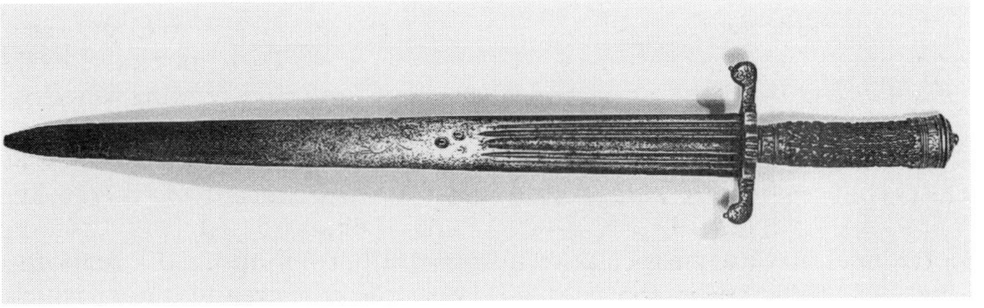

German Hunting Sword, late-1600s. The pommel and crossguard are decorated with engraving, and the grip is made of antler. The fullering of the blade is interesting in that it is contained solely to the upper section. The mid portion of the blade is stamped with the armourer's marks (the emblem of a Pincer), together with a 'running wolf'—a mark used by both Solingen and Passau. (Chris Farlowe).

England to work in the newly-established (1629) school of sword-smiths at Hounslow. In 1687 what was perhaps the most severe breach to the exclusivity of the Solingen brotherhoods occurred. A group of English merchants and financiers, determined to break the cartel of the Solingen brotherhoods, succeeded in luring nine families of sword makers—many of whom were privileged members—to leave their homeland and settle at Shotley Bridge, in northern England. They brought with them all the skills and techniques their families had developed over past generations. The inducement was financial, for not only would these sword-making families earn good money, but they would not be restricted in the quantity of weapons they were allowed to produce. The enticement which succeeded in drawing these craftsmen to England was a devastating shock to the Burghers of Cologne and Solingen. Notices and penalties decrying the action of the English merchants, and the German families who allied themselves to them, were published. Threats and penalties were suggested, but it was to no avail. The German cutlers in Shotley Bridge were there to stay; and almost as if to rub salt in the wounds of Solingen, they marked their wares with the 'Wolf' emblem which had formerly and frequently been placed on Solingen blades in the place of the traditional smith's name.

The international reputation that Solingen and Cologne had built up over the years was being challenged. Yet it was not the end of the Solingen trade. The demand for traditional weapons in the seventeenth and eighteenth centuries was continually growing. Expansion was at a level which Solingen could not have hoped to meet had the brotherhoods been allowed to produce their wares unrestricted. It created an environment of competition not only for the volume of wares required, but in the quality of product. In that respect, the craftsmen of Solingen retained their sound reputation. *ME FECIT SOLINGEN* marked on blades was still indicative of a product of reliably high quality, produced by smiths whose names were legendary in their own lifetimes.

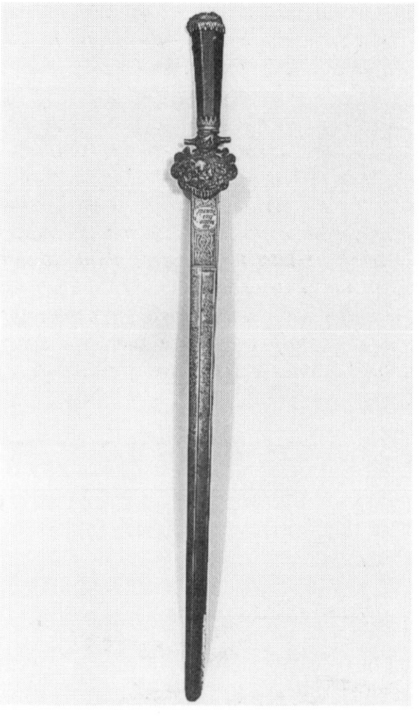

German Hunting Sword, circa 1700. The hilt fittings are made of brass, and finely decorated with floral and animal scenes. The crossguard (now removed) was probably in the form of a deer's hoof—a style which became very popular with the furbishers of hunting swords. (Chris Farlowe).

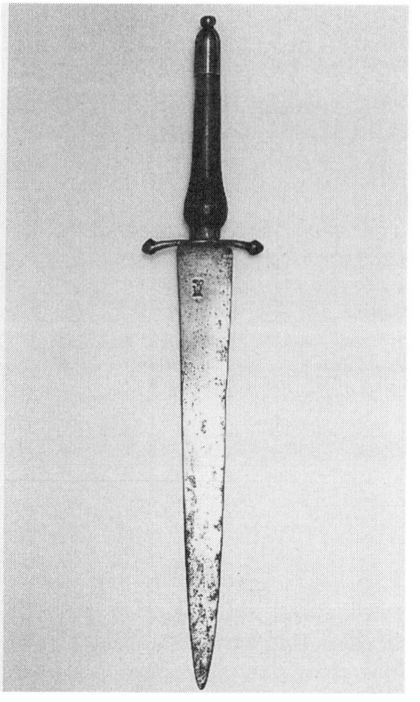

German 'plug' bayonet, circa 1680. The standard type of sidearm for all fusiliers in the latter part of the seventeenth century. The armourer's mark is that of a king's head.

The areas of Passau in northern Germany, and Toledo, in Spain, had struggled for generations to gain recognition as centres of the finest blade production. Yet despite the undoubted artisan talents which existed in these arms centres, it was the reputation of Solingen which outshone them all: the occasion of the marriage of Henry IV of France was blessed by a gift from Pope Clemens VIII of a State Sword, which was created by Peter Munsten the Elder, of Solingen. Perhaps, however, the most glowing tribute to the Solingen bladesmiths resided in a blade created by Clemens Horn of Solingen which was owned by King Philip II of Spain, perhaps in some defiance of Toledo's claims to be the premier blade-making centre of Europe.

The cutlers of Solingen, good as they were, were not the only craftsmen of their type. Bladesmiths elsewhere, in Prussia, as well as in Württemberg, Saxony, and in lands beyond, sought to emulate the quality and reputation of the Solingen smiths—some even to the extent of marking their blades 'Solingen', even though the true places of manufacture were as far away as Spain and Russia.

This pirating of the Solingen name, however, was not strictly a one-way affair. Some German bladesmiths,

The 'running wolf' emblem – a recorded mark dating from about 1464, and known to identify blades created in both the Solingen and Passau regions. The differences identifiable between the two emblems of the respective regions were highlighted in these drawings, which featured in the essay 'Zur Frage des Wolfsmarke' by Dr Magdelane Beyerling (published 1934) showing the Solingen wolf above and the Passau wolf below. It is of some interest to note that the Wolfsmarke never appeared as part of the Solingen City arms – instead the arms display (even today) the emblem of crossed swords, and an anchor. The usage of the swords as part of the heraldic device is fairly obvious, but the inclusion of the anchor seems out of context. It possibly relates to Solingen's ability to cast heavy metal items (such as the anchor), an innovative device in the Middle Ages, when the majority of ships would have used heavy stones secured to ropes as the means of anchorage in open water. (Die Klinge, 1934).

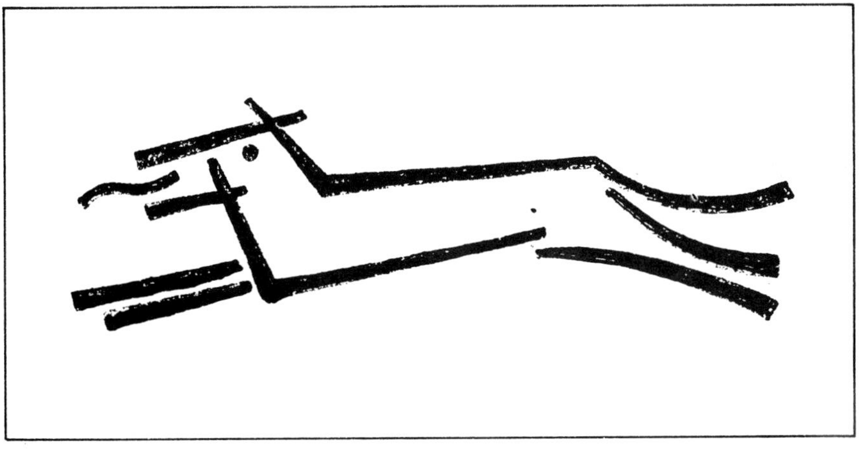

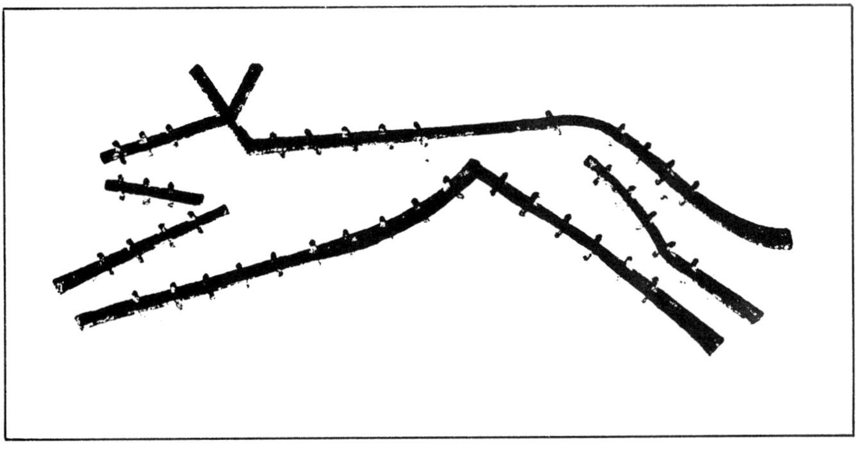

recognizing the personal reputation of some of their foreign competitors, produced pieces that were falsely marked—examples attributed to Tomas de Ayla, a revered Spanish swordsmith, were not infrequently made up. In some cases, the quality of these false blades was inferior to what the German smith would normally have produced, and leaves open to historical speculation whether or not they were the work of inferior smiths, or were poorly made for the purpose of destroying the competitor's reputation.

The demand for German quality blades, however, remained undiminished. The answer to which, for aspiring competitors, was to expand the establishment of Solingen-trained bladesmiths in new homelands.

During the mid- to late-eighteenth century, numerous other bladesmiths departed from Solingen to settle in distant lands, so great was the demand for German trained craftsmen. In 1730 a group of Solingen smiths established themselves at Tyla (Tula) in Russia, a centre which was ultimately to become famous as a gun manufacturing source; in 1772–4 another group emigrated to Eskiltums in Sweden; another group established themselves in North America in the 1794–6 period; yet another group in Danzig during 1796 (now known as Gdansk, Poland); and others moved to Klingenthal in Alsace-Lorraine (now in eastern France) in 1797. In 1814 (following Napoleon's failed campaign in Russia) a group of German swordsmiths established themselves at Zlatoust in Russia. The blade-making centre which they founded exists today, transformed, but still functioning as one of the largest weapons-manufacturing complexes in the Soviet Bloc.

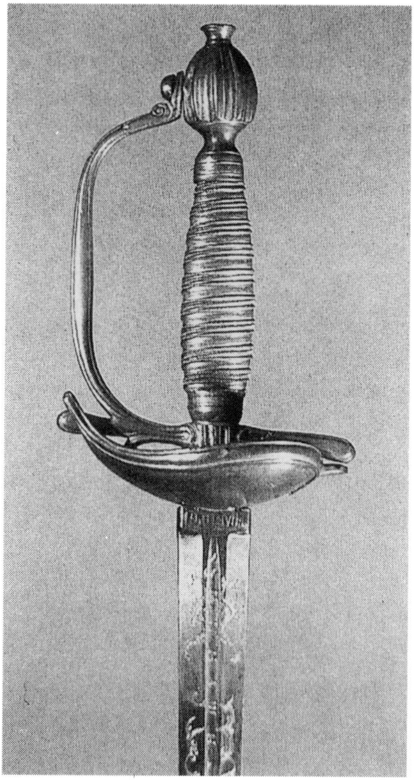

Russian infantry officer's sword from the time of Catherine the Great (circa 1770). Although manufactured at the arsenal of Tyla, the forte of this blade is marked with the cyrillic characters СОЛИНГЕН *– 'Solingen'! The reputation of the Solingen bladesmiths was so powerful that even home-producing industries in foreign lands were sometimes obliged to feature the name on their blades to make them more saleable.* (Hermitage collection, Leningrad. Courtesy Aurora publishers, Moscow).

This was the tremendous strength of the reputation of Solingen. Virtually every aspirant power and nation throughout Europe envied the skill of the Solingen smiths; and unable to compete with them, laid open the opportunities that would ultimately entice the craftsmen to new lands.

The Golden Age of Solingen had come about; but it was not to last indefinitely. New types of army were coming into existence; new weapons and technologies were emerging; and, thanks to the inventiveness of Thomas Newcombe in England, something which would re-shape military power, merchanting power, and ultimately the wealth of Europe, had come into existence. What Thomas Newcombe created was the first glimmerings of a revolution, an Industrial Revolution. Solingen was to enter a new age.

3 The Industrial Reich

The only instrument with which one can conduct
foreign policy is alone and exclusively—the sword.
Dr Joseph Goebbels, *Der Angriff*, 28 May, 1931

The eighteenth and nineteenth centuries proved to be periods of great expansionism, heralding the beginnings of endeavours and enterprises which were to have profound effects on the world as it was then; and as it was to become for the following generations.

During the early part of the seventeenth century the territorial area of Germany was composed of a number of small duchies, mainly ruled by two great Swabian families—the Habsburgs, and the Hohenzollerns. Prussia, as such, was contained in the eastern land beyond the Vistula river. It was ruled by the Hohenzollerns, but frequently dominated by Poland.

Another branch of the Hohenzollerns had gained possession of the north-central German state of Brandenburg in 1411, and although bordered by other powerful duchies (Mecklenburg, and Pomerania) there was an instinctive—as well as political—inclination for the two branches of Hohenzollerns to unite themelves, and their lands.

These gradual territorial acquisitions were mainly genealogical gains, as the Hohenzollerns intermarried with other great families, and slowly incorporated other lands within the family grouping by virtue of the laws of succession. In 1618, however, a most notable change occurred within the Hohenzollern family structure. The family branch in East Prussia died out, without a successor; yet by virtue of an agreement with other branches of the family, the duchy of East Prussia passed into the possession of the Hohenzollerns of Brandenburg. The inclination to geographically unite the two territories was given further impetus over the following two centuries, as the Hohenzollerns presented some outstanding leaders from the family ranks. Frederick William The Great Elector (1640–88) being one of them; another—perhaps the most notable of all—Frederick the Great (1740–86). These were the leaders who expanded the lands and the dynasty.

By 1795 the Prussian lands had extended eastwards into Poland (New East Prussia), southwards into Silesia;

and even into the isolated pockets of Bayreuth and Ansbach. There was some reversal to this territorial gain during a military campaign in 1807, when New East Prussia and parts of South Prussia were lost to Russia. In the west, however, other territories had been gained, to include Westphalia and the Lower Rhineland.

The concept of an 'industrial revolution' was undreamed of when, in about 1729, the Englishman Thomas Newcombe patented his 'Atmospheric Engine'. Fanciful ideas of all manner had existed, on paper, for centuries, just awaiting innovative minds to turn them into reality. Newcombe's invention—designed to mechanically pump water out from mines to prevent flooding—relied upon the principle of boiling water and causing it to expand and force itself through chambers and one-way valves. It was a form of pump; but for those who could grasp its fairly simple principles, it was a pump with far wider potential.

'Old Fritz'—the affectionate nickname given to a statue which once stood in the Market Place of old Solingen, said to be in honour of one of the legendary swordsmiths of the City, Peter Hahn, whose reputation was so notable that he was specifically requested to make swords for Frederick the Great. (Original photo by Weyerstahl; source Die Klinge).

Knowledge of Newcombe's engine was undoubtedly known to the Scotsman, James Watt, and his partner, Matthew Boulton, when in the latter part of the eighteenth century they set about developing another form of 'atmospheric engine', to which was added a condenser. Their creation allowed for the harnessing of the power of heated water—it was the Steam Engine; and it was to change society as radically and dramatically as had the invention of the wheel in ancient times.

Controllable power, traction, torque, and movement could be created without reliance upon wind or rivers. Machine energy could be produced and directed more easily, more reliably, and more powerfully than by man or horse. It was a new form of tool, which could be used to make other tools, a machine which could help create other machines. It was the beginnings of a new type of industry, which as it developed would envelop and eliminate more and more of the traditional hand-work industries of the previous centuries. The work of the swordsmith was to be no exception in the face of these new machines.

Of all the states which collectively constituted the Germanic peoples, at the beginning of the nineteenth century Prussia was by far the largest, with territorial boundaries that stretched from eastern provinces in the Baltic, to the frontiers of France, Belgium, and Holland. Prussia, by virtue of her size, and geographic location, was an empire. An autonomous power that could, and did, stand alone; and yet which at the same time nurtured a desire to unite all of the German communities that were scattered across Europe. The developing industrial age contributed to that desire in no small way.

The industrial power that was being unleashed upon Europe at the beginning of the nineteenth century, started to rapidly affect the commercial, social, and cultural aspirations of all those who recognized the potential.

Peasant workers, whose families had hitherto worked on the land, started to migrate to the cities. Railway links between cities came into being; new wealth started to be generated by a new generation. The power of Prussia, commercially, politically, and physically, was being redistributed. The wealthy landowners of the beginning of the century gave way to industrialists, who would rule at the end of the century.

During the nineteenth century Germany experienced an explosion in commerce, population, and industry. From a population of 24,833,000 in 1815, the states of Prussia, Saxony, Bavaria, and Württemberg grew to a staggering 42,518,000 by 1875. Some notable Germans of a new class would emerge, one was Otto von Bismarck, another (ironically) was Karl Marx.

The development of the steam engine opened new opportunities to the craftsmen of Solingen, although it was distrusted and disliked by many of the quality bladesmiths.

The arduous labour of forging a blade over an anvil, by hand, was slowly being replaced by mechanically driven hammers which could relentlessly pound the glowing billets of metal into shape. More dramatically, the facilities for mass production

A soldier of one of the German Lifeguard Regiments, circa 1800. The firearm of the day was still the single-shot flintlock, slow to reload. The sword, therefore, remained an indispensable part of the personal armament, despite the profusion of pistols and rifles in the eighteenth and nineteenth centuries. (Artist unknown, collection of Chris Farlowe).

were being evolved. Blades for some weapons—bayonets particularly—could be drop forged in dies; drawn and shaped mechanically, with only the finishing work left to the hand labourer. It was the beginning of the end of the traditional form of blade making; and even change to the scope of work undertaken by furbishers was to become affected by the industrialization of Solingen.

Military power, under the direction of Bismarck, had grown tremendously since the inception of the North German Confederation of 1861. The ranks of the Infantry, the Artillery, and the Navy started to swell, and all troops required weapons of one form or another. Industrial mass production made this possible—as well as developments in other areas related to steel products—and the exclusiveness of Solingen as a steelware production town gave way to the development of the whole Ruhr area as the centre of German iron and steel industries. The Ruhr was rich in coal, and iron ore, as well as other mineral deposits. Other territories such as Silesia and the Saar, dominated by Prussia and her allied states, also held valuable iron and coal deposits; and it all helped to develop the expansion of industrial steel production.

Another development during the nineteenth century which affected the German steel industry was Thomas Gilchrist's process for making steel from phosphoric ores. Phosphoric ore—of which there were extensive deposits in Alsace-Lorraine, Silesia, and elsewhere—had previously been considered unsuitable for steel production. The chemical process devised by Gilchrist altered that situation, and this too added to the increasing production of German steel. In 1880, the combined pig iron and steel production of all of Germany—or the Second Reich as it had become known, since 1871—was 4,277,000 metric tons.

By 1890 the production figure totalled 7,822,000 tons; by 1900 it was 15,893,000 tons; and in 1910 it was 27,943,000 tons—massive expansion which was only possible by means of industrial processes.

Other industries, too, had started to develop during the nineteenth century, notably the chemical and electrical industries. These developments also affected the swordsmiths of Solingen. Finely chased hilts of gold and silver work started to give way to mechanically-engraved dies for cast hilts, and electro-plating finishes to base metals gave the same appearance as the fire-gilded finish which had previously been commonly produced. It was not simply the adoption of a new and novel form of technology—fire-gilding was a hazardous technique involving the use of cyanide, and the resultant exposure to the toxic fumes had claimed casualties.

During the first half of the eighteenth century attempts were made by some of the more progressive Solingen firms to centralize their sources of labour. The forges, where steam-driven drop hammers were used to pound the billets of metal into shape, would arrange for carters to collect the raw blades, and distribute them to other workers who would attend to the finishing, polishing, and furbishment of the consignment. Many of these other craftsmen were situated in other parts of the town, and even in the outlying districts. Some had grouped themselves together as co-operative ventures to handle large orders from the blade manufacturers, but the majority were small, family-orientated artisans working as 'cottage industries'.

In a move designed to centralize and contain these outside workers, the blade forges succeeded in encouraging many of the 'cottage' artisans to move their work activities into new, custom-designed buildings that had been built by the forge owners. These were the beginnings of the new industrial family businesses which would emerge at the century progressed.

Other changes within the Solingen industries had come about by design, and as a result of the higher-quality requirements that were being demanded by some of the larger customers—principally government contracts. These contracts were not restricted to the governing legislators of the varied German states (each state was responsible for raising its own military force, and the incumbent financial burden of arming it), but also from foreign governments such as Russia and France.

The demands of these customers centred not only on large volumes of product within specified budgets, but also with the requirement that all products be produced to a uniform standard. These were requirements with which the hand-forging bladesmith could not hope to comply. It was possible only by investment in the new types of machine which were being introduced; and it added further impetus to the factory owners to bring as many of their craft workers as possible under a single, corporate roof.

4 The Road to War

I seek Prussian honour in this, that Prussia above all,
had departed from any tasteful connection with democracy.
Bismarck, 1850 (Landtag speech)

On 30 October 1848, the Guild of Solingen swordsmiths announced that their membership was ready to omit their hereditary marks from sword blades—a move which was, to some degree, motivated by the insistence of some of the emerging large factory-forge smithies that the factory name only be placed on the blade. Many of the traditional sword blade makers, their families and assistant workers, reluctantly started to leave their part of the trade, moving into allied areas, producing pocket knives, shears, and commercial implements—items which they would once have condemned as being beneath the standard and dignity of the craftsman and guild member. Others accepted offers from the *nouveaux riches* factory owners to work in the growing areas of mass-production.

The German export market, too, had started to open up again. The competitive, hand-working swordsmiths of Germany, Spain, and

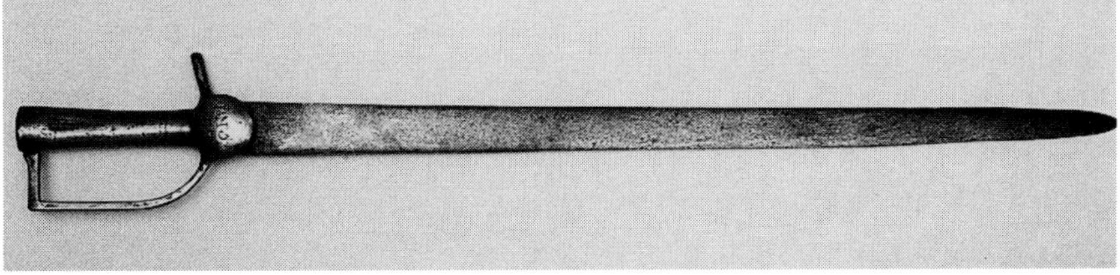

A German (Prussian) sword bayonet from about 1810. The hilt fittings are made of brass, and the langet is engraved with a regimental number.

One of the fascinating aspects of military weaponry of this period is that although hardware, such as the carbine and rifle, were more or less fully specified regarding constructional techniques, the bayonets which were to fit them varied widely—usually the result of private arrangements between the financier of a regiment and the cutler. The system for attaching the bayonet to the fusil was standardized, but the overall appearance of the weapon was wide ranging.

England who had formerly vied with each other to secure and retain the best labour, soon discovered that the new industrial developments had affected these competing centres as well. The industrial German sword and blade industry started to compete with the industrial sword and blade industries of other nations; and it did so with some remarkable effect, although not always with the prestige that was due to Solingen.

English cutlers, from about the time of the Crimea War campaign, had increasingly been sub-contracting much of their work to the competitive artisans of Solingen. This had arisen partially due to the enticingly low labour cost rates which Solingen could offer, and additionally because Solingen had industrialized many of her forges. The situation was one whereby English government contracts for the production of swords and bayonets were being issued to English manufacturing firms, who in turn contracted with Solingen companies for the production of the completed goods, or alternatively for the production of blades only, which the English contractors would assemble and finish.

This deployment of foreign labour on the traditional work of English bladesmiths had been causing increasing concern during the 1870s; questions were being asked by both the military authorities and the government of the day as to why Solingen was being offered these lucrative orders. The answer submitted by the English contractors was that the craftsmen of Solingen had already invested in machines and equipment to produce these blades, that they had the capacity to accept this work, and that if the English contractors were to likewise invest in similar machinery it would not only be costly, but time consuming. It would, it was estimated, take two years to design, build, and install the specialized machinery which would be necessary. Time was of the essence, the mighty Empire of Queen Victoria was maintaining her military presence in all corners of the globe; blades for the troops were required immediately and Solingen was there to fulfil that requirement. All, however, was not well with the products from Solingen—an event was in the offing that would subsequently be referred to as 'the sword and bayonet scandal'.

In their haste to sub-contract orders to the Solingen smithies, the English contractors, who had been enthralled by the low labour costs which were available, remained unwitting to the distinction between low-cost quality and low-quality costs; sub-contract orders had been placed with the lowest tenders submitted. The result was a disaster—the blades supplied for swords and bayonets proved to be of very low quality indeed. The raw steel was good enough, but the tempering was very thin, so that sharpened blades had the temper ground out of them.

The crisis came to a head during the Sudan Campaign of the 1880s, when reports came back of bayonets breaking and swords bending—and staying that way—when used in combat. It was a scandal of such proportions that it became a national joke, except for the luckless soldiers defending the empire in desolate wadis.

Debates concerning the poor quality of the blades for British soldiers were voiced not only in every major newspaper in England, but also in the Houses of Parliament, such was the magnitude of the scandal. The demand was that no more inferior blades be puchased from Germany, and that if reliable and professional suppliers for the sub-contract work could not be found, then the English manufacturers had better do something about the matter themselves.

As it happened, producers of quality

A Landsknecht pattern sword, but not from the Middle Ages. This sword, in appearance and general construction, could pass as an early period sword, but it is distinguished from its ancestral patterns by a number of features: the hilt fittings are made of brass instead of iron; the scabbard fittings are made of brass, and have been nickel plated; and the blade trademark – the letters A C S with an emblem of scales, is identifiable as the mark of Alex Coppel, Solingen, dating from the 1928–38 period.

The sword is professionally made, and does not appear to fall into the category of theatrical or 'ornamental' weapons, therefore its true purpose remains a mystery. What is evident from examination of this item, is that it is substantial in construction, and could undoubtedly function in the capacity for which it was originally designed – the blade is strong, rigid, and sharp.

One potential aspect for the purpose of this sword is under consideration: in 1933 the Nazis reintroduced beheading as the authorized form of capital punishment; all available reference sources checked so far have revealed that this system of punishment – reinstated in Prussia in 1929, and throughout the Third Reich after 1933 – was performed with either an axe or a sword. It is not claimed that this illustrated item is in fact an executioner's sword, merely that the item is of useable durability, and that the system of punishment would require an item of this type of construction.

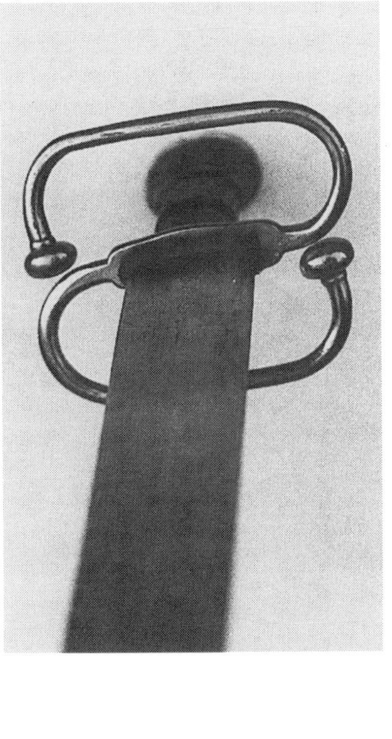

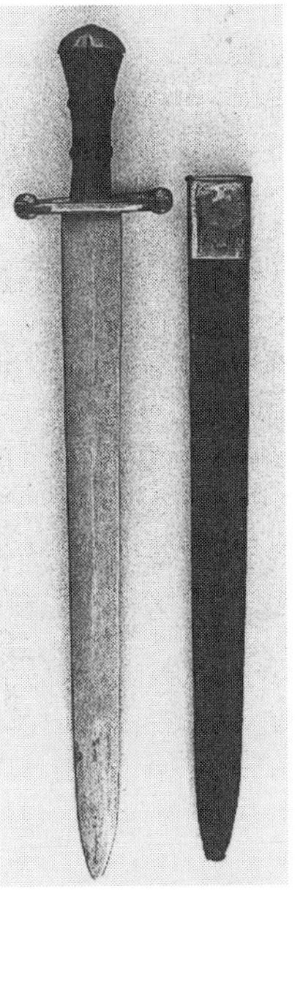

blades had been located in Solingen, and the English concern of Henry Wilkinson had indeed formed an alliance with the concern of Weyersberg Kirschbaum (W.K. & Cie) in Solingen. Their products were of reliable quality and the relationship between Wilkinson and W.K. & Cie was maintained for many years. For the other English contractors, however, who had opted for the lower prices of other Solingen concerns, the lesson learned was a costly one. An improvement in the production of home-produced English blades was authorized, and many Solingen companies lost their lucrative contracts in the tarnish of the 1885 scandal.

Two notable developments during the latter part of the nineteenth century particularly affected Solingen's competitive position. Henry Bessemer's improved technique for refining steel and controlling the carbon content was one such innovation (invented by an Englishman, but more successfully deployed by Germans); another one was the adoption in 1873 of the techniques of mechanically rolling steel blades.

The mass-production of blades accelerated into an even higher gear, and the time-honoured, traditional hand-forging bladesmiths of Solingen finally admitted defeat in the face of industrialization. Their unique role in sword and dagger making history was coming to a close. The skill of producing the hand-made blade was relegated to the production of exhibition pieces, and the few private orders from wealthy customers who wanted the hand-made article.

The anvils where craftsmen of the calibre of Peter Munch, Wilhelm Weyersberg, Johann Eickhorn, Hans Ohlig, Peter Berg, and many others, had wrought steel and iron into items of precision and beauty, would stand rusting and forgotten in some dark corners of disused forges. Only occasionally would they be seen and commented upon by an elderly craftsman showing some new batch of would-be apprentices around the factory. Tales of the great swordsmiths of the past would be retold by the old craftsman to his new charges, standing as he may with one foot resting on the anvil, dusting-off the cold facts of history whilst in the warmth of the forges of the new industrial Reich.

The Industrial Age of Solingen had finally vanquished the Golden Age, and was to be the source of Solingen's wealth for the next 50 years. Bismarck had brought the ideal of the unification of the German states into a reality—the nation was now an empire, and militarily she dominated the land mass of Europe. German armies had marched as far west as Paris in the war of 1870, and forced a humiliating defeat upon the French empire. The Kaiser, Wilhelm I, had actually held his coronation in the palace at Versailles where numerous Kings of France had once ensconced themselves in pre-revolution times.

Right *The Aplikantendolch ('Applicant's Dagger') Model 1871–90. Aspirant officers in the German Navy were permitted the right to wear a short sidearm, prior to the introduction of the Model 1890 Naval dirk. The items illustrated depict three patterns of the Aplikantendolch showing variations in the quality and workmanship of items that were available for private purchase–all based upon the same basic theme.*

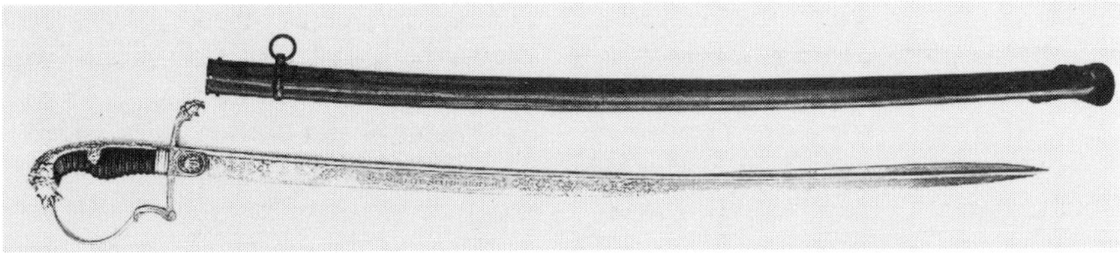

Above *A fine quality Imperial German Army officer's sabre (circa 1910), with a damascus steel blade inlaid with gold decoration. Although designed for walking out purposes, the construction style of this time reflects the fighting characteristics of the day—the blade is a 'cut and thrust' pattern. That is to say, the sabre blade, although designed for a slashing type stroke in combat, is also equipped with a double-edged tip, for thrusting. A weapon of this quality would never be used for combative purposes, but the style of the armourer's design remains, even though it is a purely decorative item.* (Wallis and Wallis).

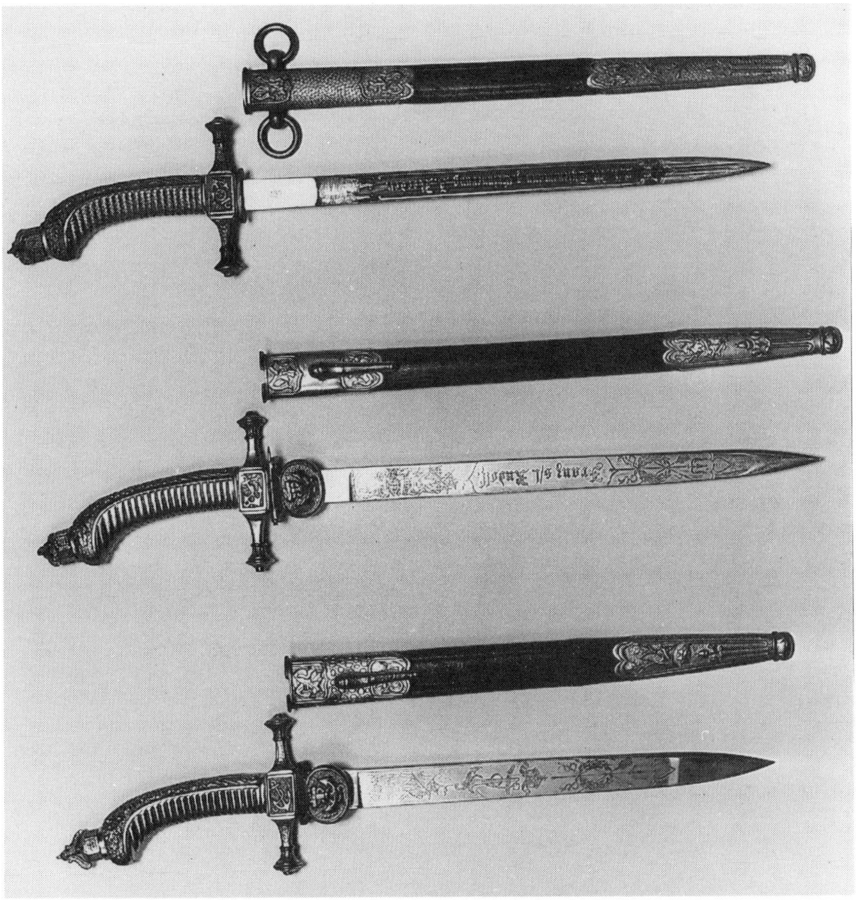

The might of Germany and the control of Prussia was seemingly unassailable in all but one respect—control of the high seas. The most powerful navy of the age was that of Britain, and Prussia envied the British maritime force almost to the point of emulation.

A detailed study of the British maritime fleet, techniques, and armaments developments, had attracted the interests of a young German naval officer for some time, and he had repeatedly submitted papers and memos to his superiors in the Admiralty for consideration. His suggestions and recommendations were continually ignored, and for this young career officer it seemed that his role in life was to be one of obscurity. His name was von Tirpitz, (later to become Admiral), but in the 1890s the foresight of this officer was overlooked by his peers. It wasn't until the early 1900s that the German Admiralty finally realized the wisdom of von Tirpitz's theories, and hurriedly rushed through the Naval Bills that would allow the expansion and development of the *Kaiserliche-marine*, as the German Navy was known in those times. It was too late, however. Turmoil within Europe, especially amongst ethnic communities, was bubbling into small revolutions. The cauldron of politics bubbled over in 1914, and Germany was drawn into a war on the side of Austria. Contending opponents on other sides saw the opportunity to show support for the minorities, and nationalists everywhere rushed to salvage national pride. It was to become the Great War of 1914–18, and it devoured the lands of Europe as voraciously as it devoured an entire generation of young men. It claimed over 7,000,000 lives, and affected millions more.

5 The Vicious Circle

What we want now is a new Bismarck to take the helm
and be the Führer of the German People.
Vice-Admiral Breusing, January 1914.

The palls of smoke had long since drifted away from the ravaged cities of northern France and Belgium; the acrid smell of cordite no longer wafted in the damp air of November, 1919; the Great War was over, it had become a part of history for almost a whole year, yet the Treaty of Peace was still to be signed.

At the Forest of Compiègne, near the great palace at Versailles, an ancient railway carriage had been trundled out from its isolation—a piece of rolling stock that had witnessed more than its fair share of momentous events. It had been in this very railway carriage, in 1871, that the French had been coerced to sign the surrender document that confirmed the end of the Franco-Prussian War. Forty-eight years later Frenchmen and Germans faced each other once again in the same carriage, only this time it was Germany that was obliged to accept the conditions of surrender.

By means of the Treaty of Peace (also known as the Treaty of Versailles) the Allied and Associated Powers levied upon the German nation the terms and conditions incumbent in the cessation of hostilities. Fifteen separate Sections constituted the basic terms of the Treaty, and 440 Articles spelled out in detail what the cost to Germany would be: the surrender of lands and territories; the dismemberment of military powers; the destruction of industries conducive to war-like activities; the payment of debts and repatriations. The well-intentioned, but humiliating, Treaty went on and on in great detail with the demands and conditions which Germany was obliged to accept.

Article 235 required, during each of the years of 1919, 1920 and 1921 payment by Germany in cash, or repatriated goods, of 20,000,000,000 (twenty billion) gold marks. Articles 27 to 309 redesignated the new territorial boundaries of Germany; the re-allocation of new domains to the seized lands, industries, and indigenous population. Articles 119 to 158 covered the limitation or surrender of former German colonial possessions. Articles 159 to 213 concerned themselves with the reduction of German military strength, personnel, equipment, fortifications, etc.

Other Sections and Articles covered financial clauses, economic clauses, ports, waterways, railways, labour, guarantees and so on.

It was, in short, an instrument designed to quell forever any forms of German internationalism; the cost for ensuring such was, naturally enough, to be borne by Germany herself. This was the bequest that the newly-formed League of Nations bestowed upon post-war Europe; in the belief that harsh, dictatorial conditions would bring the German beast under the control of the Allied Powers for all time.

The Great War had taken an immense toll from all the European nations. A whole generation of young men had been sent to slaughter, whole communities had been wiped out; and towns and villages pummelled into rubble; international economies had been sent reeling under the weight of the war effort; and yet at the end of the day there had not been a decisive victory. Germany had accepted peace demands enforced by the weight of numbers of the Allied Powers (America had joined the war in 1917, and brought considerable influence with her fresh, well-armed troops, although even so it was not possible to manoeuvre the Allied Powers into a totally conquering force). The stalemate of war produced a stagnant peace, under which the Prussians smarted with humiliation at being made to pay the cost. The Treaty of Versailles had laid fallow lands which would be ripe for revolution.

One of the facets of the Treaty of Peace, intent as it was on the prevention of war, was the inclusion of Articles that related to 'war souvenirs'. Part VIII, Section II, contained several demands, amongst which were the following: Article 245—the return to France of French Flags captured by the Germans in the war of 1870–71; and Article 246 (second paragraph) contains the following strange stipulation, that Germany 'hand over to His Britannic Majesty's Government the skull of the Sultan Mkwana, removed from the Protectorate of German East Africa and taken to Germany.'

With great solemnity the signatures and seals were affixed to the historic document. Peace was declared. The soldiers of the Allied Powers started to disband, although an Allied military presence was retained in the Saar and Rhineland—the industrial heart of the German war machine. Old German territories were taken over by new masters: Prussia was divided in two, separated by a strip of land that was to become known as the Polish Corridor. The Germans of the Sudetenland were annexed to Bohemia and Moravia in the creation of a new state, Czechoslovakia. Alsace and Lorraine were given back to France. The map of Europe had become changed.

On 31 July 1919, Chancellor Ebert (later President Ebert) headed the parliamentary regime which adopted the Weimar Constitution. The unity of German states that had been engineered by Bismarck and Wilhelm II had given way to what was considered to be a democratic republic. The Presidential post was to be filled by election, and equality of votes—be they from peasant or prince—was to be the mainstay of the new constitution.

The effects of the Great War, the divisions within society, the distress felt at being the undefeated victims of the war; the political unrest; and the resurgence of mutiny and revolution amongst the working classes, all made their impact on the emerging Weimar Republic. Germany, despite being at peace with the rest of Europe, was very much at odds internally. Paramilitary groups and old-comrades associations were springing up. The German Communist Party was beginning to make itself felt, and Socialists opposed to them were equally disruptive. It was a period of turmoil which needed a powerful figure to bond national pride back together, and at the same time counteract the unnerving influence of the extreme left-wing politicians. This new leader was to emerge in the form of a wounded ex-soldier, recruited by the post-war *Reichswehr* to spy upon some of the political gatherings which were causing so much unease. This agent was Adolf Hitler.

Adolf Hitler was born at Braunau, on the Austrian-Bavarian border, on 20 April, 1889. His father, Alois Schickelgruber, had commenced his working life as a shoemaker, and by diligence and perseverance had expanded his working potential to end up with a minor post as a customs officer for the Austrian government. He had adopted the surname of Hitler (also known as Heidler) in 1877, at about the time he married his second wife, Klara Polez. Alois Schickelgruber was 51 years old at the time of this marriage, and his bride was in her 20s.

The adoption of the Hitler name was not a random choice, there were other distant relatives in the family who bore this surname. The reason for the change of name apparently centred on a family embarrassment, Alois Schickelgruber bore only his mother's maiden name—he was illegitimate. His mother had suffered the fate of countless country girls; she had been put into service as a servant with a well-to-do Jewish family called Frankenburger, had become enamoured with a young member of the household, and in 1818 had the misfortune to find herself in the family way—and out of a job. Alois Schickelgruber had borne the stigma of illegitimacy all his life, and the knowledge that his paternal ancestor was both wealthy, and possibly Jewish, undoubtedly influenced his attitude to life, and that of his subsequent offspring.

By all accounts, the young Adolf Hitler did little to distinguish himself academically. He was educated in Linz under a teacher of history who was influenced by the activities of the Austrian Pan-Germanic League headed by Georg von Schönerer. The nationalism and anti-semitism promoted by the Pan-German followers filtered through the educational influence and undoubtedly made some impression on the young Hitler.

In 1909, following the death of his parents, Hitler moved to Vienna. He was at this time 19 years of age, without formal qualifications of any sort, although he held pretensions to being both an architect and an artist. For three years he scraped a living doing paintings, drawing postcards;

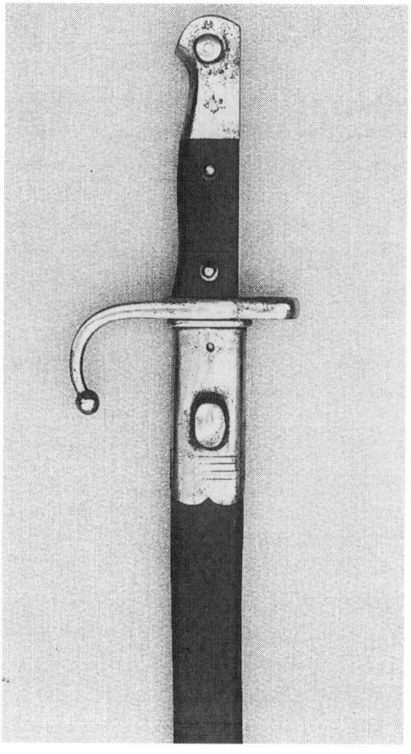

A typical example of one of the many types of weapons which were produced in Solingen for export to foreign nations. This item is the Turkish issue Mauser bayonet, which fitted on the standard Gew 98 rifle, which was standard issue to all German troops, and which additionally was exported to German allies during World War One. Although Turkey had her own arms industry, the vast majority of weapons supplied to her troops were imported from Germany.

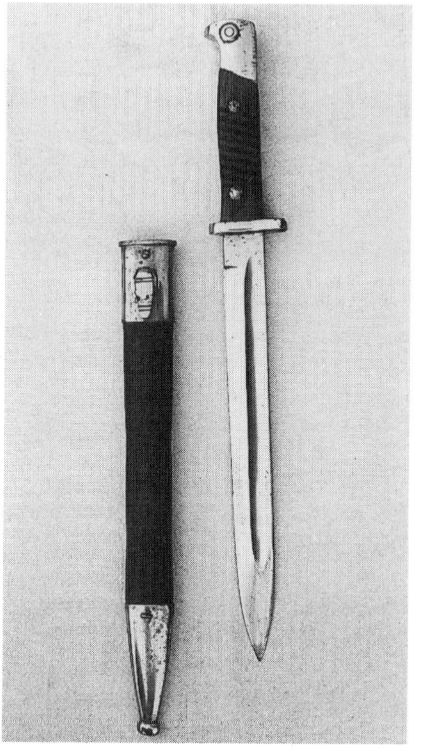

A highly unusual version of the Army dress bayonet, this example was produced by the Eickhorn concern, circa 1916. This item looks basically like the regular service-issue bayonet of the period, utilizing the pre-war (Model 1908) scabbard pattern, and a blade that was then in current service. The pommel features the press-stud device for securing the bayonet to a rifle, but does not feature the mortise slot, thus rendering the bayonet suitable only for walking-out purposes. The grip scales are made of wood, and all metal portions of the hilt, blade and scabbard are nickel plated.

sometimes sleeping rough, and at other times living in doss-houses. From a lower-middle-class background, Hitler had degenerated to the despairing levels of the poorer working classes.

In 1912, in pursuit of better opportunities, Hitler moved to Munich where, apparently, he fared marginally better than hitherto in Vienna. Times, however, were changing. Political unrest amongst minorities in Serbia and

Croatia was seething against the Austrians who dominated them, and exploded one afternoon in August 1914. Austria suddenly found herself at war with Serbia, and called upon Germany to assist. Russia, taking the side of the Serbs came into the fray; the tide of war was suddenly sweeping through Europe, dragging dissenting parties into the maelstrom. Adolf Hitler was another unknown who was caught up in the turmoil, and he was permitted to enlist in a Bavarian regiment as an orderly on the headquarters staff.

Later on, Hitler was sent into action in France, where the comforts of the orderly's life were replaced with the harsh realities of trench war, and apparently Hitler acquitted himself with some distinction. He achieved promotion to Lance Corporal, was wounded in action, was gassed and hospitalized, and finally decorated with the Iron Cross First Class—the latter award being unusual in so far as the First Class award was normally awarded to offiers, and the enlisted ranks of Hitler's standing more usually received the Second Class version.

Semi-invalided, and temporarily blinded, Hitler was repatriated to Bavaria; at the time of the Armistice he was still in a reserve battalion of his regiment.

6 The Rise of the Nazis

At the formation of the new Constitution of Weimar, the *Reichswehr*—the Armed Forces—although depleted in number, we're still expected to maintain control inside the country. Revolutionary groups were springing up everywhere, motivated by all manner of radical ideas. The *Reichswehr*, justly concerned about the extent and influence of some of these organizations, adopted a policy of investigating all these varied factions, openly showing support to those which it considered might be beneficial to the State generally, and hostile to those it considered to be otherwise—the communists in particular. In the course of maintaining contact with these radical parties, the *Reichswehr* recruited Hitler to investigate, and liaise with if necessary, a group headed by an Anton Drexler and known as the German Workers Party. This small party, with a membership of about 200, was strongly nationalistic and received the favours of the *Reichswehr*.

To Hitler, however, this small party represented ideals which were similar to his own, and in September 1919, aftering having given some inspired speeches to the party gathering, Hitler received an invitation from Anton Drexler to join the party executive. He did so, and was recorded as being Party Executive member No. 7.

As a man of some vision, and popular instinct, Adolf Hitler soon recognized the potential that this small party could offer. The terms of the Treaty of Peace were hated. The despair of millions of honest German working people was exacerbated by the conditions imposed by the victorious Allied Powers. Germany was in tremendous debt, her industries had been dismantled (and in some cases physically loaded on to trains and taken away), unemployment and hardship were rife everywhere. The Weimar Constitution seemed to be unable to redeem the standing of the new nation. Circumstances and times invited national revolution.

In the ten years that were to follow, the fortunes of Germany and Europe were to ebb back and forth in the turbulence of the 1920s. The small German Workers Party changed its name, to become the National Socialist German Workers Party (*Nationalsozialistische Deutsche Arbeiter Partei—NSDAP*). It secured an enlargement of its membership and adopted a uniform (an unsold consignment of brown tropical shirts, purchased by Party member Ritter von Epp as a job lot, and used to dress the Party faithful); an emblem was designed and adopted—the swastika—to be worn on the uniform, and borne on flags; and a bodyguard unit to protect the Party speakers from harassment at public meetings was organized, these being known as the *Schutz-Abteilung* (literally 'protection detachment'). After a short period, however, it became apparent that this protection unit could more usefully be deployed in the wider capacity of disrupting the meetings of opponents, and it changed its name to *Sturm-Abteilung* ('assault detachment)—the SA—which title it retained until the end of the Second World War.

A Fighting Knife, one of inumerable patterns which were produced by Germany, and issued as standard items to all of her troops during World War One. In the post-WWI period thousands of this type of knife remained in store, and were variously modified for resale to the general public as utility knives, camping knives, tools, etc.

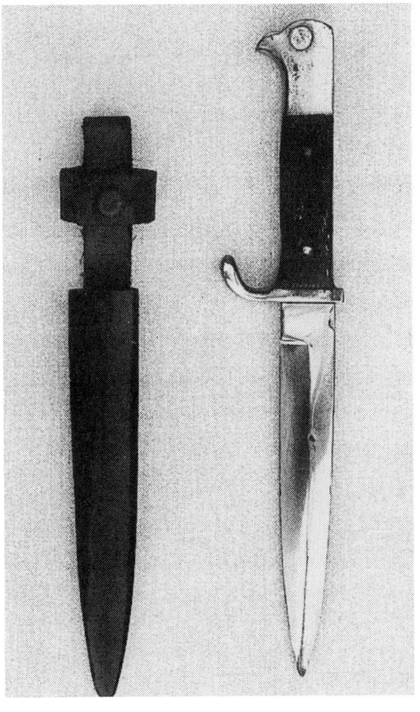

The Nazi Party grew, slowly at first, but steadily, as its nationalistic manifesto became more evident to a wider audience. Most Germans were distressed and humiliated by the terms of the Treaty of Peace, and the Nazis promised to restore German dignity and national pride.

In 1923 the NSDAP, led by Hitler, attempted a *coup d'état*, intent on overthrowing the Bavarian government and re-establishing it with a NSDAP-military alliance. Supported by the approval of national hero and military leader Erich Ludendorff, Hitler and his supporters broke into a meeting being chaired by the Bavarian Prime Minister Kahr and General von Lossow, and declared at pistol point that the national revolution had come.

The following day, 9 November, several thousand NSDAP supporters, headed by Hitler, Röhm, Goering, and others, marched through Munich in the direction of the State parliament, intent upon ensconcing themselves in the seat of power. It was not to be. The *Reichswehr*—supportive as it was of the NSDAP—was not willing to go so far as to openly revolt against constitutional power. Near the steps of the war memorial *Feldherrnhalle* the chanting army of Nazis met resistance in the form of armed *Reichswehr* and police. Shots were fired, about 12 NSDAP followers were killed, and the

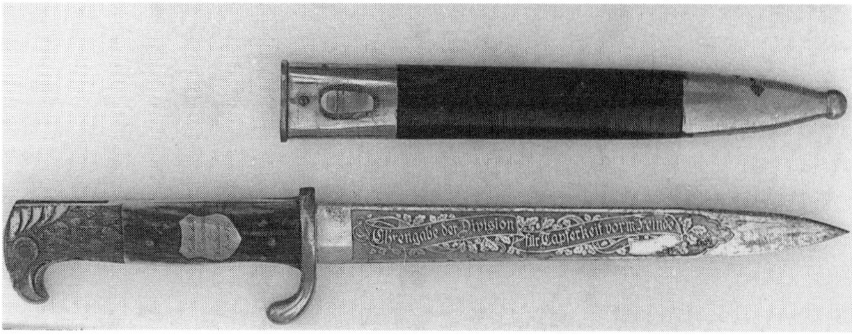

A post-WWI period dress bayonet, decorated and etched with an inscription for presentation, to a former soldier. The etching on the blade denotes: 'The Honour Gift of the Regiment, for Bravery in the face of the Enemy'. It is interesting to note that even in the Depression years of the late 1920s, the sense of style and quality was still available for the production of quality items – if the customer could afford it. (Dr Julian Milestone collection).

'revolution' (later known as the Munich *putsch*) collapsed. Hitler fled, but was later captured, and the Nazis were rounded up. Hitler was sentenced to five years' imprisonment in Landsberg fortress.

The *putsch* was over, but it had brought the actions of the Nazis to a far wider national audience. Hitler served a period of just a year in Landsberg, but the time was not spent idly. Assisted by Rudolf Hess, Hitler analysed, revised, and dictated his concepts of the principles of National Socialism. Hess took the manuscript out from the prison over a period of a few months, and the supporters of Hitler arranged to have it published – it was to be known as *Mein Kampf* ('My Struggle').

Following his release from Landsberg, in December 1924, Hitler once again set out to build up support for the Nazi cause, and to tackle the political disarray that beset the Weimar Republic. This time, however, a new approach was to be used; the ballot box. The NSDAP would appoint candidates and contest in all the electoral areas where it could find support. The rivalry with opposition parties continued, but the NSDAP succeeded in expanding and gaining seats in all the State elections. By November, 1932, of the 582 seats in the *Reichstag* (Reich Parliament) 196 (33.6 per cent) were held by the Nazis. They were a powerful party, but not yet large enough to form a new government. The other major parties were the Social Democrats with 121 seats (21 per cent), and the Communists with 100 seats (17 per cent).

Under the terms of the Constitution of the Weimar Republic, every German government of the Republic had to be formed of a coalition of at least three parties to secure the necessary majority of the *Reichstag*. A coalition of the NSDAP and the Social Democrats, and any other party who could be roped in (the Hanoverian Party held one seat, and the German Peasant Party held two seats) would possess an overwhelming majority.

Hitler and the NSDAP approved the principle of a coalition with the Social Democrats as a temporary measure to secure power; and the SDP unwittingly allowed itself to be lured into this unhealthy alliance.

On January 30, 1933, a new government, dominated by the Nazi Party, was formed. Paul von Hindenburg was installed as the President of the new government, but it was already planned by Hitler that the new coalition would have as short a life as possible. On 28 February 1933, the Reichstag building was mysteriously set afire, and Hitler saw to it that the Communists were blamed. The situation required that President Hindenburg suspend vital clauses of the Constitution; then on 23 March the Nazi-dominated Reichstag Cabinet passed the 'Enabling Act' which effectively continued the suspension of the Constitution—meaning that for the time being all state decisions were undertaken solely by the Cabinet, and not with the dissension of the elected Reichstag. This gave Hitler a virtually free hand in determining the policies of the Government, and thus the State. By the end of June, 1933, the Nazi Cabinet had succeeded in suppressing or outlawing the other opposition political parties. On 14 July 1933, the Cabinet issued by decree the law that featured the ominous words: *'there is only one political party in Germany, the National Socialist German Workers Party'*. The revolution that had been dreamed of in the beer cellars of Munich ten years previously had finally come about. The National Socialist state had secured its grip upon a whole nation. Vice-Admiral

Photograph from a manufacturer's publicity advertisement, circa 1938. The sword depicted is a special presentation piece that was commissioned by the City of Solingen, for presentation to Field Marshal von Hindenburg. Paul von Hindenburg had passed away in the summer of 1934, and the sword was, presumably, retained on display at the Solingen city hall. The workmanship of the piece is outstanding, and the manufacturing company were undoubtedly very proud to feature the item in their subsequent publicity literature.

The manufacturer was the Alex Coppel company. The sword is in the Prussian style, with the Imperial eagle displayed on the fore of the basket guard—which is finely decorated in filigree work showing figures engaged in weapons production—note the blacksmith working at the anvil, and the main figure of a classical warrior with sword. The presence of a swastika emblem is discreetly suggested in the binding of the ivory grip. (Die Wehrmacht magazine, 1938).

Breusing's comment of 1914 had been realized with a chilling reality. Germany now had a *Führer*.

The red, gold and black tricolour flags of the old Republic were hauled down, and the red, black and white swastikas of the Nazis unfurled across the towns of Germany. Portraits of Hitler were ordered to be prominently displayed in public buildings, alongside those of national heroes past. And across the streets, banners appeared bearing the legend: *Ein Volk—Ein Reich—Ein Führer* (one people—one nation—one leader).

The way was now clear for the Nazis to implement, by force if necessary, the changes essential for the revitalization of German industries, people, and the economy. A price would have

A series of photographs showing some of the operations involved in the manufacture of swords. These illustrations appeared in the 1940 publication Leisten und Dienen, which was published to commemorate the 75th anniversary of the Carl Eickhorn company.

A blade grinder: the sword blade is held clamped on to a wooden base, and held to the heavy, revolving millstone which ground the final shape of the blade.

The blade proofer. Completed blades were stored in racks, according to length and style. The blades were required to meet specifications regarding temper, hardness, and flexibility—the latter requiring that the blade be bent crosswise, and still able to spring back to true without distortion.

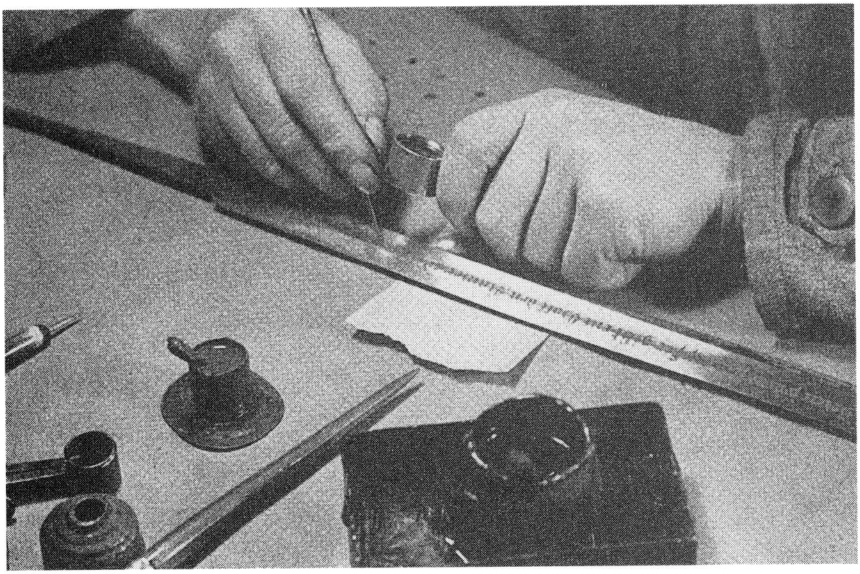

Above *Mass-produced decoration on blades was effected by means of a template, which produced a design in an acid-resistant material (usually a wax) which was applied on to the blade surface. Personalized designs such as presentation inscriptions were applied on to the blade by hand. The photograph shows an etcher preparing a blade by penning an inscription on to the blade surface. When the inscription was completed, the blade was then immersed in acid, and the exposed areas of the blade were eaten away. The result was that the design (or dedication) remained intact, and proud of the surface. Etched blades were sometimes further enhanced by polishing, and plating with colourants to highlight the decoration.*

Right *Assembling a sword blade in a hilt. The hilt was usually formed in four main portions: the crossguard and knuckle bow; the backstrap and pommel; the ferule; and the grip. Each portion locked together with its adjoining pieces, and the blade was assembled with the tang passing through the inside of the grip, and out through a hole in the top of the pommel. The exposed tang would then be peened over to lock the assembly together, and any excess metal protruding would be filed off and then polished.*

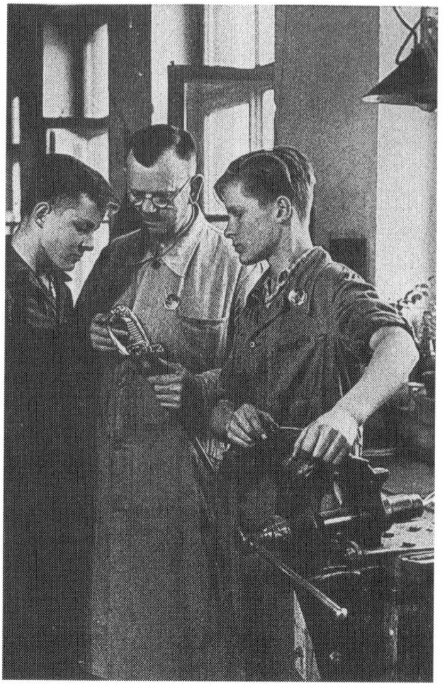

The Scheidenschmied – the Scabbard Smith. The skill in producing a sword scabbard – even some of the less interesting, common patterns – was a good deal more complex than many collectors currently realize. Even a 'one-piece' all-steel scabbard was subjected to several operations, all demanding a keenness of skill to produce an acceptable product. The scabbard starts out as a flat sheet of metal, which was cut, and shaped over a mandrail – a carefully shaped device that formed the insert area that would eventually accommodate the blade. The exposed edges of the scabbard body were then joined together by brazing, resulting in a curved, flattened tube. The lower end of the scabbard was sealed, with a specially shaped piece of steel that formed an extending lip around the side edges of the scabbard and underneath the tip – known as the 'drag'. At the upper end of the scabbard, the 'throat', a reinforced steel lip – the 'mouthpiece' – was inserted in the throat to cover the raw edges of the scabbard top. This fitment was usually secured in position by screws sited on the edge sides of the scabbard body. A pre-formed suspension band was usually slid over the scabbard body just before the mouthpiece was added, and secured in position by brazing, some two to three inches beneath the throat area. This suspension band frequently displayed two features: on the reverse side of the scabbard it comprised of a flat bar, which would mate with a clip on the bearer's belt strap, to suspend the sword vertically; it also featured a suspension ring on the back edge of the scabbard, which likewise could be used to connect the item to the belt strap clip – but allowing the sword to swing more freely.

The illustration (left) shows the scabbard smith in the process of filing off the excess metal from the brazing on the scabbard band. Following this operation, the scabbard would be polished, and then sent off to the enamelling shop for coating in a hard wearing, protective black enamel.

The completed sword (above). Two apprentices pose with the Master Sword Smith, who indicates to them the fine points of workmanship on a naval sword.

to be paid, of course, but that was unthought of in terms of reality. It seemed only that Hitler was the answer to the prayers of the people. In recounting the achievements and benefits that the new system was bestowing upon the German people, Minister of Propaganda, Dr Josef Goebbels, illuminated the Messiah-like status of the Leader with the immortal words: 'You my Führer, have given us our daily bread this year also.' (National Festival, 1st May 1935.)

7 Solingen and the Third Reich

Revival of the Solingen industries
The effects of NSDAP influence on the cutlery trades

Our enemies did not use their victory of 1918.
Dr Robert Ley, Speech at *Kraft durch Freude* anniversary, 27 November, 1940.

The flow of political events had escalated in the closing days of 1932. In the elections of November of that year, the NSDAP had lost 34 seats in the Reichstag, and Hitler, fearful that even more losses might erode the dominant position of the Party, had sought compromises and coalitions in an attempt to stabilize the Nazi position. A new government had to be formed, and it was essential to ensure that the impetus favoured the NSDAP.

Twelve years previously, in the early days of the Party, NSDAP had announced a 25-point manifesto. It was a *précis* account of what the NSDAP promised to achieve once it had attained power. It was highly pro-nationalistic and anti-semitic; yet it also promoted industrial and economic concepts which made some sense to the (then) impoverished industrialists of the post-war years. Item No. 7 in the manifesto commenced: *We demand that the State shall make its first duty to promote the industry and livelihood of the citizens of the State.* *

The need to honour that promise of industrial revitalization (and its inherent benefits to the workers) was clearly one Party promise which Hitler could not default upon. On the 4 January 1933, at the Cologne house of the banker Baron von Schröder, Hitler had a meeting with Chancellor von Papen and Schröder himself, at which the benefits and opportunities to be offered to the industrial and financial community were outlined—providing the new government received the support of the business institutions.

On 30 January 1933, Hitler was appointed to the Chancellorship by Hindenburg, a move which undoubtedly influenced the business community's appreciation of the standing of the NSDAP, and in the eyes of the Prussian monarchists. In the aftermath of the Reichstag fire (27 February 1933) at the multi-party Reichstag elections on 5 March, 1933, the NSDAP recouped its previous

* Translation quoted from *Nazi Germany*, Erwin Leiser, Pelican Books, 1962.

losses by gaining 288 seats (44 per cent). Three weeks later the NSDAP dominated Cabinet passed the Enabling Law (the Constitution had been suspended because of the Reichstag fire)—it was a *coup d'état*; the Communists had been prevented from voting, and the Social Democrats voted against the law, but all the other parties voted in its favour with the NSDAP. Hitler had got what he wanted, it was only to be a matter of time before the physical banishment of opposition groups was to become a reality. In the meantime, however, Hitler had to ensure that the support of the industrialists was rewarded.

The fortunes of Solingen had been somewhat lean since the end of the Great War. The whole of the German economy and industry had been in a demoralized state, and Solingen was but one section of it. Through the apparatus of the NSDAP, and the paramilitary formations which it fostered, some attempt was made to regenerate the vitality of the Solingen industries: Solingen could produce knives for the Party formations.

The vision of the vast army of brownshirts bearing swords and daggers had probably not been appreciated in 1933, but it was a potential market which could be probed, and if successful, catered for. In Italy, Mussolini's blackshirt formations (the MVSN) had adopted the wearing of dress daggers in the early 1920s, a feature which undoubtedly was not unnoticed by the NSDAP, and by Solingen companies looking for outlets to supply. Some of the Solingen companies had been successful in securing orders from the Italian Fascist state, not only in the supply of swords for the armed forces, but also in the limited production of some dress daggers for the Italian political formations. What Solingen needed, however, was a home-based market to cater for. It just needed something to encourage the situation.

In 1928, the NSDAP had sponsored the creation of a young persons' organization—the German Youth—for the families of the membership. It had paralleled in some ways the Boy Scouts Movement, although it differed in that it was politically motivated. Nevertheless, the healthy aspects of the outdoor, clean-living life in the Nordic culture, and the camaraderie of belonging had made the German Youth movement popular, and a valuable source of future NSDAP membership. Shortly after coming to power, the NSDAP ensured that the German Youth, now to be known as the *Hitler Jugend* ('Hitler Youth') would replace all other youth organizations throughout Germany. The political objective was obviously to eliminate all forms of opposition groupings, and to school the membership in the ideals that the Nazis needed to foster in order to increase their grip upon the nation. All other independent youth organizations, including the Boy Scout Movement, were banned. Membership of the Hitler Youth organization was to become compulsory. To identify members of the organization, uniforms and badges were to be worn, and therefore they had to be created. Part of that uniform was to be the *Fahrtenmesser*—the Hiking Knife. In reality, this knife was nothing more than a scouting- or camping-type knife, except that it was

Massed ranks of buglers from the Hitler Youth organization, overlooking the crowded Nuremburg Stadium during the 1936 Party Rally. The Hitler Youth Fahrtenmesser knife is seen in wear. The HJ knife was one of the first mass production orders made to Solingen by the National Socialists – a simple knife but one of such importance to the businesses of Solingen that the cutlery industry was deeply grateful for the commercial benefits that this order, and others like it, bestowed upon the businesses of the city. (The late A. S. Walker photo collection).

Minister Goering meeting one of the trade officials of a mining community. The miners' organization (the Bergbau) had, since Imperial times, accepted the right to wear a sword for dress occasions. This attribute, together with a dress uniform, was not as bizarre as might seem at first sight. Coal, and the importance it played in the economy of the Imperial empire – as well as during the Third Reich – was a valuable contribution to the national economy, and mining communities were afforded a great deal of respect both for the importance of their product, and the dangers they faced in order to provide it. The photographic study depicts one such mining official resplendent in his Imperial-style uniform complete with sword.

of a particular design and bore the Hitler Youth emblem.

The requirement that all eligible members of the Hitler Youth organization were obliged to purchase a Hitler Youth *Fahrtenmesser* to wear with their uniform was no doubt a welcome surprise to the businesses of Solingen. In 1934 the Solingen trade magazine *Die Klinge* ('The Blade') reported that trade orders for the production of 2,100,000 examples of the Hitler Youth knife had been placed as of July, 1934. It was a vast order, and would require over 37 tons of processed steel for the blades and scabbards alone; and additionally there were the hilts to make, the scales (the slabs that formed the grips of the hilt), the badges (made of copper, with red, white and black enamel work), the leather belt loops and button fastenings.

The promises made by Hitler and the NSDAP did have some real value to them. It was to be the same throughout the other German industries, and the orders for production placed with Solingen were but a reflection in microcosm of the new business that was to be generated throughout the nation. In Solingen,

An illustration taken from the Eickhorn kundendienst of 1938, showing the (then) current production pattern of dress sword for members of the Bergbau. The sword is a plain hilted version, decorated on the langet with the emblem symbolic of the mining organization – crossed hammers, the tools with which the miner laboriously chipped away the coal from its seam deep beneath the earth's surface.

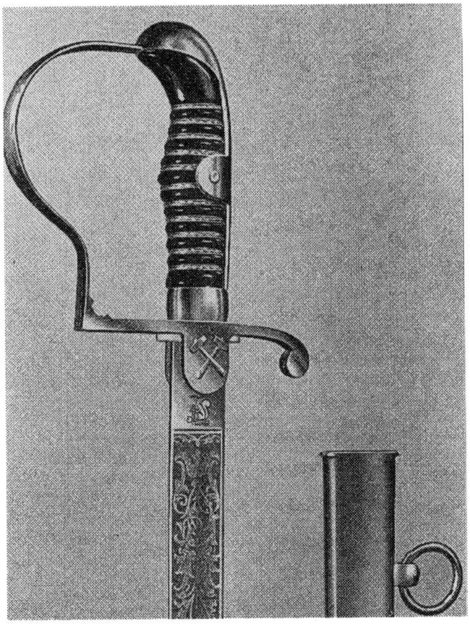

workers were being taken on to cope with this impressive order. Business was starting to move, finances were starting to flow. A new age of prosperity started to dawn, and it became evident that in the new order of the NSDAP state there existed other vast organizations who likewise might seek the adornment of dress daggers or swords. The NSDAP was encouraging a self-regenerating home economy that would keep the industries of the nation afloat; whatever personal misgivings the burghers of Solingen may have had about the Nazis and their radical policies, it was clear that Hitler believed in implementing the dignity of labour as a prerequisite to the dignity of the nation. The workers of Solingen had something to look forward to, and, it was believed, something to be grateful for. The new Führer would be recognized for the benefits he was offering.

The City of Solingen, in demonstrating its gratitude for the commercial benefits the NSDAP system had brought the finances of the city, marked the occasion by presenting Hitler with a unique sword, a stylistic pattern of broadsword, with a blade of Damascus steel, and gilded inscription denoting the occasion. This sword, known primarily from photographic documentation published at the time, is now known to have been captured as war booty and shipped to the United States at the end of World War Two. It is currently in a private collection in Texas.

The gesture of the presentation of a sword to Hitler was not a singular one – the City of Nuremburg, anxious

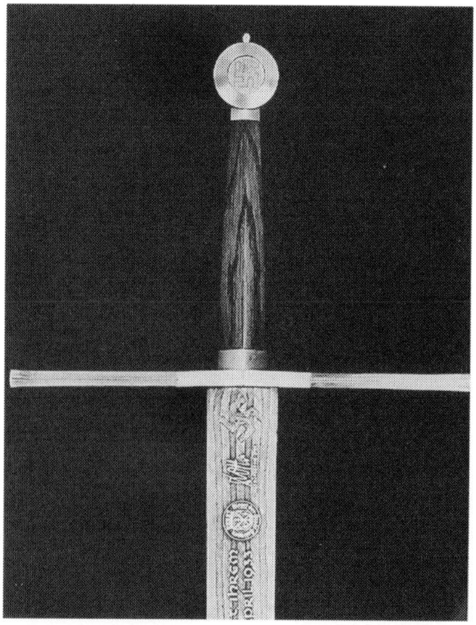

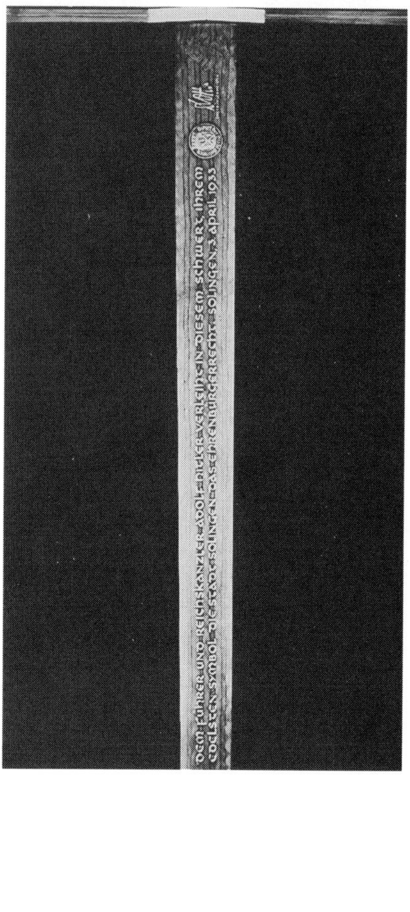

In April 1933, in appreciation of the new Führer's continued support to revive the Solingen steelware industry, the City of Solingen presented Adolf Hitler with a unique pattern sword, which was the product of several concerns who worked jointly together to create this magnificent gift.

Styled in the form of a medieval crusader's sword, this massive sword was contained in a solid oak display case which had been specially created by Otto Arnold and Friedrich Schaaf.

The hilt was comprised of a plain, oak grip, with a polished steel disc-shaped pommel bearing the swastika. The crossguard was lozenge shaped, and on the underside bore the mark of the Industry Trade School for Steelware Products of Solingen. The steel portions of the hilt were made of V2A Kruppstahl, to a design presented by Professor Woenne of the Solingen Trades School, and the metal work was executed in the Gottlieb Hammesfahr factory.

The blade was a magnificent example of the damascus smith's art, being in Maidenhair damascus pattern, and with the swastika emblem moulded into the damascus graining. The damascus work of the blade was created by the blade masters of Ernst Gämlich and Paul Voss. A gold-finished dedication adorned the obverse of the blade, denoting that the item was presented to Adolf Hitler by the City of Solingen on the occasion of the bestowing of the Freedom of the City upon the new leader. The reverse of the blade featured a nationalistic poem extolling the virtues of the Bergischland (the mountain region which surrounds Solingen). The decoration and etching of the blade was performed by Karl Broch.

The sole information concerning the existence of this sword had, until recent years, been known through the historical account recorded and published in the journal Die Klinge in February, 1936. In 1984, two American collectors succeeded in tracing the sword to its post-war owner who had kept it, and were successful in purchasing it. It was displayed at an American Militaria Show, an awe-inspiring example of the Solingen cutler's art—and testament to the fact that rarities of this magnitude can still be located. (Jeffrey J. Roth).

to extol the virtues of the leader, bestowed the Freedom of the City upon him, and marked the occasion also by the presentation of a sword specially created for the occasion—this example being in the style of a sword once possessed by Charlemagne. Photographs of this sword were published in the trade press at the time, and the *Illustrierter Beobachter* (the Nazi-sponsored newspaper) published a photograph of Hitler receiving the sword from the Lord Mayor of Nuremburg. The present location of this sword is unknown, but it is possible that it survived the war, and awaits rediscovery.

Individual arms manufacturing companies also took advantage of the opportunity to honour the Führer with gifts, and constructed knives and daggers of elaborate form for presentation to Hitler as tokens of their esteem and gratitude. It was a time of rising prosperity. The initial order of vast quantities of knives for the Hitler Youth organization had also been complemented by orders from other organizations—the brownshirted SA, and the SS organization, had also presented hefty orders for the production of bladed weapons. Other organizations, which had not existed in any major capacity before the formation of the Third Reich, were soon to become increasingly more apparent, as the total restructuring of NSDAP society brought them under the wing—and added to the uniformed echelons of the Fatherland. The spread of economic stability in Solingen reflected a general trend in national economics. Businesses were starting to function efficiently, people had money to spend, and consumer

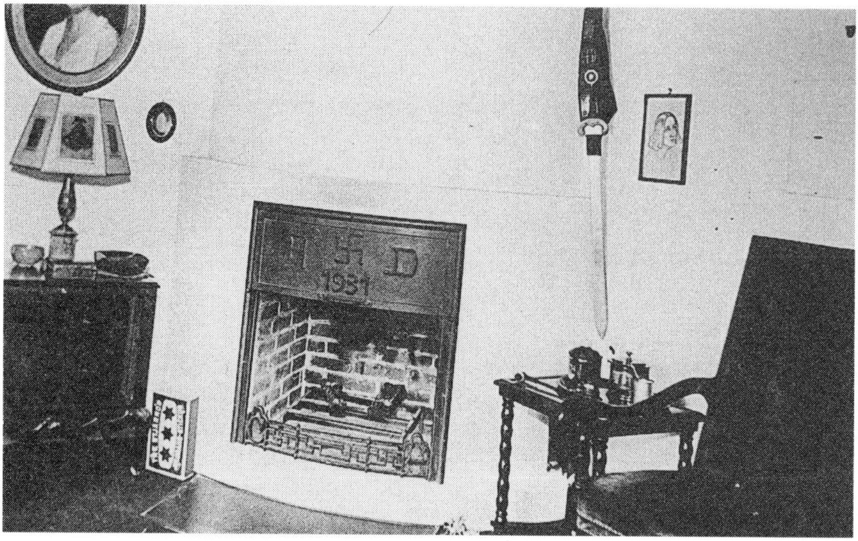

Above *A photograph taken inside one of Goering's country homes, showing by the wall decorations Goering's penchant for swords. Note the swastika on the belt. The sword pattern is based on a classical medieval German style.* (Göring collection, Library of Congress).

Left *Detail view of a photograph taken inside Goering's hunting lodge Carinhall. A stylistic sword of Crusader pattern, but of modern (i.e. 1930s) construction, displayed suspended from an oak beam. There is a swastika in the pommel. The production patterns of the Luftwaffe Fliers' Sword are reminiscent of this display iitem, and may well have been based upon it.*

goods were being turned out to satisfy those needs. A rising economy is, potentially, a self-regenerating system. With money to spend, more goods have to be supplied, and with more goods being sold more finance changes hands. The wealth of Solingen was not founded solely upon the sword and the dagger. There were countless other steel products that were turned

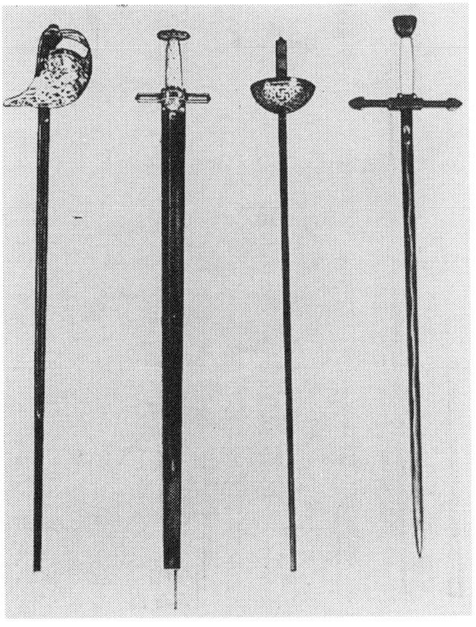

A selection of swords that were featured as part of a display assembled in Paris, in 1938, promoting the craftsmanship of Solingen. Left to right: an unidentified basket hilt sabre; a sword styled upon a medieval executioner's sword, and created by Professor Woenne of the Solingen Industrial Trade School – this sword may be seen today, on display, in the Deutsche Klingenmuseum, Solingen; a rapier pattern sword, with swastika prominently featured in the basket design of the guard, present location unknown; a stylish sword manufactured as a display item by the Eickhorn company, and which also featured prominently in the company's 75th anniversary book. The sword was last seen in the mid-1970s when the Eickhorn company exhibited some of their products at a German trade fair. (Die Klinge 1938).

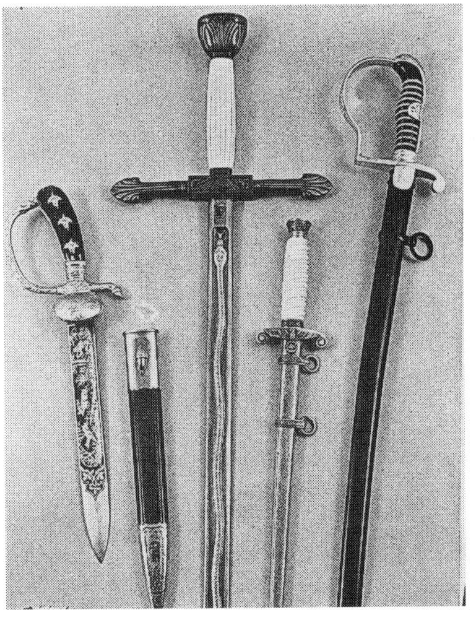

A photograph from the Eickhorn publication Leisten und Dienen, 1940, depicting some of the company's products. Note the sword in the centre of the display, which was the one exhibited at the Paris exhibition (see previous photo).

out by the workers of Solingen: shears, needles, razors, manicure sets, cutlery, tools, metal fittings of every description. It was not only Solingen that benefitted from new wealth of the consumer market. Other industrial towns throughout the Ruhr area, such as Ludenscheid, Wuppertal, Dortmund, all of which were producers of goods for industry, commerce and the private purchaser, experienced the demand for products, and more products. All this, however, was only the tip of the iceberg. The German armed forces (in 1934 restricted to a defensive token army and navy), were soon to be given the revitalization treatment. And when that day came, Germany would have finally shaken off the 'shackles of Versailles' to stand once more, aggressively apart from the remaining, downtrodden, nations of Europe. The metalware industries would soon be astonished to discover that they would have a full-time job just coping with the existing demands,

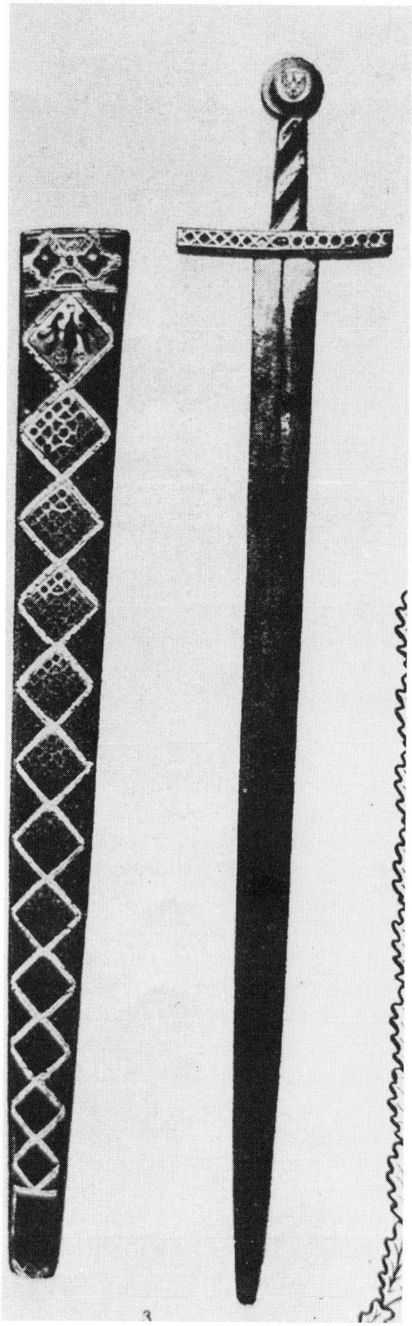

Left *Detail of a photograph published in the February 1936 issue of Die Klinge, showing a medieval pattern sword. An article published in the magazine described this item as the First Reich Sword, relating to the fact that an identical example had been created during the twelfth century as an official sword of the nation. This duplicate example was created to commemorate that first national sword, and was presented to Adolf Hitler by the City of Nuremburg. The article describing the sword noted that the scabbard featured the decoration of 4,000 genuine oriental pearls, and 18,000 gold pins. The last recorded documentation of the sword was pre-war, when it was on display in the State Museum at Aachen. Present location unknown.*

Below *SA Gruppenführer, and Lord Mayor of Nuremburg, Willy Liebel, presenting the Reich Sword to Adolf Hitler.* Illustrieter Beobachter, special edition, 1938).

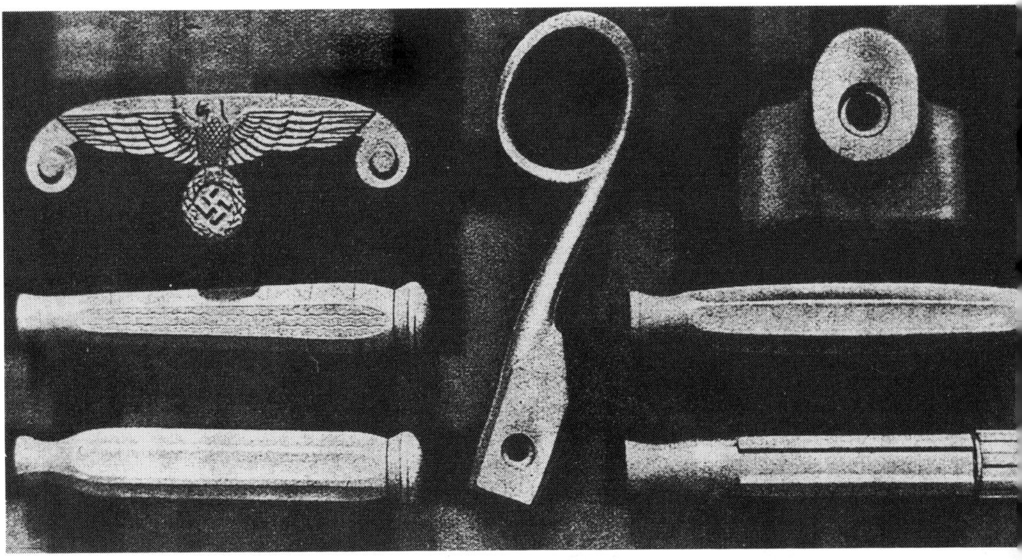

The effect of modernization on the Solingen industries. This photograph, published in a 1936 issue of Die Klinge, was part of a feature about the widespread introduction of injection-moulding techniques into the Solingen trades, and showing some of the items which were currently being produced by this method. The items depicted are handles for safety razors, scissors parts, and – of interest to the dagger collector – crossguards for Army daggers.

The Army dagger was not the only edged weapon to have its production modernized in this manner. It is obvious from the article that some producing concerns concentrated solely on injection-moulding processes, and mass produced parts for sale to other manufacturers. It can be deduced that, with a volume production item such as Army or Luftwaffe daggers, some parts were probably created by contract suppliers, and then sold to the arms companies who assembled them on the blades which they fabricated. Other companies are known to have specialized in the injection-moulding of complex items such as the hilts for dress bayonets – which if constructed in the old style manner (milling out of a solid block of metal) were both time consuming and very costly.

let alone the requirements of even further expansion.

An advertisement published in *Die Klinge* underlined this potential situation in a simple, yet dramatic way. It was becoming necessary to start to *import* raw materials. One company even published advertisements to show that they were able to supply steel from Sweden. The massive foundries of companies such as Bochumer Verein, the major suppliers to the Ruhr steel industries, were unable to meet the demand. From being a nation unable to export goods, Germany, by the mid-1930s, was obliged to import raw stock just to keep the level of domestic production on line. Whatever history might have to say about the evil of the Hitler regime, it will have to acknowledge that it pulled an inspiring commercial mountain out of an economic chasm. The National Socialist revolution could be seen to be working.

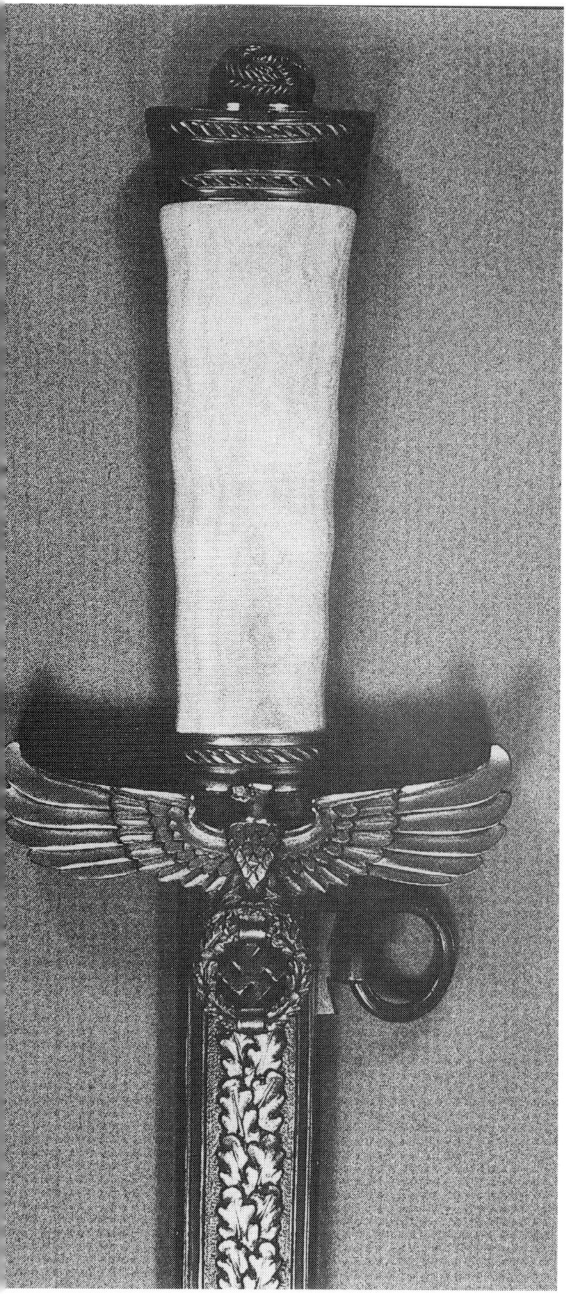

In 1938, the leaders of the industrial community in Solingen afforded an honour to another of the remarkable personalities of the Third Reich – Hermann Goering, when the flamboyant Reichsmarschall was presented with a special sword, which had been commissioned from the famous damascus blade smith Paul Müller. At about the same time the industrial leaders of Solingen commissioned the sword from Müller, they also commissioned a dagger, which was also to be presented to Goering. The company appointed to undertake this work was the concern of Alex Coppel, who upon instruction created two examples of the dagger – one for presentation purposes, and the other to be retained as a pattern/exhibit piece in the company works' showroom.

The dagger pattern was of unique form, having a smooth white, undulating ivory grip and gilded fittings, the crossguard bearing a modernistic version of the national eagle and swastika. The scabbard design was decorated with a continuing line of overlapping oakleaves.

The presentation pattern of the dagger was most certainly created, and duly presented to Goering. The second example was retained at the Alex Coppel factory, and was there when members of the Allied Occupation Commission visited the factory in 1945. On seeing the dagger, they issued instructions that it was to be destroyed. The dagger subsequently was defaced by having the blade broken in two. In 1964, the American collector/researcher, Major James P. Atwood (later Lt.-Col.) visited the Alex Coppel company, and having been shown the dagger – still complete with broken blade – succeeded in purchasing it from the (then) owner of the company. Major Atwood then contacted Paul Müller, who was still living in the Solingen area, and had the master blade smith recreate a new damascus blade for the dagger. The restored dagger subsequently found its way to the United States, and at the last account (1978) was believed to be in a private collection in the San Francisco area. (Lt.-Col. (retd.) T. M. Johnson).

8 Party and State

Political and governmental organizations: SA, SS, NSKK, NPEA, Hitler Youth, Diplomatic and Governmental Services

Where a Hitler leads, a Hohenzollern can follow.
Prince August Wilhelm, June 1931.
(Son of Kaiser Wilhelm II)

The creation of the National Socialist State was embodied in the re-awakening of a feeling of *Weltanschauung*—a 'philosophy of life', which presented itself in a spirited contrast to the disarray that had been evident during the period of the Weimar Republic. The new Germany of the NSDAP was seen, and felt, to have a vibrancy that permeated everywhere, from the highest offices of the land down through all the echelons of society to the most humble peasant. It can perhaps be best described in the German expression *Volksgemeinschaft*, meaning in definition an enthusiastic hybrid between tribal clanship and fervent national pride, a community of the people. The idea appealed enormously to the millions of Germans who had gone through the hardship of defeat, followed by economic depression; and who suddenly saw the promise of a restoration of national dignity; of meaningful employment; of a nationalized institution that offered to restore and care for its every subject. It was to be the 'cradle to grave society' quoted by Robert Ley, Leader of the DAF (*Deutsche Arbeits Front*—German Labour Front).

There were, of course, exceptions who were to be excluded from these impressive benefits. The National Socialists had made those decisions early on in the 1920s; their policies decreed that Marxists, Communists, alien nationals, and Jewish persons were not to be invited to share in the new Germany that the NSDAP desired to build. In the case of the Jewish community, the initial directives determined that they were to be deprived of public office, prevented from maintaining business interests, property, wealth, and ultimately their Statehood. They were to be classified as aliens, unwelcome in the Third Reich.

The blatancy of this discrimination passed by the majority of Germans, who doubtless considered it unjust, but were far too preoccupied with their own recent misfortunes to pay any great heed to the problems of the Jews. It was something which it was felt, probably, would resolve itself in

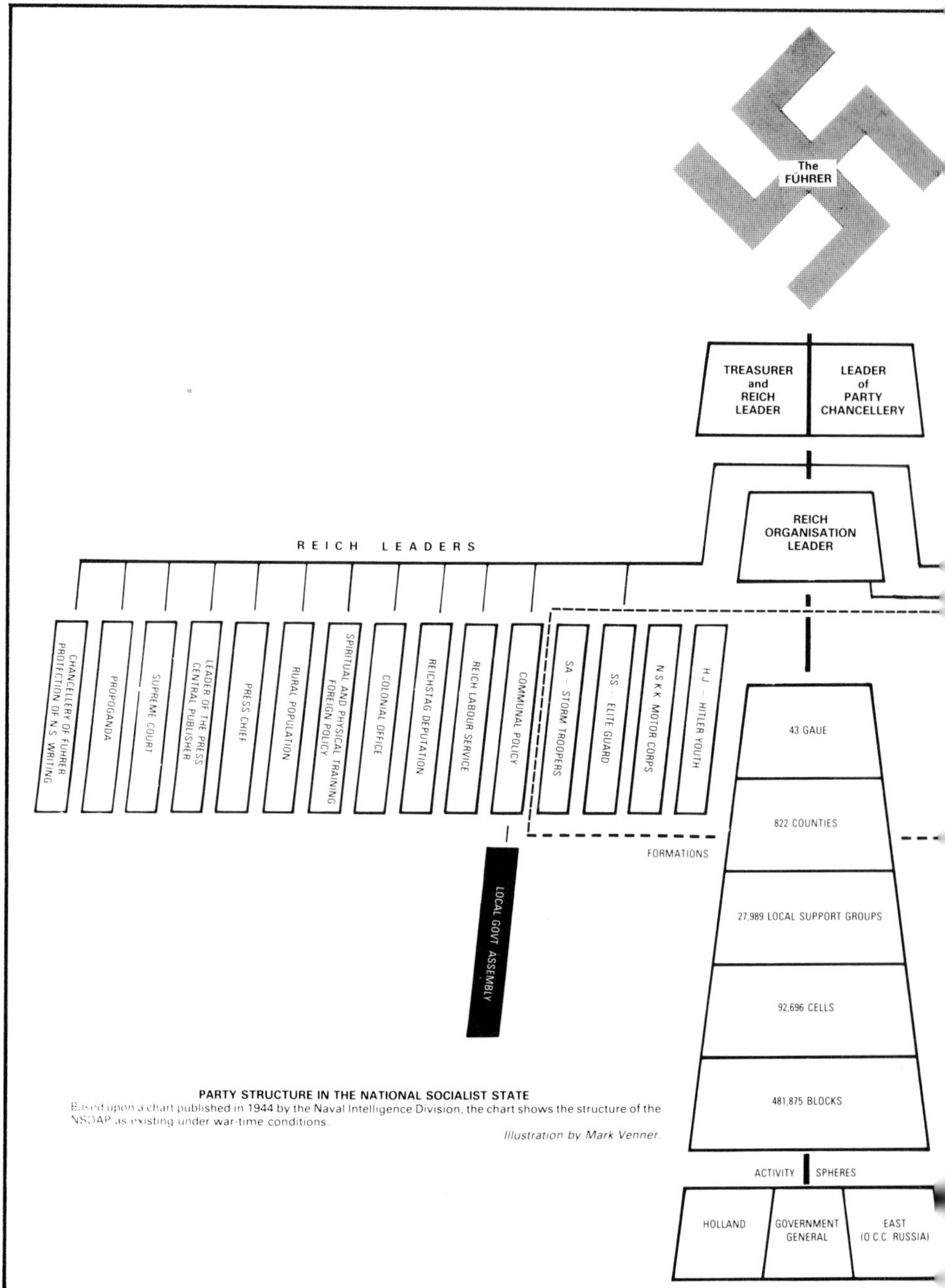

PARTY STRUCTURE IN THE NATIONAL SOCIALIST STATE
Based upon a chart published in 1944 by the Naval Intelligence Division, the chart shows the structure of the NSDAP as existing under war-time conditions.
Illustration by Mark Venner.

Chart showing the sub-division of the National Socialist State and the respective ministries, departments, and Gaue regions.

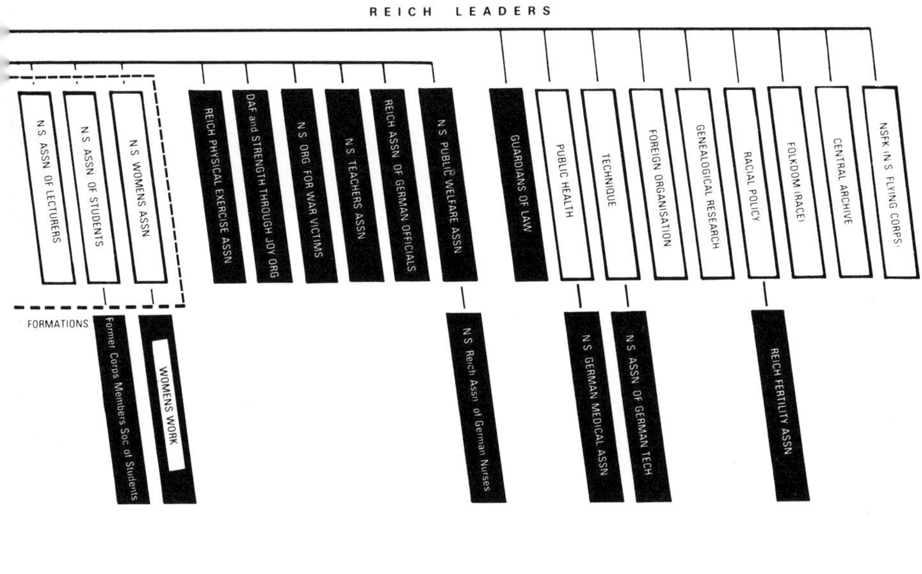

good time. It would be difficult to conceive that the honest working German had any real conception that the discrimination against a minority of nationals would escalate into an intensive programme of genocide. Had the forthcoming awfulness and inhumanity of the *Konzentrationslager* been evident to the German in the street, it is debatable as to whether or not the new Reich government would have survived more than a few months. The hostility that the NSDAP whipped up against ethnic minorities and political opponents was something that would, it was probably believed, tone down once the Nazis realized the error of their ways and the response of world opinion. The internal economic and social problems of Germany were more than enough to keep the new political system fully occupied.

The immediate political problems that the NSDAP had to overcome were those of the national economy, and the firm entrenchment of the NSDAP system in the amalgam of Party and State. The essence of that combination was personified in Adolf Hitler and the *Führerprinzip* (leadership principle). In the words of Hans Frank, during his tenure as Reich Commissar for Co-ordination of the States: 'Our constitution is the will of the Führer!'*

The organizational structure of the Nazi Party functioned in two basic spheres—the Reich level, which determined all the national policies; and the Gaue level, which implemented those policies on a regional basis.

* Quoted in 'The National Socialist State—Fundamental Principles', *Germany*, Vol. II, Naval Intelligence Division, March, 1944.

The supreme deity above it all was Hitler, and to whom was answerable the office of the Party Chancellery (whose Chief Administrator was Rudolf Hess, until he departed on an abortive peace mission to England early in the Second World War, later being replaced by Martin Bormann); supported by the Treasury (leader Franz Xaver Schwartz). Beneath these overlords the Party structure divided into two main spheres; the office of the Reich Organization Leader which dealt with NSDAP affairs from the Party top directly down into the Gaue (approximating the territories of the old German states), and thence into Kreis (districts), Orstgruppe (local groups), Zellen (cells—neighbourhoods), and Blockwart (streets or small communities); while on a parallel level with the office of the Reich Organization Leader existed the departments of the Reich Leadership, which was comprised of the various governmental ministries (see chart). Six of these agencies sponsored uniformed formations whose mode of attire is pertinent to this chapter, for they carried dress weapons; they were the Sturmabteilung (SA), Schutzstaffel (SS), Nationalsozialistische Kraftfahrkorps (NSKK), the NAPOLA (NPEA) organization, Diplomatic and Government Service, and the Hitler Jugend (HJ).

Some of the other organizations in the Party structure carried bladed dress weapons (the NSDAP leaders were authorized to carry a pistol), but because of their nature and status in the overall structure of the Reich, they are discussed elsewhere in this work in the sections more pertinent to their standing.

Right *The second example of the Goering Industrial Dagger manufactured by Alex Coppel.* (Lt.-Col. (retd.) Thomas M. Johnson).

Below *The Eastern Peoples' Leader's Dagger, First Model. Full length view of the obverse of the dagger, and detail view of the reverse of the hilt. The obverse langet bears the emblem of three lions, and the reverse langet is decorated in enamel in the national colours of Estonia. It is believed that these daggers were introduced for adoption by German Political Leaders throughout the Occupied Territories, and differed only from each other in the form of the arms on the crossguard and the national colours. A revised pattern having the eagle and swastika emblem was designed for production in 1941, but it is believed that this Second Model never actually went into production.*

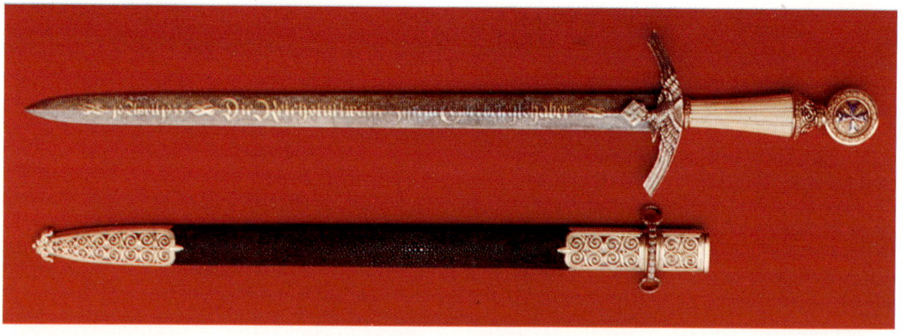

Left *The magnificent sword presented to Hermann Goering by the Luftwaffe, on the occasion of his marriage, in April 1935. The sword is a unique example of the bladesmith's art: the pommel is solid gold, with highly detailed enamel work depicting the Pour le Mérite award which Goering won in the First World War, and the family coat of arms on the reverse side. The grip is made of solid ivory, with gold bars segmenting it longitudinally.*

The damascus blade was produced at the Eickhorn factory under the guidance of the damascus smith Paul Dingler, and bears a raised and gilded inscription denoting that the sword was the gift of the Luftwaffe to Goering – the Luftwaffe came into legal existence concurrent with the occasion of Goering's marriage. The scabbard body is made of blue sharkskin, with gilded fittings. (Private collection).

Above right *Left to right: The dress bayonet of the Hitler Youth Wachgefolgschaft; an etched-blade presentation sidearm for the Fire Department; a dress bayonet of the RLB Organization (Reichs Luftschutz Bund – Reich Air Defence League). The bayonet is in reality a standard pattern dress bayonet with the RLB emblem mounted on the obverse grip.* (Dr. Julian Milestone collection.)

Right *Publicity advertisement for the company of E. u. F. Hörster, promoting the Hitler Youth Fahrtenmesser knife.* (Die Klinge, 1938.)

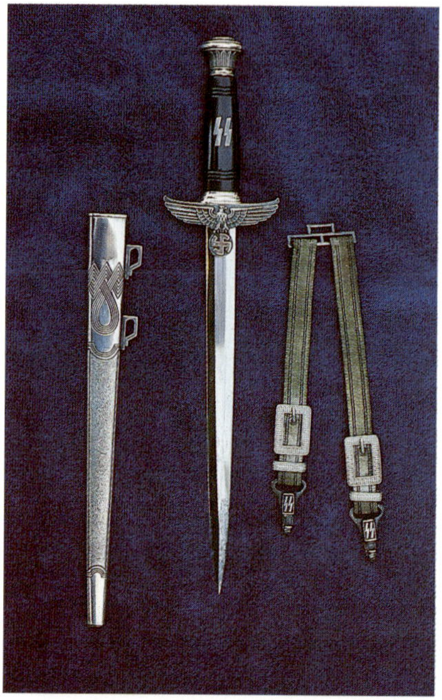

Left *Unique prototype SS dagger manufactured by the Alcoso company. The item is believed to be unique, as no other example of this pattern has been identified. Details regarding this item, and the circumstances which brought it to light, are discussed on page 76.* (John E. Pepera collection.)

Below *A rare example of the Hitler Youth Leader's dagger, complete in its original presentation red leatherette case.*

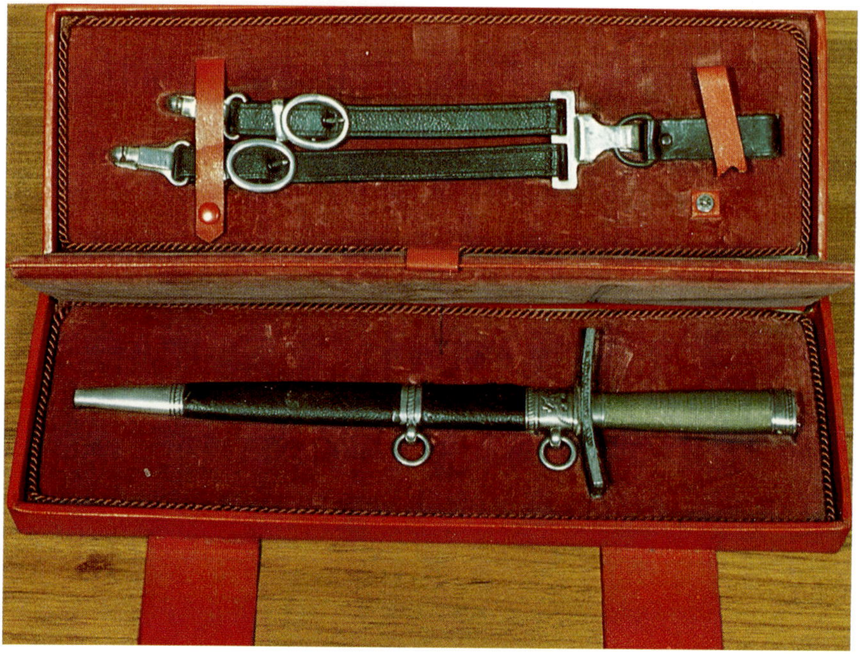

The usage of a boy scout type camping knife by youth organizations was, perhaps, the most common example of a knife carried visibly on a uniform. Sheath knives were commonly produced by Solingen manufacturers, and when the Nazi-sponsored youth organization came into existence in the late 1920s, the membership undoubtedly equipped themselves with the regular types of camping and sheath knives that were popularly carried by other organizations.

Although the knife manufacturing industry was going through a depressed time (the creation of new designs was a rare event), manufacturers throughout the Solingen region had in stock quite a considerable quantity of bayonets and fighting knives left over from First World War production. There was not much in the way of an outlet for these items in the late 1920s. Millions of examples had been consigned to scrap and the metal re-used where possible for other products. The cost of dismantling a completely formed knife, however, was often greater than the original cost of first producing it, and many manufacturers could see little wisdom in throwing good money after bad. The only practical option, in many cases, was to re-use the same product in another capacity. Knives and bayonets which had been destined to serve as trench fighting weapons were subsequently resold as camping knives, souvenir items, utility tools, or in whatever capacity made them acceptable to a customer. The cutlery industry of Solingen had, in effect, been reduced to selling its scrap material.

The German Youth of the NSDAP organization became just another grouping to whom some of the surplus stock of the Great War was recycled. At some time before the creation of the National Socialist State, however, some inspired individual in either the Solingen industries, or in the Nazi hierarchy, conceived an idea which was to have far-reaching effects. The idea was a knife especially for the Hitler Youth organization, as the German Youth Organization of the NSDAP had become known. A plentiful supply of complete, or partially constructed, knives already existed. All that was required was that they be made a little more distinctive. The answer was to decorate them with emblems indicative of the organization. Fighting knives (*Nahkampfmesser*), which had never been despatched to the front, were unearthed from storerooms and cleaned and polished. The hilts and blades were made of good steel, and with a little innovation and skill could be turned into something nicer than a weapon for killing—they could be transformed. The pommels and blades could be etched and decorated, and oak leaves and swastikas could be featured on the design. The Hitler Youth was a growing market and there was capital to be made out of it, and so with a bit of ingenuity a quantity of potentially unsaleable stock was turned into an attractive item—a knife for the Hitler Youth. The idea caught on, and it was a concept which would have far-reaching effects.

One of the characteristics of the Nazi creed, which made it and the whole movement at large, stand out from the drabness of the crowd, was the usage of the uniform and the flags. The adoption of the swastika emblem in the early 1920s and its prominent display on flags and armbands did more than afford an instantly recognizable emblem for one faction of the political scene, it provided a rallying point. It was an instantly indentifiable emblem, strong in colouring and almost hypnotic in form, that was ideal to challenge the Red Star sported by the other militant political party, the communists. As a form of corporate identity, the swastika made an impact that still causes an effect today, almost half a century after the demise of the Third Reich. In the late 1920s it was still a relatively new emblem on the political scene but, combined with the appearance of the men in brownshirt uniforms, with their polished boots and shining buttons and buckles, clearly gave an impression of an authoritative force of apparently military standing. That these uniformed ranks should complete their military appearance by the adoption of a sword or dagger was, perhaps, not an altogether unexpected development.

The conversion of First World War trench daggers for the Hitler Youth was a commercial success, and it was not long before other knife manufacturers, keen to exploit the commercial end of this market, started to enhance a lot of their products with the swastika emblem. Commercially available sheath knives with small brass or silver swastika badges inset in the grip were soon being offered for sale. There was no limitation on the purchase of these items, anyone who wanted to buy one could do so; they had no real organizational significance other than that they featured a political emblem.* That freedom to use the emblem for commercial gain was to be short lived, however.

Shortly after the NSDAP swept to power in the 1933 elections, the new government introduced legislation concerning the new national emblem (i.e. the swastika, and the eagle and swastika) determining that it would, henceforth only be produced by official permission on items of direct relationship to the State, or State-sponsored organizations. Overnight it became illegal to manufacture goods bearing the swastika without permission; and concurrently—as far as the manufacture of knives was concerned—regulations were hastily implemented to effect some control, over such items as were already in production and destined for the use of Nazi-affiliated organizations. The first of these to come under scrutiny were those of the Hitler Youth organization.

The modification and production of remaindered stock knives into camping knives for the Hitler Youth was promptly legislated. The production or conversion of non-official variations was halted, but in its place came an approved design for a new knife pattern which manufacturers

* That the swastika has a pedigree dating from ancient times is not disputed, and even today it retains a religious significance in India. It has variously been used in modern times (non-politically) as a good luck charm, company logo, and even as the emblem of an American motor car manufacturer. To the European observer, however, it is almost impossible to view the emblem as anything other than the device indicative of the Nazi, so prolific was their use of it, so emotive are the memories it has fostered.

could produce, if they were licensed to do so. The design was simpler and lighter than the old-style converted *Nahkampfmesser*. It meant financial investment and re-tooling to produce the knife exactly according to the specification, but the approved knife pattern was declared to be a mandatory part of the full uniform of the Hitler Youth member, and therefore purchase of the item was virtually compulsory. The fortunes of Solingen were about to take a sharp turn upwards when the first orders for the new Hitler Youth knife were received by the factories.

In late 1933 the High Command of the SA decreed the institution of a dagger pattern for members of the SA and SS organizations. As strictly political organizations, the SA and SS had no real practical use for a knife, but the adoption of one was viewed as a fitting complement to the uniform. A publicity illustration published in the cutlery trade press at the time showed a squad of SA men, with their daggers prominently displayed suspended from their belts, with the emotive slogan: 'The SA Dagger, the Symbol of the Fighting Spirit!' This then was the dual purpose in the orders for political knives with the factories of Solingen; on the one hand the dress dagger was being used to afford a status, as an emblem of authority, and of comradeship; and on the other it fulfilled the role of creating new business for a depressed section of industry. Where the SA and the SS were to lead, other organizations were soon encouraged to follow, and the cutlers of Solingen were to witness a new era of prosperity.

SA

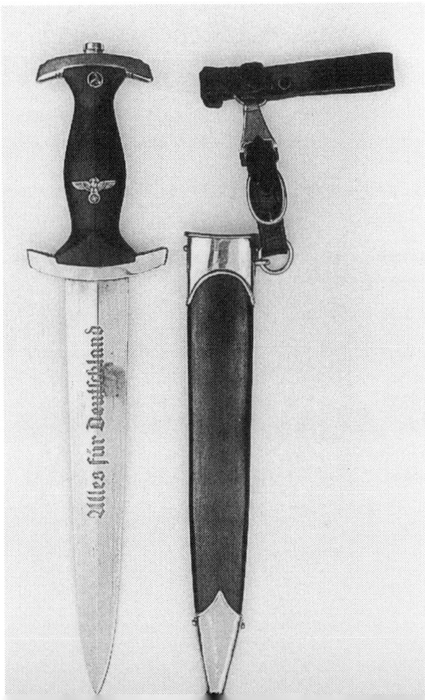

SA Service Dagger, Model 1933. The dagger pattern is based on a medieval pattern (the 'Holbein') which was popular in South Germany and Switzerland in the fifteenth century, and follows the original style very closely, although it is modified in keeping with the National Socialist period. The hilt is made of dark brown wood, with nickel plated crossguards. The SA runic insignia is set in the top of the hilt, and the national eagle and swastika emblem midway down. The blade is broad, straight and double-edged (it does not have sharpened edges). On the obverse of the blade the SA motto is etched: 'Alles für Deutschland' – Everything for Germany.

The scabbard is made of steel, enamelled or anodized a dark brown colour, and with nickel plated fittings.

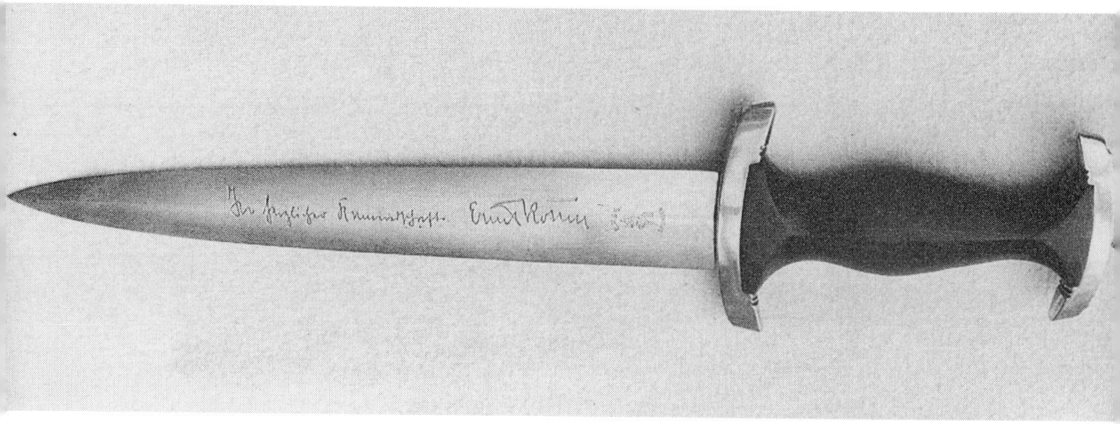

Above *In February 1934 the (then) Commander-in-Chief of the SA and SS, Stabchef Ernst Röhm, instituted an Honour Dagger for selected members of the SA and SS. This 'Honour' was in the form of an inscription which was to be placed on the reverse of the SA and SS Service Dagger blade. The wording of the inscription, which was in facsimile of Röhm's handwriting, stated: 'In herzlicher freundschaft Ernst Röhm'–In heartfelt friendship Ernst Röhm.*

In the summer of 1934, following internal political events, Ernst Röhm was arrested and executed on charges of treason, together with several thousand other Nazi officials. Orders were given that members of the SA and SS possessing daggers with the Röhm inscription were to have the inscriptions removed forthwith. As a result of this directive, examples possessing a complete and unaltered Röhm dedication are rather rare.

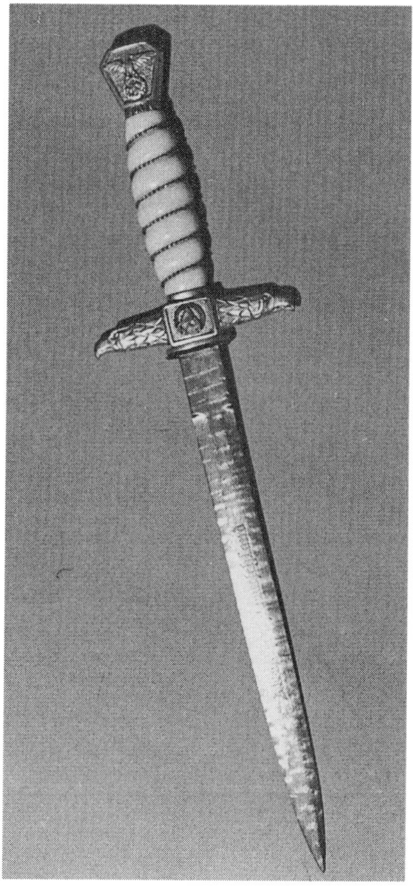

Right *A highly unusual SA presentation dagger, details of which were first published in 1965 in The Daggers and Edged Weapons of Hitler's Germany by Lt.-Col. James P. Atwood. The only information offered by Lt.-Col. Atwood about this pattern is that there were about six recipients of the piece. To date there are three known examples identified in collections, but no further information regarding the actual award or the recipients.* (Bob McCarthy collection).

Below *SA Dagger Model 1933, with ornated crossguards engraved in the form of an oakleaf design. An Honour Dagger of similar styling had been authorized by the new (after Röhm) SA chief, Viktor Lutze. This new dagger had crossguards which were cast in the form of decorative oak leaves. This illustrated item is a privately-made piece, with the engraved decoration clearly based upon the official pattern; it also has a dedication inscription etched on the blade.* (Dr Julian Milestone collection).

Right *In 1937, an élite formation of the SA, the Standarte Feldherrnhalle was authorized a new pattern of dress dagger for its leaders. This new style, which broke away from the traditional appearance of the Model 1933 Service Dagger, was constructed of aluminium, and finished in a reddish-gold wash. The grip was formed in the style of the Model 1933 dagger, and was made of wood on the early production examples, and out of bakelite on the later production. Very few details governing the 'Feldherrnhalle' dagger are known, other than that it was exclusively manufactured by the Eickhorn company, and the total production run is thought not to have exceeded 100 examples.*

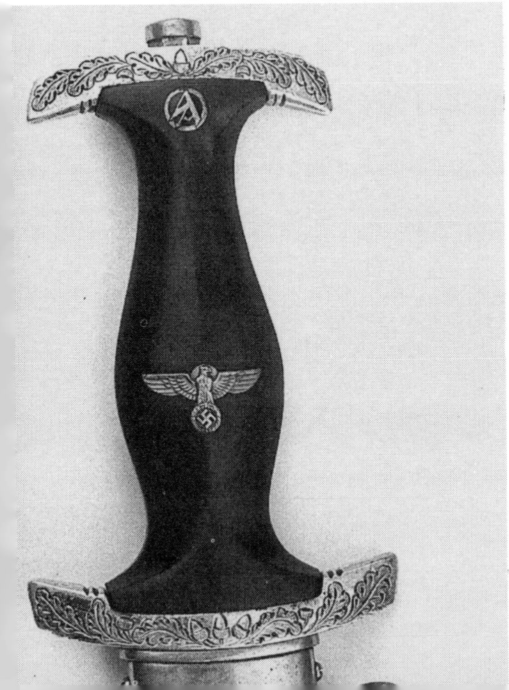

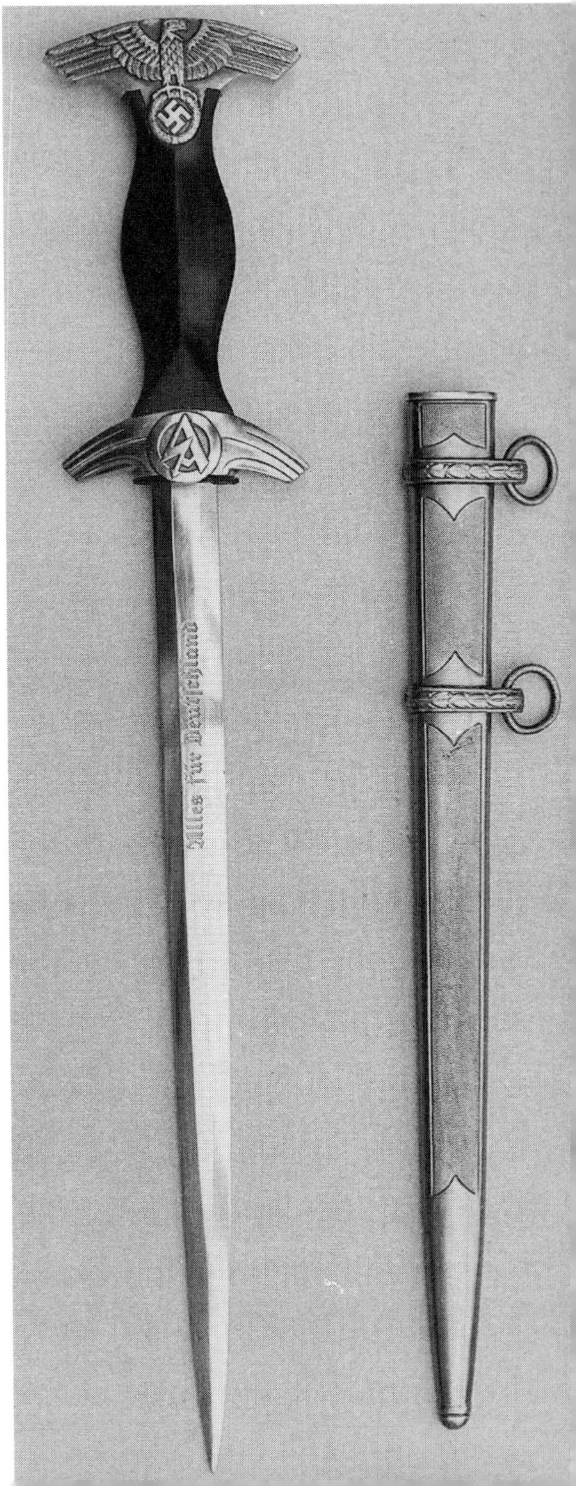

SS

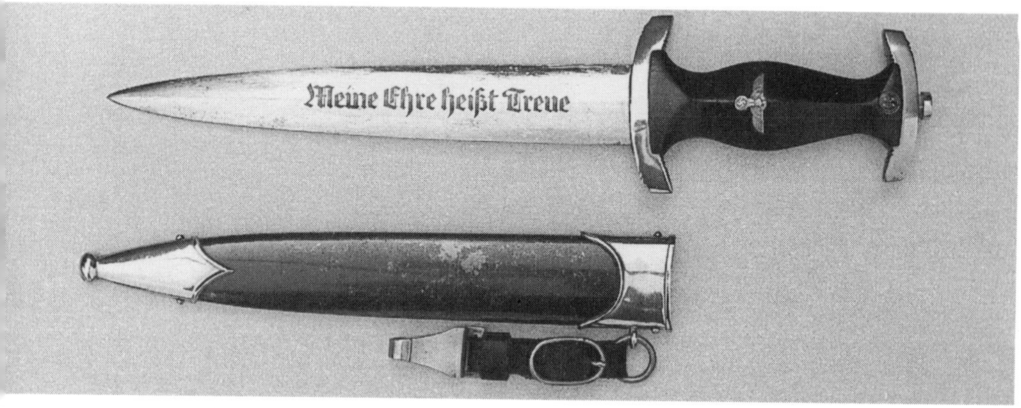

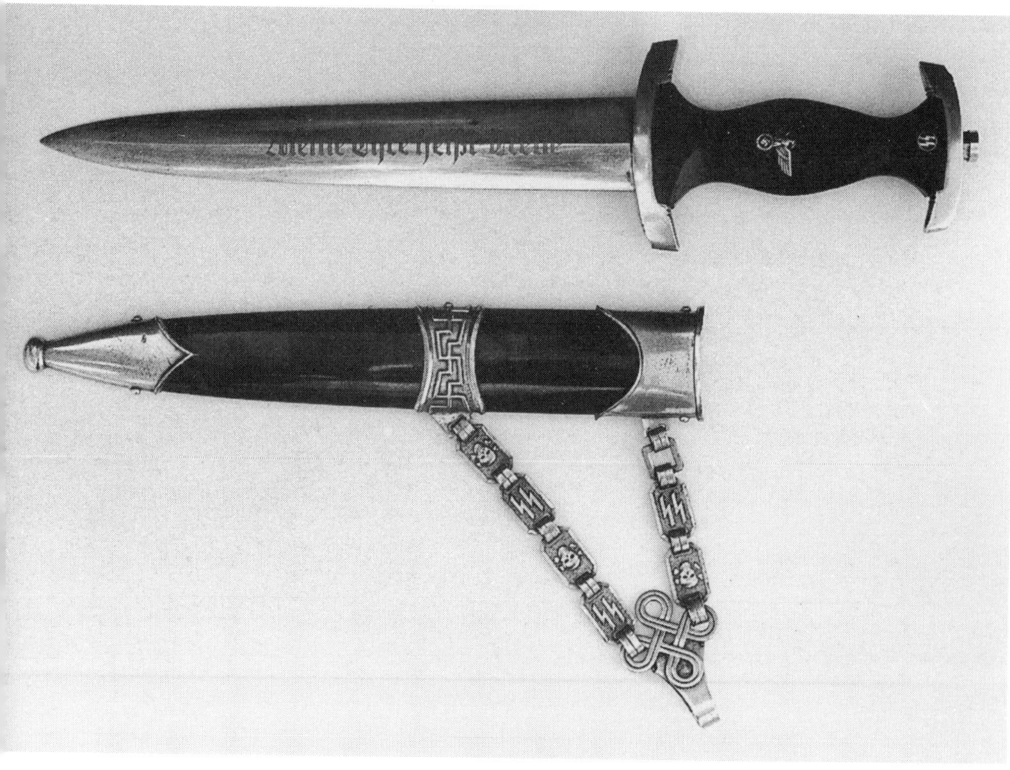

Left *In 1933, at the introduction of the SA dagger, a similar pattern was concurrently introduced for members of the SS. The dagger followed the same 'Holbein' style as used by the SA, but differed in that the grip was made of black wood, inset with the SS runic insignia at the top; the blade motto was 'Meine Ehre heißt Treue' – My Honour is named Loyalty, and the scabbard was finished in black.*

Below left *In 1936, a new pattern of dagger was authorized for long-serving and senior members of the SS, the Model 1936. It utilized the same basic Model 1933 blade and scabbard, but the scabbard had an extra refinement – a double chain suspension. The links of the chain alternately show a Death's Head device (the emblem of the SS), and the SS runic insignia. The centre scabbard band was decorated with a design of continuing swastikas.* (Barry Brown collection).

Below *SS Honour Dagger, Model 1934. The distinguishing features of the Honour Dagger are that the crossguards (which are made out of German Silver instead of the usual nickel-plated brass) are decorated in relief with a design of oak leaves. The scabbard fittings are also decorated with a panelled outline.*

The example shown also features a damascus steel blade, with the SS motto shown in raised and gilded letters, with an oak leaf pattern at the terminal ends. (Barry Brown collection).

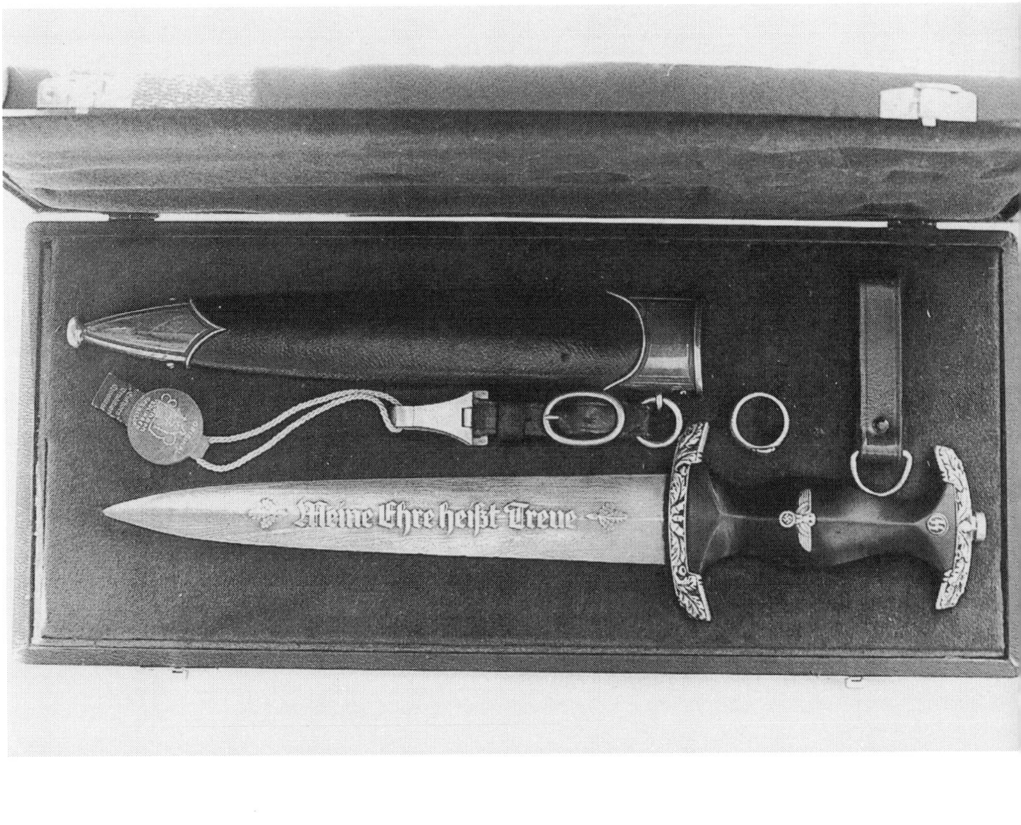

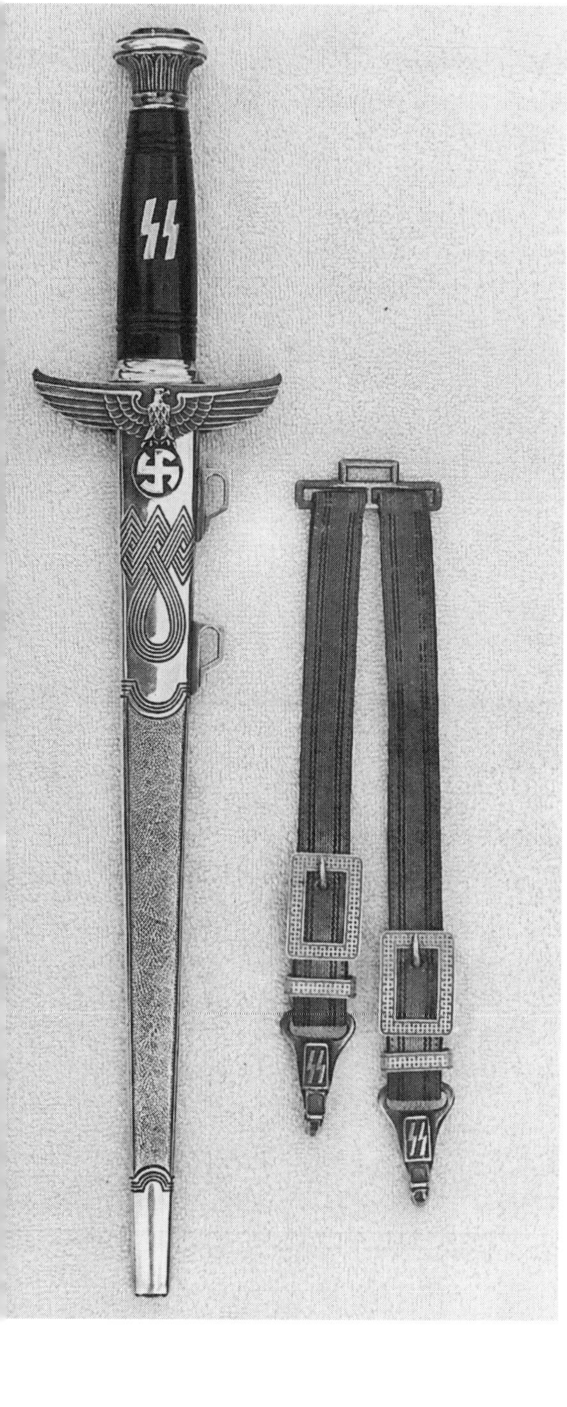

Left *A mystery SS dagger. This unusual item, so far the sole known example of its kind, was first recorded in a 1975 publication, after the dagger appeared at an American Gun Show – brought in by a collector who had received it from a neighbour. Since then the item has changed hands several times, and the present owner, Mr John Pepera of Ohio, supplied the author with this photograph and several others. The dagger bears the trademark of Alcoso, Solingen, and as far as can be ascertained, the item appears to be a prototype pattern which was never adopted by the SS. Research has also shown that several companies and individuals submitted dagger designs to the SS authority as proposed designs, but few of them ever progressed from being artwork designs to reach the state of a physical example.*

In the pursuit of further information, Mr Pepera succeeded in tracing the family of the original owner of the dagger at the time it entered the USA, and they have provided a sworn affidavit to Mr Pepera to the effect that they recall seeing and handling the dagger when it was in the family's possession in 1946. With this documentation now available, inquisitive researchers can now reasonably satisfy themselves that this dagger, whatever it really is, is at least an authentic, pre-1945 German product. It is presented here as an example of one of the unique, one-of-a-kind war souvenirs, which may still be discovered by collectors today. (John E. Pepera collection).

Right *A standard pattern Service bayonet, bearing an inscription by the original owner, denoting service in the crack SS 'Adolf Hitler' Division. The bayonet itself is a standard pattern, but the engraving on the blade was done by the original owner, who probably kept the bayonet separate from his service issue equipment.* (Lt.-Col. (retd.) J. R. Angolia).

NSKK

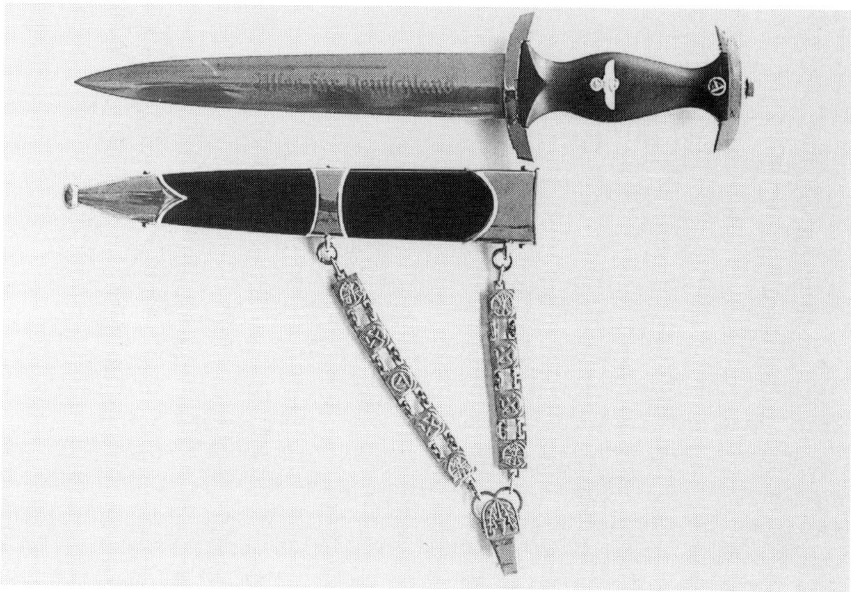

Left *Model 1936 Service Dagger of the NSKK. The NSKK organization functioned to supply the Party with a fleet of motor transport, and to supply drivers, mechanics, and traffic control officials. In 1936 members of the NSKK adopted the wear of the SA dagger Model 1933 to complement their uniforms. The dagger was identical to the SA pattern, differing only in that it was sheathed in a black-finished scabbard. At the same time of adoption of the dagger pattern, Leader Officers in the NSKK were authorized their own distinctive pattern of dagger, which yet again was in the style of the Model 1933 SA dagger, but having a double chain suspension system. The chain decoration was in the form of an NSKK eagle and swastika, a swastika, and a triangle – the international motoring emblem. The blade inscription was the same as that on the SA dagger – 'Alles für Deutschland.'*

Below left *A highly rare NSKK dagger variation. At the time of writing this specimen is the sole example of its type which has been identified in a collection, but photographic research has revealed the existence of at least two other examples on historical photographs, although the precise conditions for the award of the dagger have not yet been identified. The dagger was manufactured by Eickhorn, and the metal portions of the hilt are aluminium. The grip is made of phenolin resin, which originally was white in colour, but has now darkened to a deep orange.* (Robert McCarthy collection).

Right *A unique variation NSKK dagger, basically in the form of the previously described item, but differing in that this example has an Honour-pattern upper crossguard, and the lower crossguard is in the form of the NSKK eagle and swastika. The straps shown with this dagger appear to be regulation pattern Army dagger straps. No details to account for this dagger pattern have been discovered, other than that an identical example – possibly the self-same example – was photographed being worn by Adolf Hühnlein, Commander in Chief of the NSKK.* (Private collection).

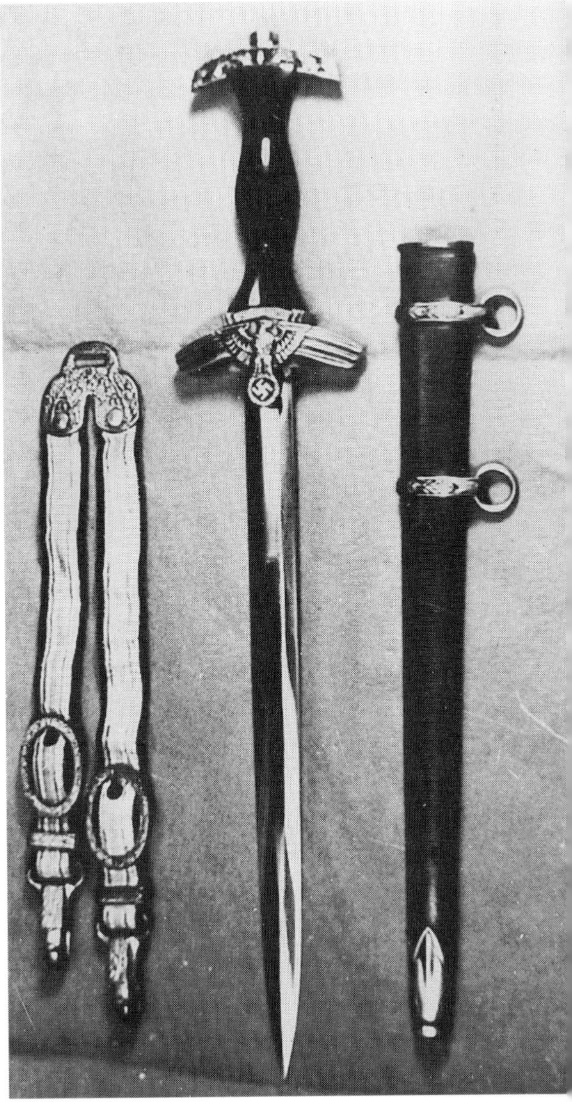

Overleaf *Senior members of the Nazi hierarchy congratulating Hitler on the occasion of his 50th birthday in 1939. On the right of the photograph is Konrad Huhnlein (with arm raised): note the dagger pattern being worn, compared to the previous illustration.* (Library of Congress collection).

NPEA

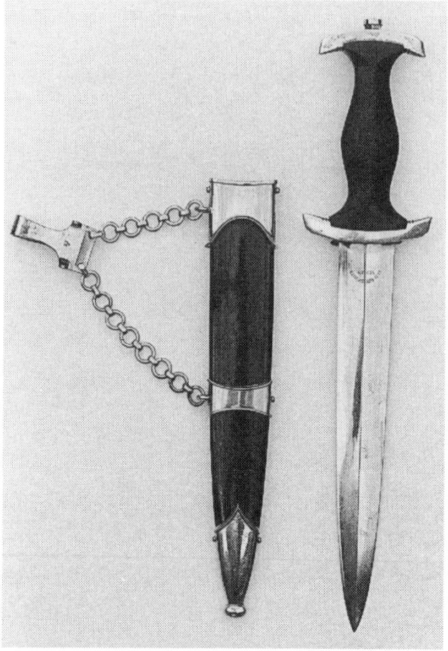

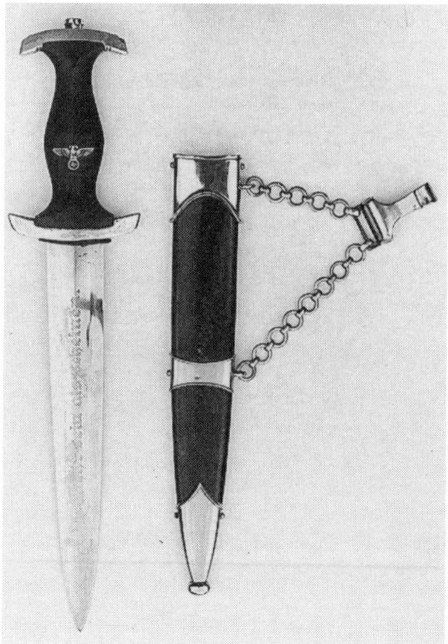

Left *Leader's Dagger of the NPEA. The NPEA (or NAPOLA) organization was a series of schools and educational institutes designed to mould suitable young persons into the psychological Nazi ideal. The NPEA schools were run in the manner of military cadet boarding schools. Staff Officers and Leaders were authorized the right to wear a dagger, the design of which conformed basically to that of the 'Holbein' pattern. The blade inscription was different, however–'Mehr wein als scheinen'–Be more than you appear to be.*

The example illustrated is a Leader pattern, which has a double chain suspension on the scabbard. The Junior Leader pattern was identical, but was carried in a plain scabbard without metal tip or throat, and suspended vertically from a leather frog like a bayonet. (Steward Wilson/The Old Brigade).

Above *Young members at a NAPOLA institute. The youngsters are all dressed in Hitler Youth winter uniform, and wear the HJ-pattern knife. The Junior Officer instructing them (on the far right) wears the NPEA dagger in the vertical hanger.* (Das Illustrierter Blatt newspaper, Frankfurt, 1938).

Hitler Youth

In the early 1930s, Leader members of the National Socialist German Youth (which soon became known as the Hitler Youth, or HJ (i.e. Hitler Jugend)) adopted the wear of a dress knife. In reality, this knife was intended to serve as a hiking or camping knife, and in view of the economic circumstances of the day, many companies saw the opportunity to create these knives out of surplus stock of First World War fighting knives. To make the item more appealing to the intended purchaser, attempts were made to decorate the hilts of these fighting knives with emblems and decoration associated with the Nazi cause (i.e. the swastika), and blades etched with the motto 'Blüt und Ehre' – Blood and Honour, which had become the motto of the organization. The original pattern knife was short, and with an iron hilt that had been nickel plated. The grip was made of wood, chequered in finish but devoid of any emblems.

Two versions of the early pattern HJ Knife, shown with a 1934 pattern (centre) for comparison. (Tony L. Oliver collection).

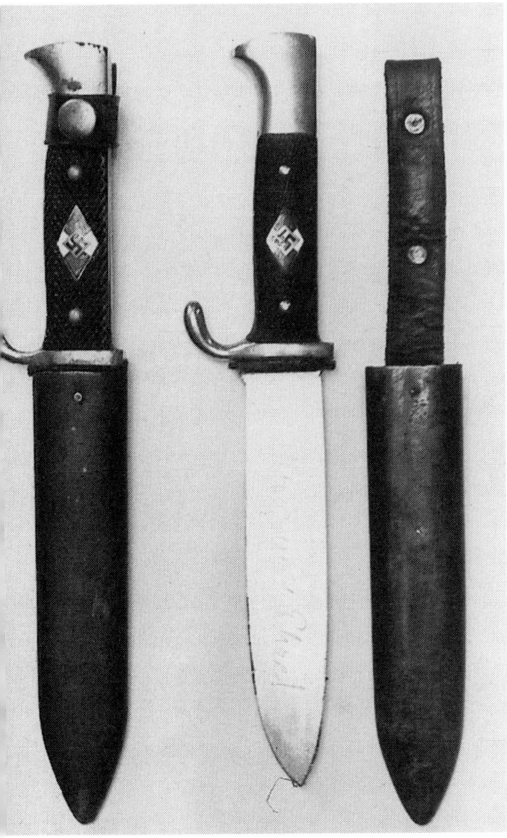

The ubiquitous Hitler Youth knife – the Fahrtenmesser – 'Hike Knife' of 1934. The composition of the metal portions of the hilt range from iron and steel, through to zinc-alloy. The grips are made of an early type of plastic, and decorated with a chequered design, and inset with the red, black and white enamel diamond-shaped swastika emblem of the organization. The blade on pre-1930 examples is etched with the motto 'Blüt und Ehre!', but examples manufactured after this date appear to be devoid of motto. The scabbard is made of steel, stove enamelled black. The knife was probably the most mass-produced knife of the Third Reich, estimated production from 1934 to 1945 being in excess of 20,000,000; and yet, today, mint condition examples are extremely hard to find.

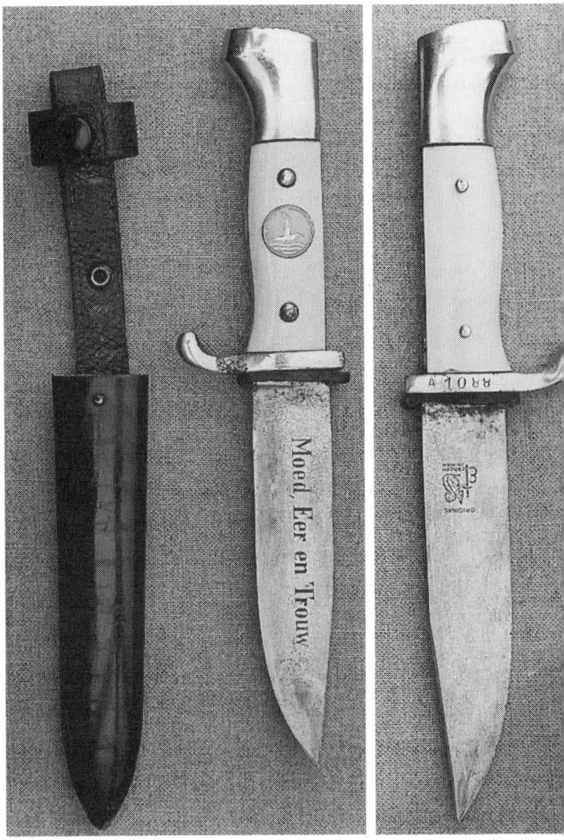

The Dutch Hitler Youth knife. Fascist and Nazi-like organizations existed in other countries as well as Germany, and in Holland the Nazi Youth movement there emulated their German counterparts by adopting their own knife pattern. The knife is similar to the HJ pattern, but smaller. The grip is made of bone, and bears an enamelled emblem of a white gull over waves, on a sky blue field. The blade is etched with the motto 'Moed Eer en Trouw'. All examples of the Dutch Hitler Youth knife were manufactured in Germany by the Carl Eickhorn company.

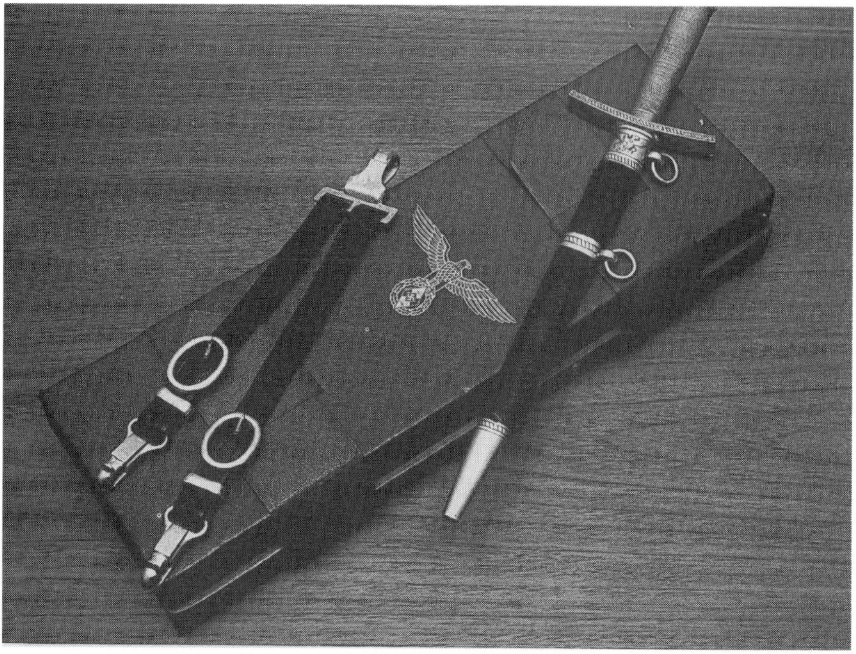

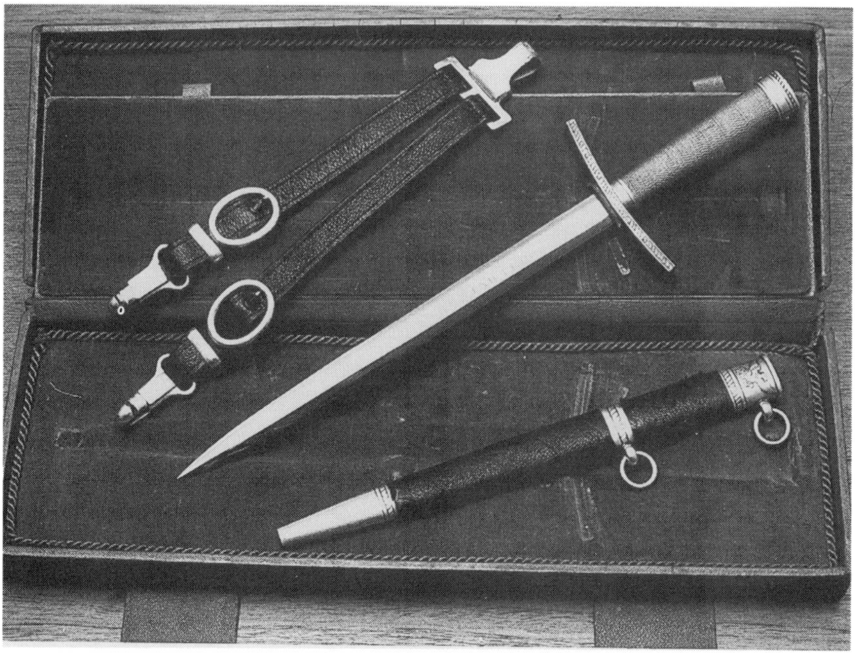

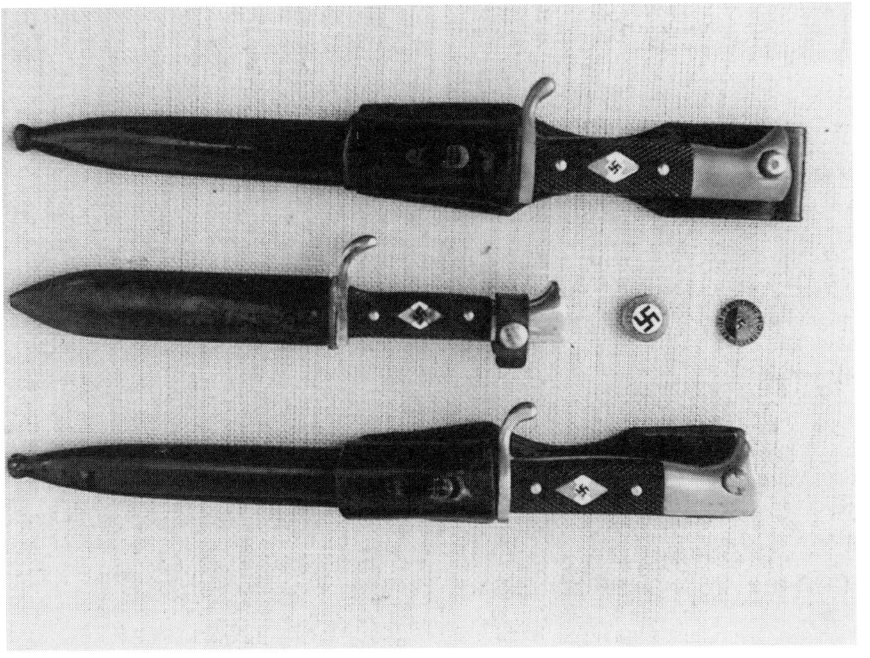

Left *The Hitler Youth Leader's dagger, Model 1938. Until 1938, leaders of the Hitler Youth organization carried the same small knife as their young charges. In 1938, however, a new dagger was introduced for the leaders, in the form of a slim stiletto. The blade was etched with the Hitler Youth motto. The metal finish of the dagger was in silver, with the HJ diamond emblem on the top of the pommel, and a simple grooved design on the crossguard beneath the wire-bound grip. The scabbard was a metal body bearing a dark blue/black leather wrap, with silver-plated fittings. The upper fitting, the locket, bore the emblem of a flighted eagle bearing a sword and lightning bolts, with the swastika emblem on its breast.*

The dagger is shown together with its original leather straps, and presentation case. The case is made of red PVC over a wood base, with red velvet liner. An alternative version is known to exist, comprising a blue finish case, but otherwise identical in construction.

Above *In 1943, members of the Hitler Youth organization were placed on a war-footing, to assist with the war effort and to help relieve manpower from the homeland for service in the Wehrmacht. In the 1943 edition of the Organizationsbuch der NSDAP an illustration was published identifying a new dress weapon that was to be worn by these wartime Hitler Youth members. They were to become known as the HJ Wachgefolgschaft, and their dress weapon was a special bayonet.*

The bayonet pattern was basically identical to the small dress bayonet carried by some of the Wehrmacht for off-duty occasions, but was distinguished by having the Hitler Youth diamond-shaped swastika badge inset in the obverse grip. As production items from a relatively late period in World War Two (the majority of arms-producing companies had been turned over to exclusively essential products for the war, and dress weapons were more or less out of production) the HJ dress bayonet is a comparatively scarce item.

The two examples illustrated are shown together with a regulation pattern HJ knife for comparison. (Tony McCall collection).

Diplomatic and Governmental Services

Right *In 1938 a new style series of dress weapons was authorized for the German Diplomatic Service, and also for the State Ministries.*

For the Diplomatic Service, a sword was prescribed for wear. The item was a handsome and stylish Degen pattern sword, and fulfilled the role that a court sword would have provided in earlier times. The style of the item was of a finely chiselled hilt of brass, with a heavy silver plate, in the form of an eagle head, and a flat knuckle-bow. The grip scales were made of mother-of-pearl. The crossguard comprised of a large pattern national eagle and swastika device with – of importance to collectors interested in detail features – the head of the eagle facing dexter (i.e. looking towards the right of the observer when viewed from the front).

The blade was thin and tapered, with an oak leaf etching design with the national emblem shown in a central panel.

The scabbard was made of a blue/black leather, with silver plated fittings.

Far right*A dagger pattern was also prescribed as an alternative item for dress wear, the style of which was identical to the sword, differing only in that it was smaller, and did not have a knuckle-bow. The scabbard was made of silver-plated steel, with a stippled design on the body surface, and suspension bands that were decorated with an oak leaf design. The crossguard, like that of the sword, featured an eagle and swastika, with the head of the eagle facing towards the right.*

To complement this range of items, a dress bayonet was also prescribed for wear. Introduced in 1941, the bayonet was devised by the Alcoso company of Solingen. It too featured the same stylistic pattern of eagle head pommel, with ivory grips, and a crossguard decorated with an oak leaf design. No eagle and swastika appeared on the bayonet pattern. Of all the bayonet patterns produced during the Third Reich, the Diplomatic bayonet is apparently the most rare. Only two authentic examples have ever ever been discovered to date. (Formerly Dr Julian Milestone collection).

Below right *The dress dagger of the State Ministries. The Staatsbeamte were the state officials who were concerned with the running of the internal apparatus of the Reich, whereas the Diplomatic Service was concerned mainly with foreign policy. No sword or bayonet was prescribed for wear by state officials, only a dagger. The dress dagger is virtually identical to the Diplomatic pattern, except that the eagle and swastika emblem on the crossguard faces to the left side, when viewed from the front.*

The state officials' dagger is known to have been produced in three categories: gold-finished examples for the most senior ranks of the state administration; silver-finish for the remainder of the ranking officials; and an example which was of a blackened finish – *carried by members of the Ministry of Fisheries. No example of this particular pattern has been located to date, and the sole information concerning its existence is from a description published in the official German periodical Uniformenmarkt.*

One other state officials' dagger which has so far been the subject of speculation is that for the Ministers of Eastern and Occupied Territories. A dagger pattern for these officials did exist, and it is depicted in the colour section.

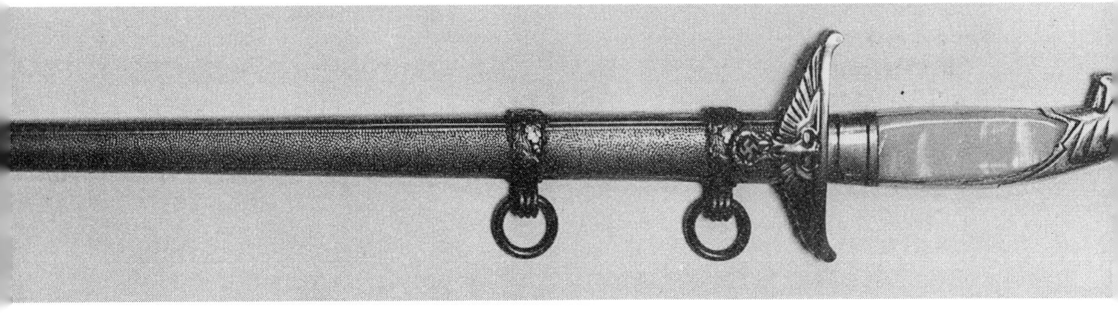

9 The Wehrmacht
The Army, The Air Force, The Navy

The ever present threat of war is of the greatest benefit to the human race.

Adolf Lasson, 1882

In March, 1935, military conscription was reintroduced in Germany, and on 21 May of the same year a *Wehrgesetz* (defence law) was passed which provided for all Aryan male Germans the requirement that they submit themselves for one year's compulsory military duty. The following year (24 August, 1936) the term of service under conscription was raised to two years.

The role that the army had played in the rise of Hitler had been highly important, inasmuch as it had given submissive support. Following the terms of the Treaty of Peace, the German armed forces had been reduced in size to a full-time force of 100,000 personnel—barely enough to defend the nation, to ensure, as far as the League of Nations was concerned, that Germany would not henceforth engage in expansionist warlike activities.

Although merely a token force entrusted with the role of maintaining internal order within the nation, compared to the relatively small, and ill-equipped Brownshirts, the *Reichswehr* would have been more than sufficient to quell any internal revolution. That the army—under the guidance of the military command—chose not to do so revealed the complicity that the military high command had covertly afforded to the NSDAP. To the Prussian militarists and the German officer corps, the nationalistic aspirations of the Nazis were preferable to the Marxist-Leninist intentions of the *Rote Front* ('Red Front', i.e. the communists).

To Hitler, who was keen to gain ultimate control over the army and the military caste, there were two main obstacles in 1933 when the Nazis achieved power. One was the restricted status of the armed forces, which had evolved through the period of the Weimar Republic; the other was the knowledge that Ernst Röhm, head of the SA, had personal aspirations to absorb the army within the SA. Röhm, the scarred street fighter with lofty ambitions and dubious morals, together with his close associates of fair young SA men not truly in the wholesome German spirit, evoked revulsion and resentment amongst the real officer class.

The general dislike of Röhm, and the strong suspicion that Röhm might ultimately usurp Hitler's position and oust the Party Leader, did not go unnoticed.

In 1933, as part of his campaign to revive the spirit of military dignity, Hitler restored the system of military courts which had been abolished during the Weimar period. The armed forces were, once again, to become a separate part of the overall State system.

In June 1934, following schemes devised by Goering and Himmler together with the trusted SS, the mighty power of the SA was savagely cut down to size in the operation now known as 'The Night of the Long Knives'. Röhm, together with numerous cronies, was rounded up and shot; and a new leader for the SA, Viktor Lutze, was installed in the place of Röhm. The SA threat to the control of the army was eliminated overnight, along with various other political thorns whilst the opportunity remained.

The Commander-in-Chief of the *Reichswehr* was General von Blomberg, a position he had held continuously since the Great War. It was a Ministerial position (Defence Ministry), and von Blomberg retained his position until he was dismissed in February, 1938. That event, however, was some time in the future, and Hitler's continued objective was to secure his position of control over the armed forces.

Within six weeks of the massacre of Röhm and his allies, President Field Marshal Paul von Hindenburg died in his sleep. With the passing of this elderly statesman and war hero, Hitler automatically assumed the Presidential powers within those of his Chancellorship. On 1 August 1934 Hitler became the supreme commander of all German armed forces. The *Reichskanzler* immediately revoked the former military oath of loyalty to the Constitution, and had it replaced with a loyalty oath to Hitler himself. All members of the armed forces were required to swear this oath, which declared:

> I swear by God this holy oath that I will give unlimited obedience to the Führer of the German Reich, Adolf Hitler, supreme commander of the armed forces, and that as a brave soldier I will be ready at any time to stake my life for this oath.

In accepting and adopting this oath, the German officer corps pledged their unremitting support for Hitler and his great intentions. The promises to shake off the shackles of limitation enforced by the Treaty of Peace, and to restore fully, firmly, and finally a militaristic system that was to be a combination of the old Imperial regime and the new National Socialist State, gave to Hitler the military machine required to care for the protection of the Third Reich.

The Army was not the only consideration in this grand scheme of events; there existed, illegally, a secret Air Force which would now be developed openly; and a Navy—so far limited to a few ancient vessels and no submarines whatsoever—which would also benefit from what the Nazi government had in mind.

The reintroduction of conscription was but the first, basic move in actively generating the programmes of growth and rearmament. In 1936 the combined forces of the *Reichswehr* were renamed as the *Wehrmacht*; a new flag was adopted, styled like the old Imperial battle flag, but bearing the red, black and white colours of the new Reich and the ubiquitous swastika emblem; new uniforms and equipment were devised.

Once again, the industries of Solingen were to receive another injection of commerce and business, as dress weapons and service weapons for the reborn armed forces were promptly decreed. The mills and presses, the grinders and polishers, the cutlers and knifemakers, who had hardly got over the first benefits of mass-producing knives for the SA, SS, and Hitler Youth, were now to be swamped with orders for swords, daggers and bayonets for the Army, *Luftwaffe*, and *Kriegsmarine*. The promises made by Hitler to restore the national wealth and industries were undoubtedly real. The economy was booming, Germany had awoken. The protestations of the French and the British, the Russians and Poles, the Czechoslovaks and the Belgians, and all the other Allied Powers, were all to no avail. The defeated empire of the Hohenzollerns had emerged from the ashes, industry had been rebuilt, the standard of living for the working man was better than anywhere else throughout all of Europe. It was no wonder that the ordinary German in the street, experiencing the heady vibrations of the industrious new Reich, was beguiled into believing that this was truly the magnificent home of the Master Race. Another concept which was soon to become aired, was the right and justification in reuniting the German communities who had become separated from the Reich after the Great War. German nationals as well as German ethnic stock (*Volksdeutsche*) were scattered widely across the European map. In the terms which had made up the Treaty of Peace, many of these communities now found themselves being designated as resident nationals of new states—in consequence of which they found themselves regarded as an ethnic minority within their new homelands. The very basics of racial prejudice, which Hitler and the Nazis were ultimately to deploy, were already festering in opposition to the German communities which since 1919 had suddenly found themselves designated as Polish nationals, in Silesia and parts of old East Prussia; and as Czechoslovaks in the former Sudetenland territory, and elsewhere within the redesignated national boundaries that the Treaty of Peace and League of Nations had established.

The sense of common cultural identity of German ethnic groups across Europe was not a new phenomenon; the need to maintain a positive link with the Fatherland was an intrinsic part of German thinking in the past, and indeed in 1920 Sartorius von Waltershausen had stated:

> Pan-German imperialism was invented and attributed to us by others, but, as the designation

> shows, its aim was only a national, ethnographic one—designed to embrace all the Germans in the world.*

The severance of German communities from their homeland, whatever the intentions of the League of Nations, ultimately worked in reverse because of the great impetus to bring them back within the German national fold; or alternatively to expand the fold to encompass them. Either objective was impossible without an aggressive foreign policy, and a military force to back it up. A quotation by Hitler in the *National Sozialistische Monatshefte*, issue No. 3, 1930, propounded that aggressive instinct in the clearest of terms:

> It is impossible to build up an army and give it a sense of worth if the object of its existence is not the preparation for war. Armies for the preservation of peace do not exist; they exist only for the triumphant exertion of war.

By 1936 National Socialist Germany was actively rearming, harvesting manpower and equipment; as a storm will gather clouds before the tempest breaks.

The depletion of the *Kaiserlichmarine* in the 1919–21 period by the Allied Powers, replacing it with the tokenforce known as the *Reichsmarine*, had reduced the German fleet to a few, ancient vessels; and the situation had been furthered by the express forbidding of the construction of any further vessels which could be deployed for military use.

The limitations enforced under the terms of the Treaty of Peace had relegated German marine power to the situation it had experienced in the 1860s—the nation was to all intents and purposes land-locked. The only seaboard which Germany possessed was a fairly lengthy strip along the Baltic Sea, and even this was divided by the territorial coastline of Poland which separated West Prussia from Danzig and East Prussia. Further west, another division in the German coast line occurs—along the coast of Schleswig-Holstein, the exit from the Baltic Sea into the North Sea passes through a narrow passage which is dominated on the western side by Denmark, and on the eastern side by Sweden. At one point the international waterway between Zealand (Denmark) and the Swedish coast is barely 14km wide. Navigation through these waters was, at all times, at the discretion of Sweden and Denmark.

Beyond the promontory which the land mass of Denmark occupies, a further short stretch of German coastline faces on to the North Sea, barely 200km in length, and the only navigable rivers which flow into the North Sea are the Elbe and Weisel.

It was these limitations of access to the open sea which were deployed by Hitler as excuses for an expansion of the German fleet beyond the limitations imposed by Versailles. The breakthrough came in the Anglo-German Naval Agreement of 1935, by which instrument Germany gained the co-operation of England in being allowed to lay down the keels for a few

*Quoted in *Thus Spake Germany* by W. W. Coole and M. F. Potter, Routledge, London, 1941.

more warships; they were to be the cruisers *Scharnhorst* and *Gneisenau*, and the battleships *Bismarck* and *Tirpitz*. Concurrent with the growth of the fleet came the expansion of the personnel to run it, and Solingen would once again benefit from orders for dirks and swords for the emerging Navy.

During the late 1920s, Russia, despite her signature and agreement to the Treaty of Peace, commissioned from Germany the construction of a number of factories to produce aircraft for the Soviet Air Force. The construction was to take place in industrial centres within the Ukraine, and technicians and workers were contracted from the Weimer government to work inside Russia at the assembly of these plants, and additionally to train Russian workers in the technology required to build good, workable aero-engines. The opportunity was too good to miss. Germany was totally forbidden by the Versailles Treaty to possess any warplanes of any sort, or to even contemplate producing them, and yet here came a heaven-sent opportunity. The Weimar government contracted a second agreement with Soviet Russia, that went beyond the commercial aspects of showing the Russians how to build planes—this agreement was an undertaking by the Soviets to allow Germany to build a few aircraft of her own whilst on Russian territory, and to train a small force of Germans to fly them. Far away from the prying eyes of the rest of the Allied Powers, German fliers were being given the opportunity to develop a few craft, and test them in the lonely skies of Russia. It was an arrangement which Stalin would have gladly vetoed had the opportunity occurred, but Russia was in a potentially worse state than Germany, and badly needed the capability to mass-produce aircraft to defend her immense domain, so the agreement went through. A tiny *Luftwaffe* was already in existence before Hitler had achieved political power.

In 1936, when the Navy and the Army had just been formally commissioned by the Reichs Ministry of War, the creation of an Air Force to defend the Reich was announced. The basis of this new *Luftwaffe* was already established, not only by the clandestine training and building which had taken place in Russia over the preceding years, but also through the auspices of another organization which the Nazis had fostered—the *Deutsche Luftsports Verband*, or DLV, a supposedly peaceful organization which had concentrated on bringing the recreational pursuits of air sports flying to air-minded enthusiasts. The peaceful activities of the DLV were merely a sham to cover up another objective, the mass training of personnel in airborne-related activities, forming a cadre of trained airmen who were prepared to step into the cockpit in the role Hitler had destined for them. Within weeks of receiving official recognition, the first of these pilots were on their way to Spain to assist Franco in the civil war in that country. Before the German Army and Navy had had any chance to put their training to the test in war-games, the newest arm of the armed forces was already testing out bombing strategies for real.

Bayonets

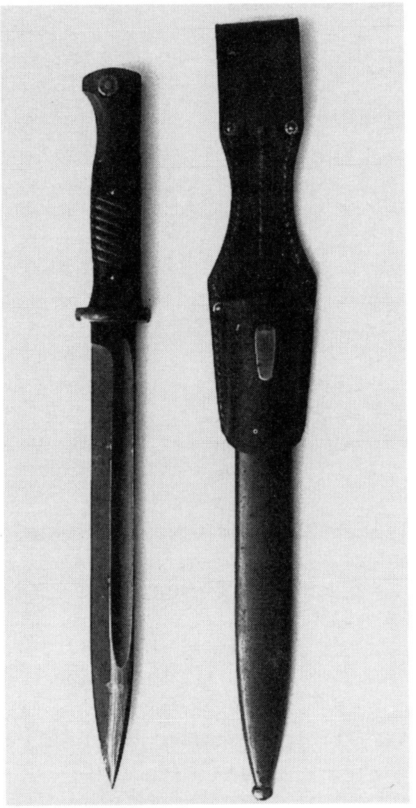

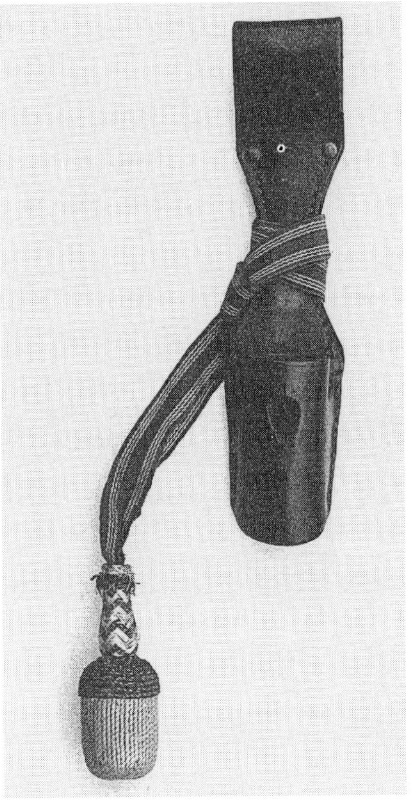

The most prolifically produced edged weapon of the Third Reich was undoubtedly that of the service bayonet (Dienstseitengewehr). The full production volume is not known, but it clearly went into many millions of examples. Known as the S.84-98, the bayonet pattern was developed from a pattern produced originally in 1884, modified in 1898, and maintained in volume production from that time. Refinements to the pattern were further implemented during the First World War, and the version which emerged was, more or less, the standard form which saw service during the Second World War.

Minor modifications in the form of the flash guard, the construction of the grips, etc., did occur in the intervening period, but the basic bayonet pattern remained practically unchanged. The bayonet was issued to all branches of the Wehrmacht, as well as the Waffen-SS.

Detail view: service pattern bayonet suspension frog, shown with walking-out troddel knot.

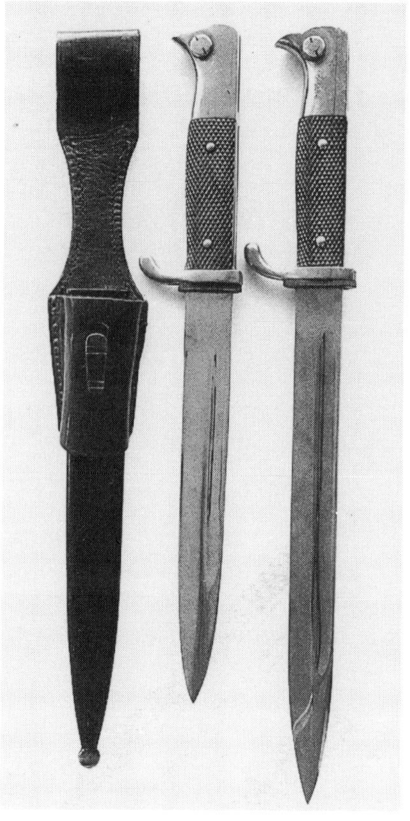

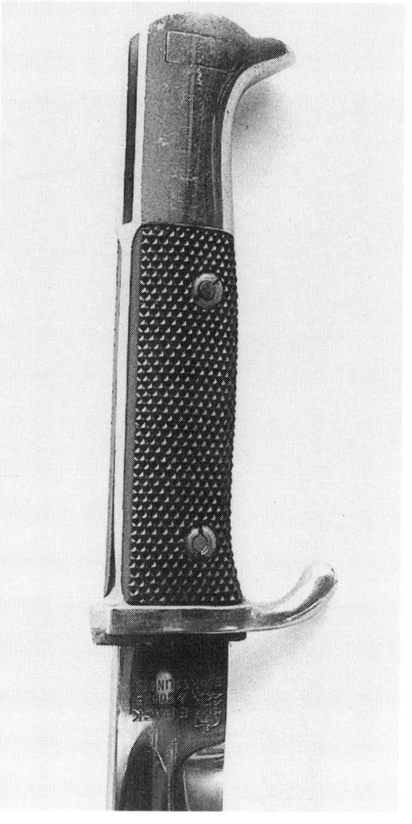

Dress Bayonets. All members of the Wehrmacht could obtain, as a private purchase, a dress bayonet for walking-out purposes. Virtually every manufacturer in Solingen featured the dress bayonet as part of the standard stock production. A great deal of latitude in the style and quality of such items was permitted – some are so ornate as to be highly collectable items in their own right.

The illustrated examples are two of the more typical patterns, being the long, and short versions (the shorter pattern allegedly being more favoured by cavalry troops). The hilt fittings range in construction materials from steel (more usual on the early, pre-1935 pieces) to later refinements utilizing injection-cast zinc-based alloy. The metal portions were highly polished, and then nickel plated; blades were similarly nickel plated. The grips are made of a black, plastic type material, with a chequered finish. The press-stud and mortise slot in the pommel were fully functional, although it was never intended that the dress bayonet should actually be fitted on to the rifle. (Collection Thomas Gorman).

Detail view of the reverse portion of the hilt of a dress bayonet, this example being manufactured by E. Pack und Sohne of Solingen, and dating from about 1934. The grip scales on most dress bayonets are secured by rivets, but the Pack company during the early period utilized nut and bolt fastenings – features which are quite evident on this example. (Collection Thomas Gorman).

Dress bayonet with a Wehrmacht eagle and swastika badge affixed to the obverse grip scale. A commercial concept, designed to boost sales, the features of the emblem on the grip scale was a reintroduction of a practice which had occurred during WW1. Die Klinge magazine in 1937, illustrated an example of a dress bayonet with the Wehrmacht emblem mounted on the grip, confirming once and for all that the practice was most definitely known in pre-WWII days, and was not simply a war-time development.

De-luxe variations of dress bayonet. A page from the catalogue of the Paul Weyersberg concern, circa 1940, showing some of the more ornate dress bayonets that the company was promoting. Etched blades were a popular feature available to all who could afford the extra cost. The examples illustrated in the Weyersberg catalogue bear etched inscriptions denoting that they were suggested as prize gifts for skills in marksmanship.

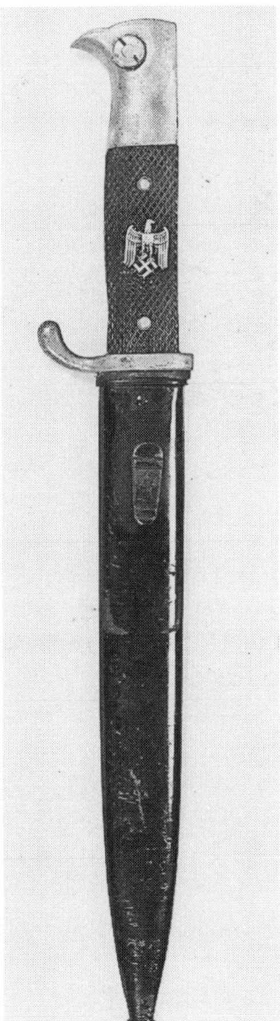

Daggers

Below *Studio portrait of a German Army Officer, with dress dagger.*

Below right *Photograph from an unidentified wartime magazine showing a Greek partisan leader. The original caption to the illustration is: ' "Ares", the Guerrilla Chief, took his name and beard from the ancient Greek God of War.' It is not the only thing that he took, the German Army dagger hanging from the belt suggests that 'Ares' took war souvenirs from the defeated enemy.* (Mike Bassett photo collection).

Right *Wartime photograph taken in the billet of Hauptmann Joachim Uebe formerly of the 12th Artillery Regiment, subsequently serving in the Luftwaffe. Hauptmann Uebe's Army dress dagger can be seen displayed upon the wall, together with his Artillery Officer's spurs. One feature evident on this period photograph is that the dagger suspension straps feature the buckles very high up the strap, close to the belt catch.* (Joachim Uebe, via the late A. S. Walker photo collection).

Below right *German Army Officer's dagger, Model 1935, manufacturer Carl Eickhorn, Solingen. The grip of the dagger is made of phenol resin, which originally was white in colour, but has – due to chemical breakdown – started to discolour to a deep orange hue. All metal portions of the hilt and scabbard are silver plated.*

Below far right *The reverse of the German Army Officer's dagger.*

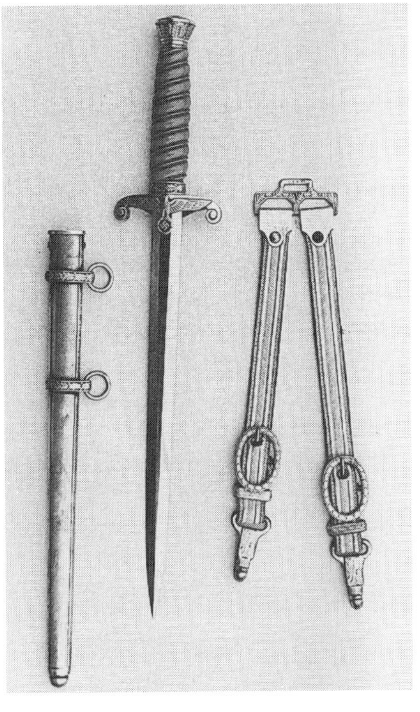

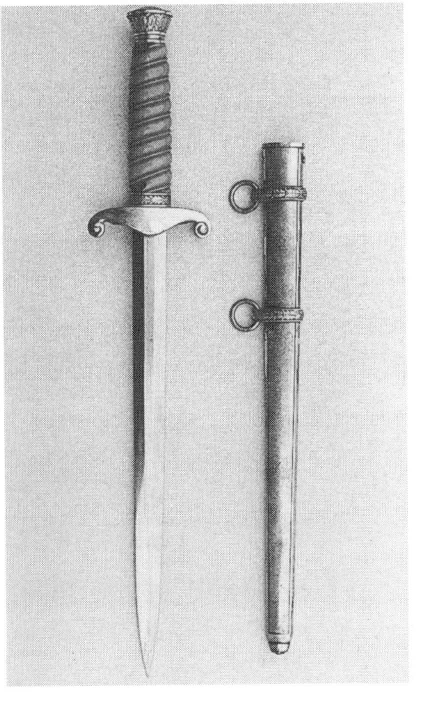

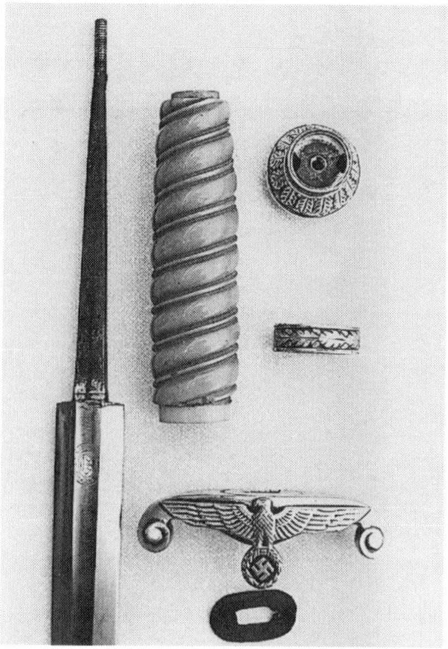

Above *Detail view of the hilt of the Army Officer's dagger, dismantled to show the assembly portions. Note the style of the crossguard.*

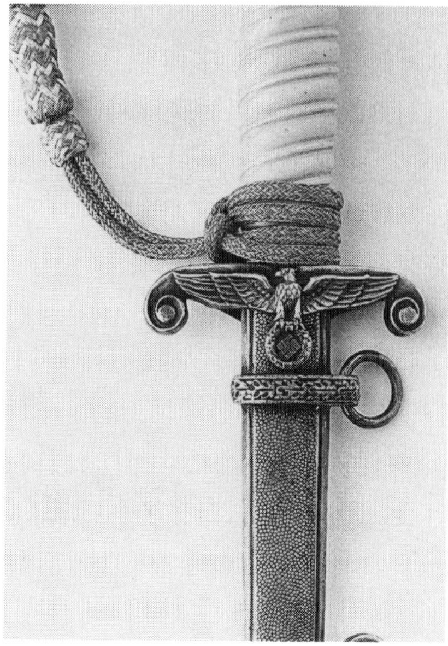

Detail view of the crossguard of a German Army Officer's dagger, Model, 1935. This example was produced by the Alcoso (Alex Coppel) concern. The crossguards of virtually every Army dagger, even though from differing manufacturers, are almost identical. Minute variations are known, but these tend to be small detail differences. This example, however, reveals one of the more extreme variations – the eagle and swastika pattern is quite distinctive. This variation has been observed only on Alcoso pieces, and apparently dates from about 1941.

Below *Detail view of an Army dagger blade, with presentation inscription. The etching proclaims: 'For good Comradeship. The Junior Officer Corps of the 7th K-J Regiment 107'.* (Dr J. Milestone collection).

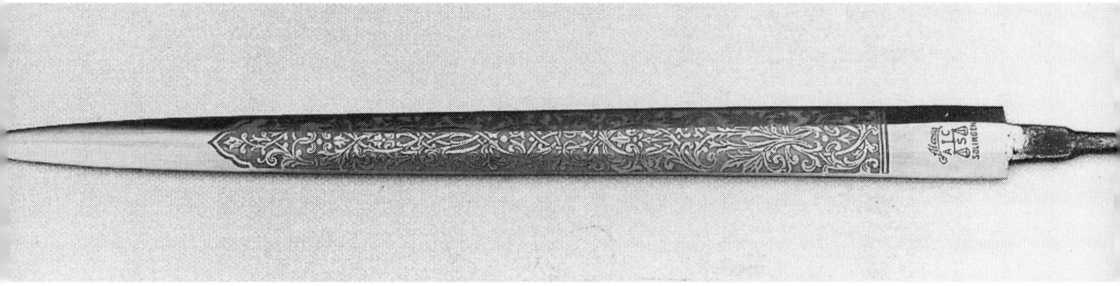

Above *Obverse and reverse of a de luxe quality Army dagger blade, with etched decoration. Etched designs on blades were available to all purchasers at a moderate cost, if one of the stock template patterns was acceptable. Personalized etching, and presentation inscriptions, were considerably more costly as they were one-off items of workmanship.*

Below *Detail view of an etched Army dagger blade, manufacturer Robert Klaas, Solingen. The etching pattern is one of the Klaas standard template designs, but the feature which is interesting with this blade is the presence of the hole in the tang. This feature is common on many (but not all) etched blades and its purpose is a mystery to most collectors. The reason for the hole apparently was to allow the blade to be hooked on to a wire and suspended in a plating bath – to impart a hard nickel plating over the etched decoration to afford protection to it.*

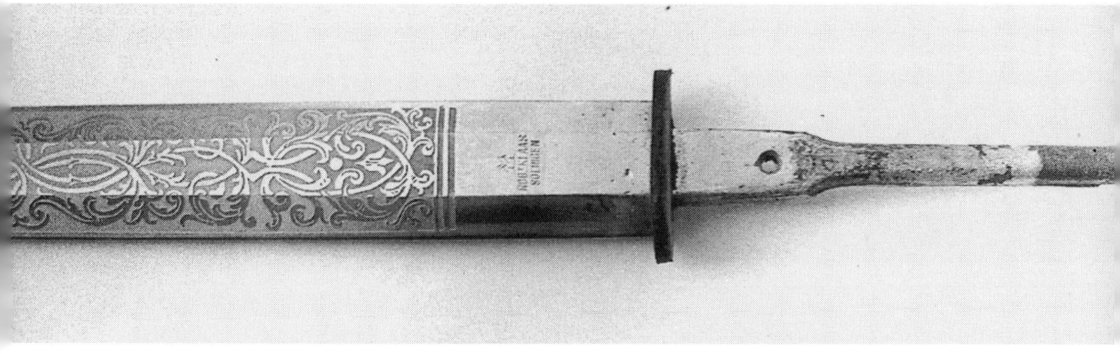

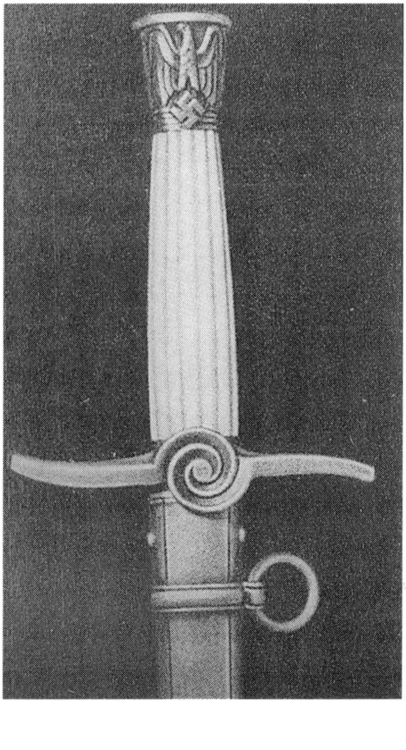

Above *Presentation inscription engraved on the reverse of an Army dagger crossguard. Most officers seeking to personalize their dress dagger elected to have the fittings engraved, as this was considerably less expensive than etching; and some presentation inscriptions were also produced in this manner. The illustrated example denotes the presentation as: 'With best wishes on the occasion of your promotion, from the officers of Staff 339, 1st June, 1942'.* (Lt. Col. (retd.) J. R. Angolia collection).

Left *Army dress dagger – probably for a Field Marshal. All hilt metal portions are made of silver plated bronze, and the grip is of fluted ivory. The crossguard is extremely stylish in featuring upswept and downswept quillons, conjoined to a scroll design on the central quillon block.*

This piece is considered not to have been developed beyond the stage of an artwork rendition. (Blank Waffen, via Lt. Col. (retd.) J. R. Angolia).

Above *Obverse and reverse views of a rare example of the damascus work produced by the SS smithy at Dachau. The basic dagger is a Model 1933 SS Service dagger, but there the similarity ends. The crossguards are finely engraved, and the damascus blade (Turkish damascus grain pattern) bears an inscription in raised and gilded letters, denoting that it was produced by the Sword and Dagger Blade Smithy (which was under the direction of Paul Müller) at Dachau (adjacent to the infamous concentration camp of the same name). The daggers were not intended for wear, but were created as examples to prove that the skill of damascus workmanship was being preserved under the guidance of the SS, for the heritage of the nation.* (Dr. R. Distelhorst collection.)

Right *An example of the SS Honour Dagger, Model 1934. The dagger in basic form is identical to the Model 1933 Service Dagger, but has silvered fittings decorated with an oak leaf and acorn pattern – this style of decoration dating from about 1941. This example is complete with a damascus steel blade.* (Dr. J. Milestone collection.)

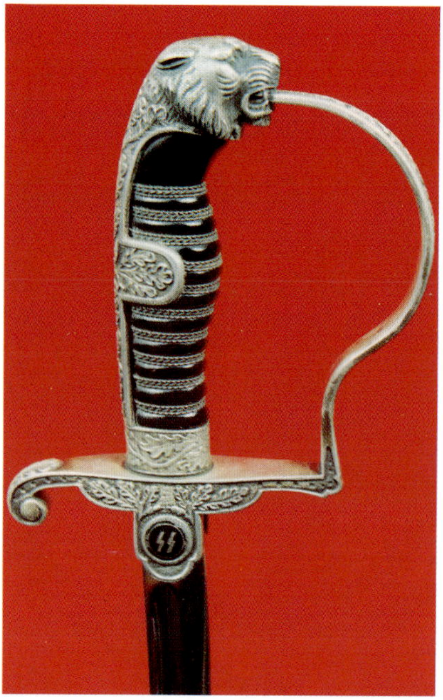

Obverse, reverse, and blade detail of the SS Honour Sabre. Produced in 1934 by the Eickhorn company, these swords were in wear and service for a short period, before being replaced by the adoption of the SS degen pattern in 1936. The hilt is of silver finish over steel, and the SS insignia is sited in a cartouche on the reverse langet. The blade is etched with the SS Service motto, 'Meine Ehre heisst Treue.'

Above *Obverse and reverse detail views of the hilt of a most unusual Model 1937 Luftwaffe dagger. The eagle and swastika emblem of the service does not appear on the crossguard, which instead features the emblem of an anti-aircraft gun. The whole piece is totally original, and the crossguard appears to be a skilfully executed modification of a standard crossguard, with the ornate design of the anti-aircraft gun being machined out of the solid metal. No reason to account for this variation is known, but it has been suggested that this might have been a special, one-off gift: perhaps to a General in command of an anti-aircraft regiment.* (Lt.-Col. (retd.) J. R. Angolia.)

Right *Publicity advertisement for the Puma concern, showing an example of one of the company's hunting cutlasses, and a special version of the Naval dirk which the company produced.* (Die Klinge, 1938.)

Left *De-luxe quality German Naval dirk, with highly decorated scabbard, shown against a background composed of the front cover of a Knights Cross award document.* (Lt.-Col. (retd.) J. R. Angolia.)

Below *Obverse and reverse views of the hilt of the Luftwaffe General Officer's sword.* (The late A. S. Walker photo collection.)

Army swords

As the traditional weapon of all Army and Cavalry Officers, the sword retained great popularity during the Third Reich, despite some of the cumbersome limitations occasioned by its size. In terms of style, the only real areas which permitted variations of refinement and quality in a visible form, were primarily the hilt, and also the blade, where etched designs could be featured. Nevertheless, despite being limited to a basic style for the form of the hilt, the number of variations in decoration and finish is quite astonishing—in excess of 200 variations of hilt decoration are known, and there are undoubtedly many more. The following selection is a brief, representative example.

Right *Adolf Hitler and Field Marshal Werner von Blomberg, September 1937. The Field Marshal wears a Cavalry pattern sabre which bears the emblem of crossed swords on the reverse side langet. The langet—the short projecting plate on the lower side of the crossguard—was commonly used for the display of emblems. Although most Army swords produced in the Third Reich featured the eagle and swastika emblem on the obverse langet, the reverse side langet was more usually left blank to allow for the option of the owner having his initials engraved upon the surface.*

Some manufacturers utilized the space to feature military service emblems, such as crossed swords (Cavalry), crossed cannon (Artillery), etc.

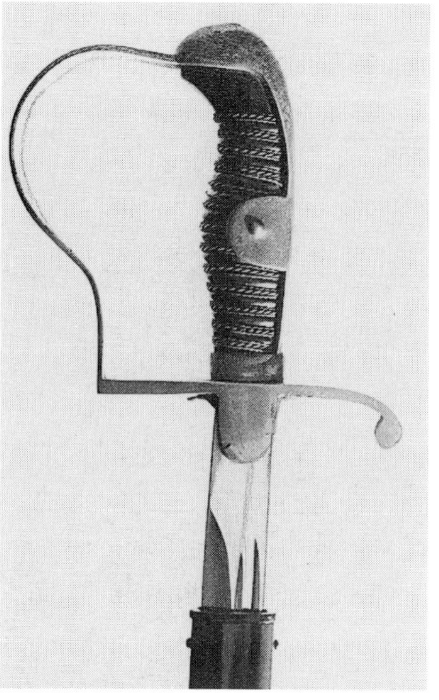

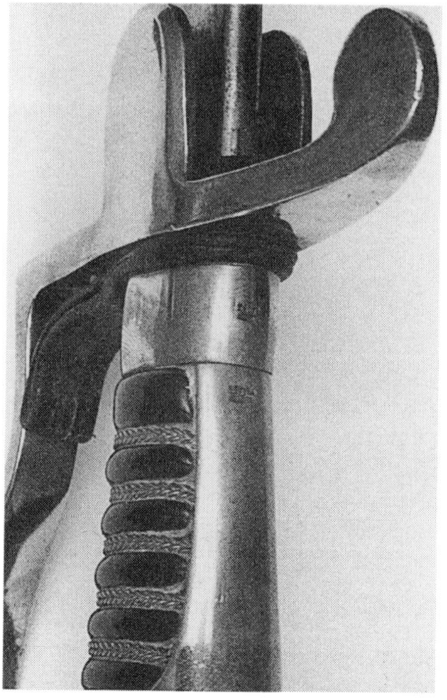

Above *The Mannschaftsabel. This plain, P-shaped hilt is typical of the basic pattern of sabre that was most commonly purchased by NCOs in the Army, in preference to a dress bayonet. Their basic pattern was not, however, restricted to NCOs; any officer of any rank could wear the sword pattern if so desired. As the most simple and basic design, the Mannschaftsabel is also known to have been purchased by the Ordnance department of the Army, for occasions where a sword was a mandatory requirement of wear for certain personnel (such as for cavalry parades), and where the personnel involved did not actually own their own sword, then a sword could be drawn from stores for use at the event – to be returned afterwards. Such swords were inevitably Waffen-amt stamped.*

Above right *Detail view of the hilt of a sword which had been accepted by the Army Ordnance Department, the stamping of the Waffen-amt mark indicating that this item was official government property, and not a private purchase item.*

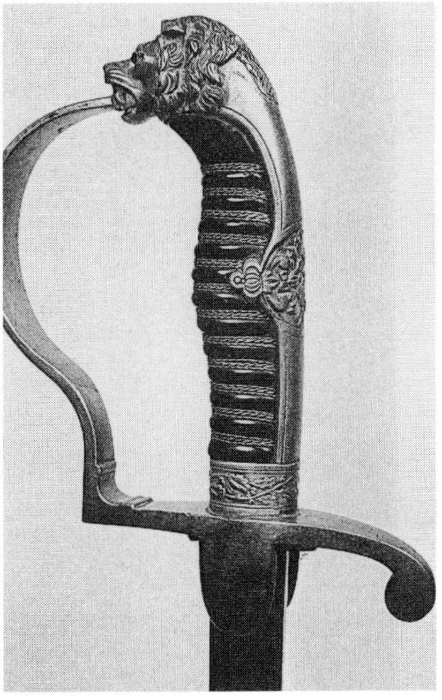

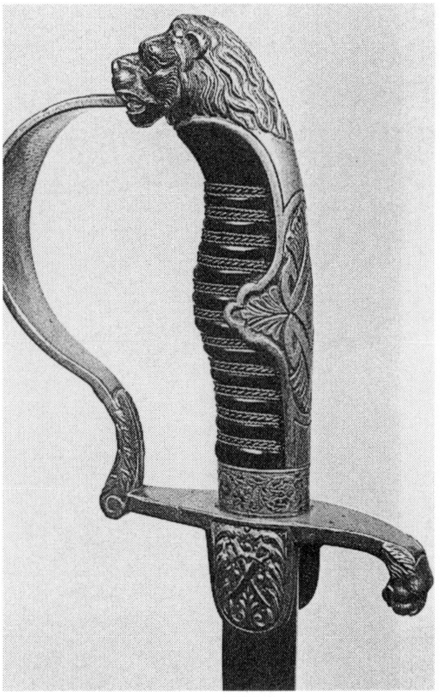

Left *A General Staff Officer at a political parade – the presence of Hitler Youth, SA, and Allgemeine SS personnel indicates that this was not a purely military gathering. The officer can be seen wearing an Imperial period style of sword, possibly the bearer's personal property from service in the Great War.* (Brian L. Davis collection).

Above *Army pattern sword, dating from the Third Reich period, not only devoid of the eagle and swastika emblem, but unusual also in that the knuckle bow and crossguard are completely plain.* (Lt. Col. (retd.) J. R. Angolia collection).

Above right *German Army Cavalry sabre produced by the Eickhorn concern, and known as Eickhorn Model No 1324. The crossed sabres emblem of the langet are sculptured in high relief.* (Lt. Col. (retd.) J. R. Angolia collection).

Right *A stylish sabre for an Artillery Officer, with ornate lionhead pattern pommel, and the crossed cannon emblem on the langet.* (Lt. Col. (retd.) J. R. Angolia collection).

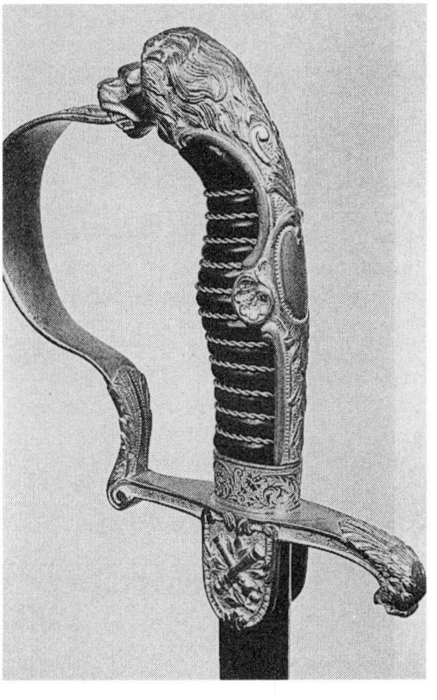

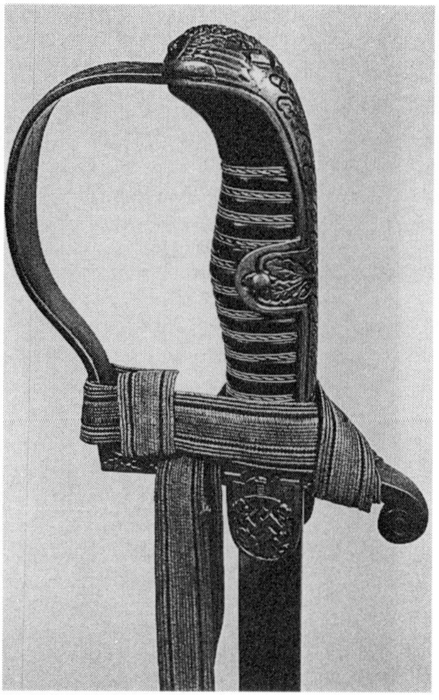

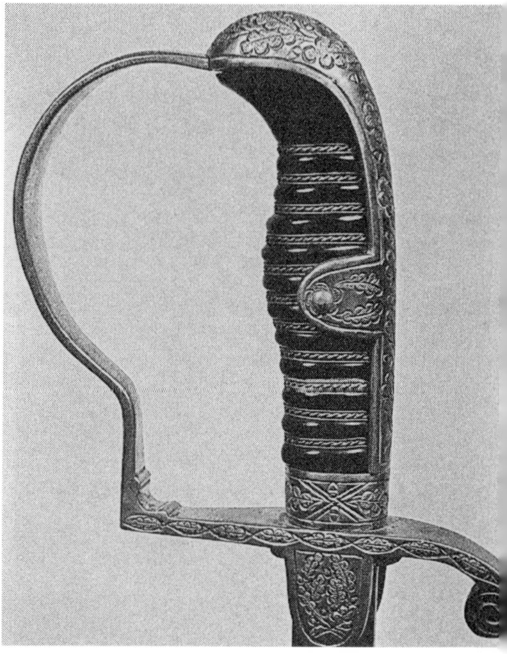

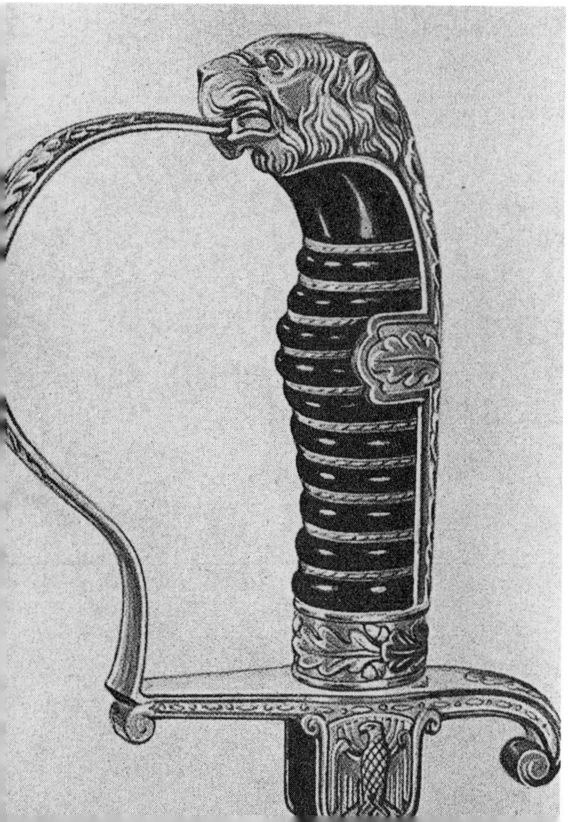

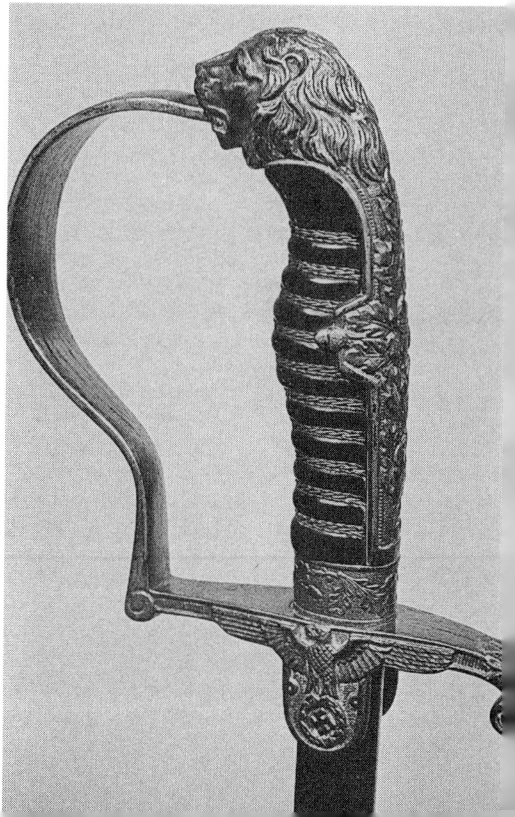

Far left *A sword produced by Eickhorn, from the 'Field Marshal' series – a range of specialized designs which were patented by the Eickhorn company. This example was known under the name of 'Lutzow', Model No 1767. The feature of the sword and swastika emblem on the langet is unique to this sword pattern.* (Lt. Col. (retd.) J. R. Angolia collection).

Left *A plain hilted sabre, with the added refinement of hand-engraved decoration. Many of the companies who produced the basic plain sabre offered the additional refinement of engraving to decorate the item.* (Lt. Col. (retd.) J. R. Angolia collection).

Below far left *Illustration taken from the 1938 Eickhorn sales catalogue, showing item no 1706 – the sword pattern 'Scharnhorst'. The design was patented by Eickhorn as another of their 'Field Marshal' series.* (Eickhorn Kundendienst).

Below left *Army lionhead pattern sabre manufactured by the concern of Richard Herder, Solingen. All hilt fittings, as is common for Army swords, are finished in a gilt wash.* (Lt. Col. (retd.) J. R. Angolia collection).

Below *A selection of three Army sword blades, showing some of the etched decoration designs which can be encountered.* (Lt. Col. (retd.) J. R. Angolia collection).

Bottom *Detail view of a sword blade etching, depicting horse-drawn artillery pulling a gun and limber. Note at the top end of the etching the feature of an emblem comprising a German steel helmet with crossed swords; and the Wehrmacht eagle and swastika emblem lower down the blade towards the hilt.* (The late A. S. Walker photo collection).

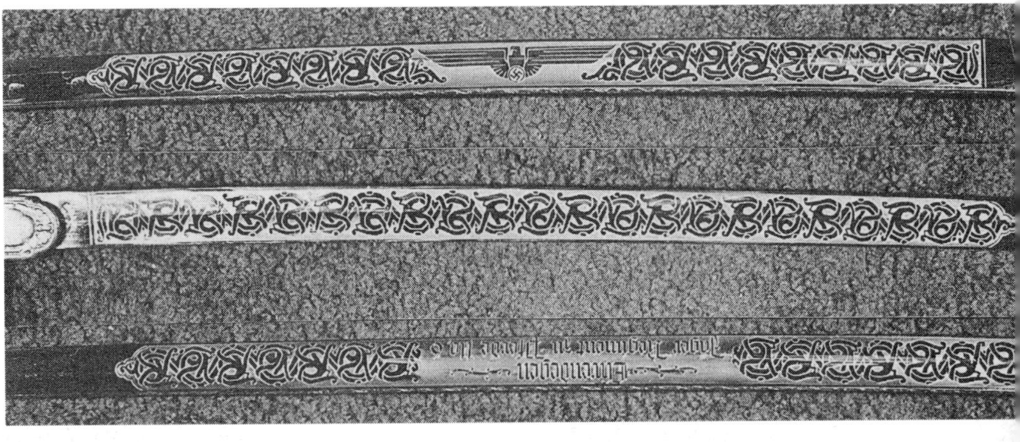

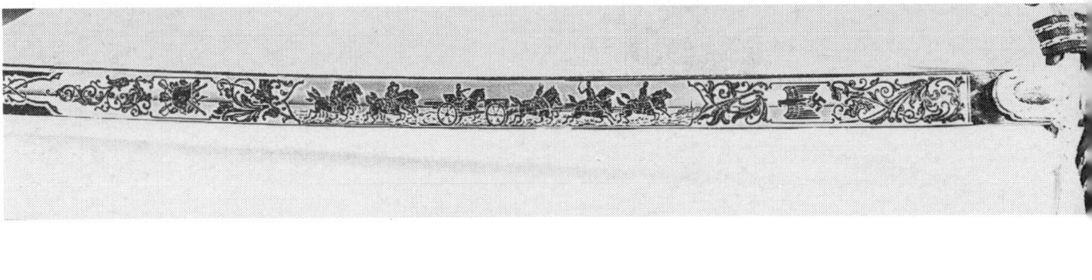

In 1941, Hitler appointed twelve new Field Marshals to the Army High Command, and each was presented with his distinctive badge of rank—the Field Marshal's Baton. In the autumn of the same year the Solingen Chamber of Commerce published a book entitled *Blank Waffen* ('Edged Weapons') in which a number of proposed designs for swords and daggers were displayed—amongst which were a sword and dagger specifically for Field Marshals. The designs were never adopted, although several of the proposed designs were indeed hand-crafted to prototype stage. The fate of these extraordinary weapons, in the aftermath of the Second World War, has never been discovered.

Below left *Army Officer's sabre in stainless steel. The design is a stylized pattern bearing the old Prussian sword characteristic of a curved backstrap, but presented in a modern form. The Wehrmacht eagle and swastika is made of gilded brass or bronze, and mounted on the upper surface of the fore-quillon. The grip is made of a grooved plastic material.* (Blank Waffen, via Lt. Col. (retd.) J. R. Angolia).

Below *Officer's sabre with basket-style guard. The hilt fittings are of bronze, or an alloy of zinc and copper, and feature the Wehrmacht emblem within the frame of the guard. The hilt is made of rosewood.* (Blank Waffen, via Lt. Col. (retd.) J. R. Angolia).

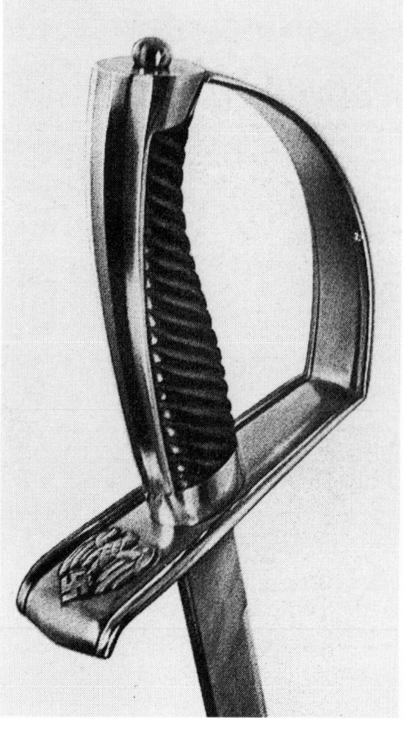

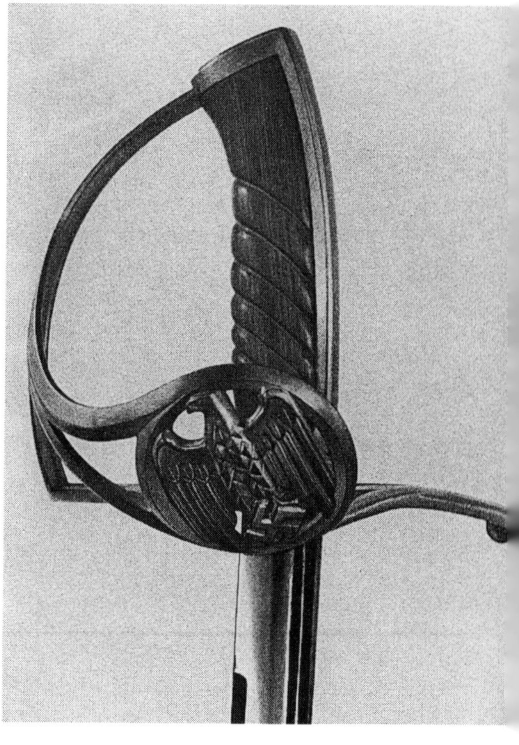

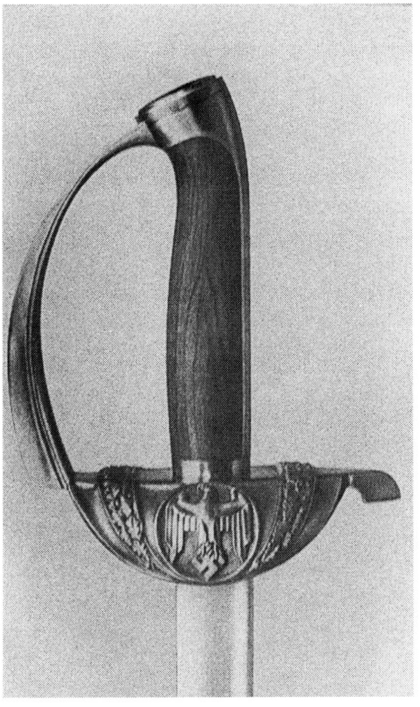

Officer's sabre with a shell guard bearing the Wehrmacht *emblem. All hilt fittings are made of cast bronze, and the grip is made of a smooth finished rosewood.* (Blank Waffen, via Lt. Col. (retd.) J. R. Angolia).

Above right *Sword for a Field Marshal. All metal portions of the hilt were to be of stainless steel, with decoration and eagle and swastika applied as gold inlay. The grip is made of smoke coloured topaz. The blade is etched within the deep fuller with the legend 'Alles für Deutschland', and bearing the swastika at opposing ends of the inscription.*

This piece is considered not to have been developed beyond the stage of an artwork rendition. (Blank Waffen, via Lt. Col. (retd.) J. R. Angolia).

Naval dirks

The German Naval dirk of the Third Reich was the continuation of a tradition which had existed since pre-Imperial times, although the practice had originally been re-adopted only in 1890, after a period during which the Naval dirk had been disused.

In 1848 the Prussian Royal Navy—in emulation of a practice adopted by the British Navy of the time—had accepted the introduction of a Naval dirk to be worn by midshipmen officers. The dirk had remained in favour for some years, until the 1860s when, following riots in Kiel and the misuse of bladed weapons, the Naval dirk was suspended from service.

In 1871, following the formation of the Second Reich, Cadet Officers in the new German Navy, the *Kaiserlilchmarine* which was formed around a nucleus of the old Prussian Navy, bolstered by financial input and manpower from the other German States, had been given permission to wear a sidearm which reflected their status. This was the *Aplikantendolch*, a short cutlass-length weapon that was midway between being a dagger and full-sized sword. Officers in the Navy continued to wear the regulation sword pattern of the day.

In 1980, the German Admiralty approved the introduction of a dress dagger for wear by Officers, Officer-Cadets, and Midshipmen. Known as the Model 1890, this dagger pattern—in various refinements, and at the whim of private purchase deluxe options—became the standard form of dress dagger for Naval personnel for the next 55 years. It was withdrawn from service in 1945 at the cessation of the Second World War.

Following the First World War, the Model 1890 Naval dirk was withdrawn, and the more discreet Model 1919 version—having a black grip and black scabbard—was introduced. This pattern remained in service, with slight modification, for ten years.

In 1929, a radical modification was

German Naval and Army troops taking up position at the Royal Castle, Berlin, 9th November 1918, during the riots which were taking place in the capital. Note that the sailor in the centre is carrying a boarding cutlass.

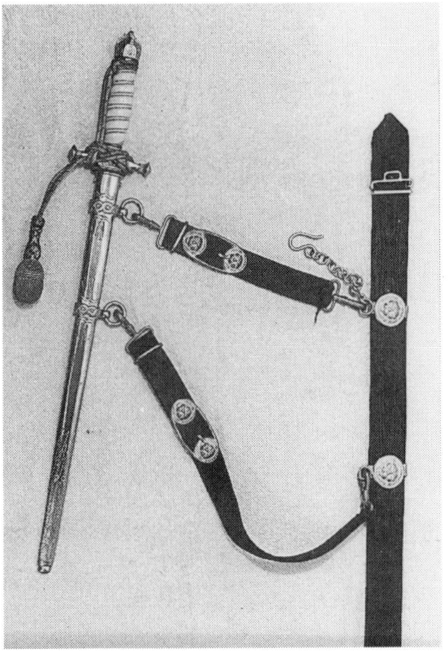

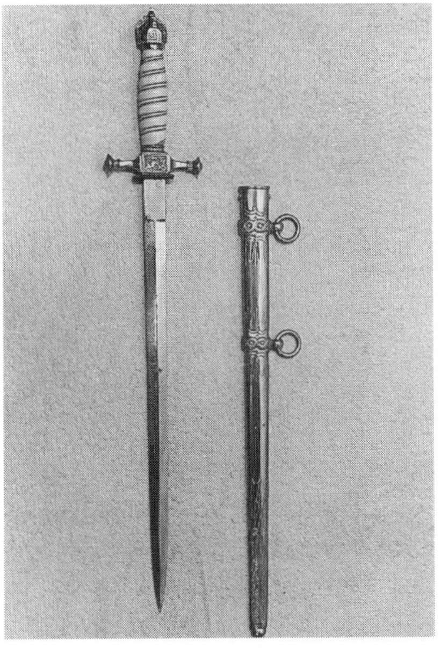

Above *Model 1890 Naval dirk, shown complete with its tunic belt, suspension straps, and portepee knot. All hilt fittings are made of gilded brass, and the grip is ivory. Overall length in scabbard: 19 in (48 cm).* (J. P. Puype collection).

Above right *Model 1890 dirk, shown out of its scabbard. The long blade (14 in) is lightly etched on both sides, depicting a three-masted sailing ship, rope and fouled anchor with the Imperial Crown, a laurel wreath and a trident, and a gun-sponge and boat-hook.* (J. P. Puype collection).

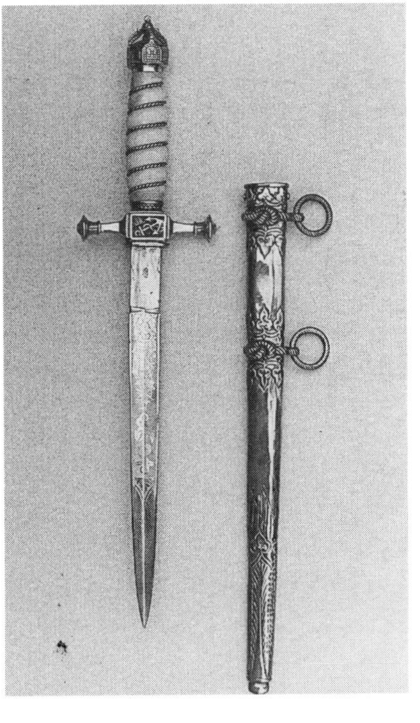

Right *A de-luxe quality Model 1890 Naval dirk. A short pattern dirk, which has some extra refinements–the scabbard, which has the standard pattern 'lightning bolt' design also features some additional engraving around the scabbard bands. The long pattern dirk (described previously) remained as the regulation pattern, but shorter patterns, which were more convenient to wear, especially at mess dress functions, gained rapid popularity and eventually replaced the longer pattern.*

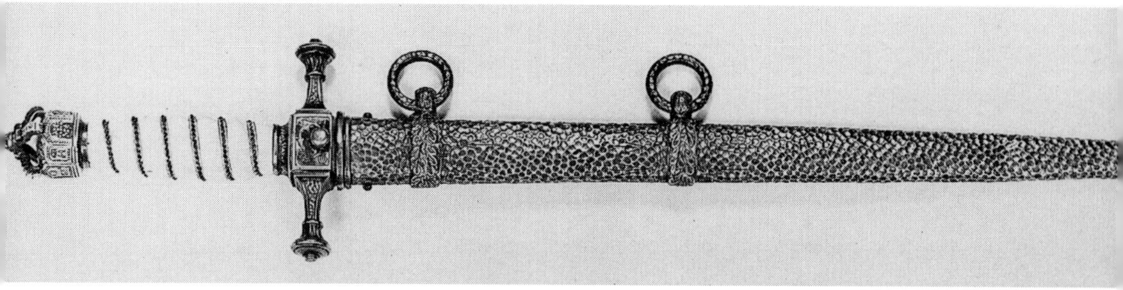

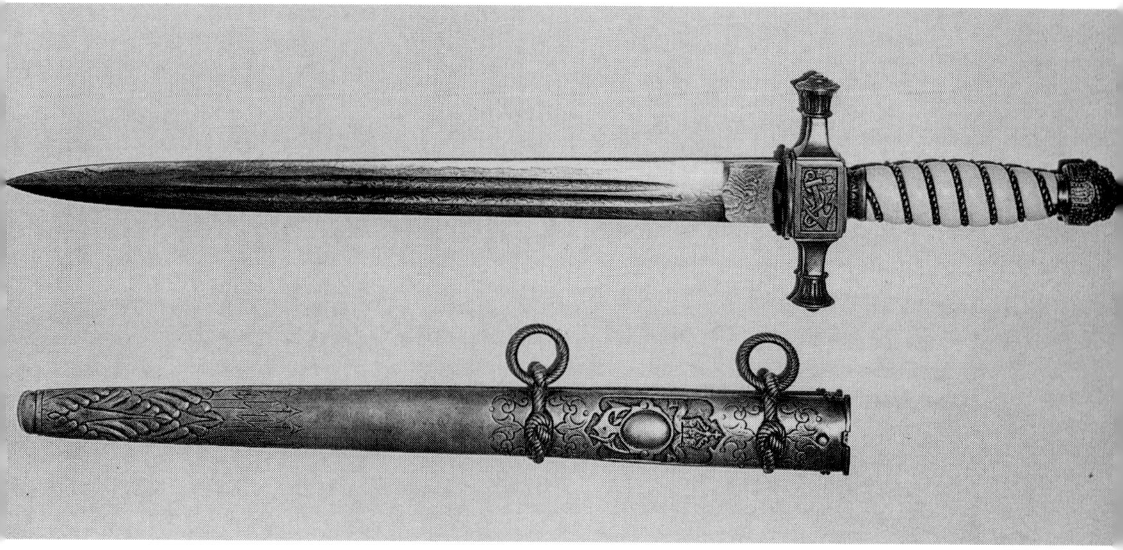

Top *De-luxe quality Model 1890 Naval dirk, having additional engraving to the crossguard, and a hammered pattern scabbard. The dirk dates from about 1910.* (Weller & Dufty, Birmingham).

Above *The 'Heavy Dirk', a de-luxe pattern Model 1890 dirk which came into production about 1900. The dirk follows the general style of the Model 1890, but is distinctive in that it is, overall, much larger than the regulation pattern. The blade and scabbard are distinctly fatter and wider. This example is complete with a damascus steel blade and ornately decorated scabbard.* (The late A. S. Walker photo collection).

Above right *The Model 1919 Naval dirk. On the formation of the Weimar Republic in 1919, a new pattern of dirk was authorized for the officers of the smaller Navy permitted under the terms of the Treaty of Peace. Emblems and style reminiscent of the old Imperial period were prohibited, and the Crown pommel of the 1890 pattern was replaced with the flame pommel (also considered to be representative of a globe encompassed with waves). The grip was made of black horn, and a new crossguard pattern was introduced.*

The most distinctive feature of the Model 1919 dirk was the plain, black steel scabbard with single suspension ring. This illustrated example features a brass scabbard band and suspension ring. (J. P. Puype collection).

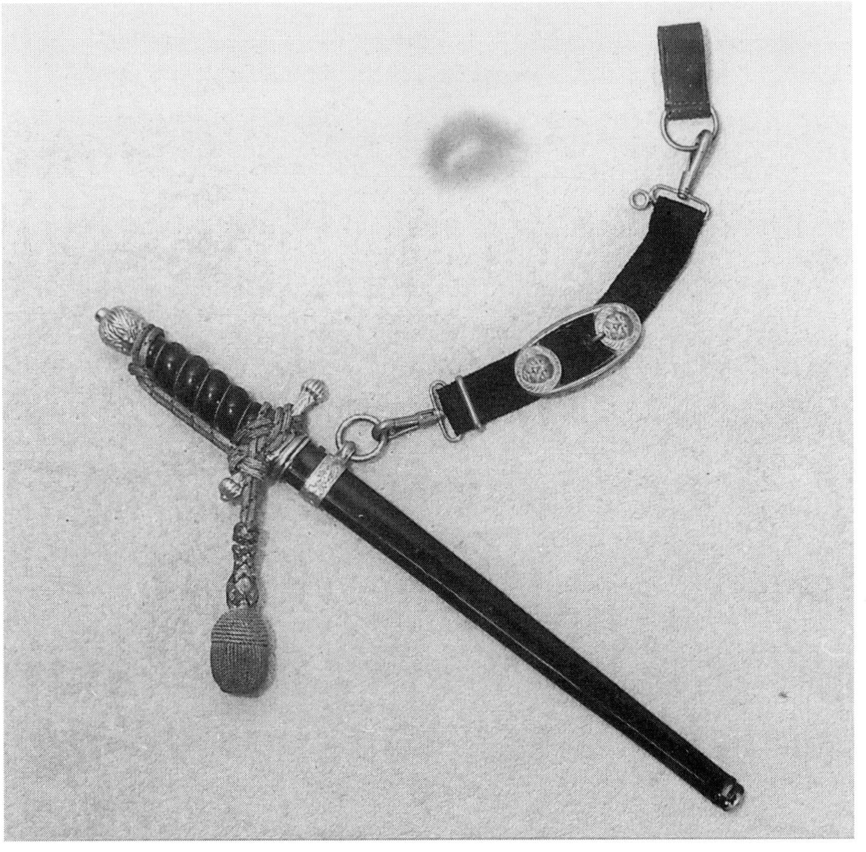

Below *Model 1919 Naval dirk. A regulation pattern having the feature of a frog stud on the scabbard to facilitate vertical suspension, as well as a movable scabbard band to allow the dirk to be suspended from a strap for dress purposes.* (J. P. Puype collection).

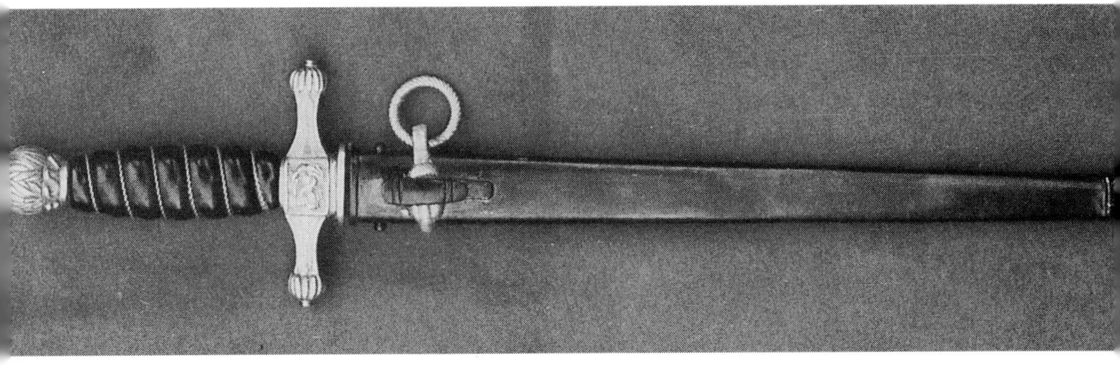

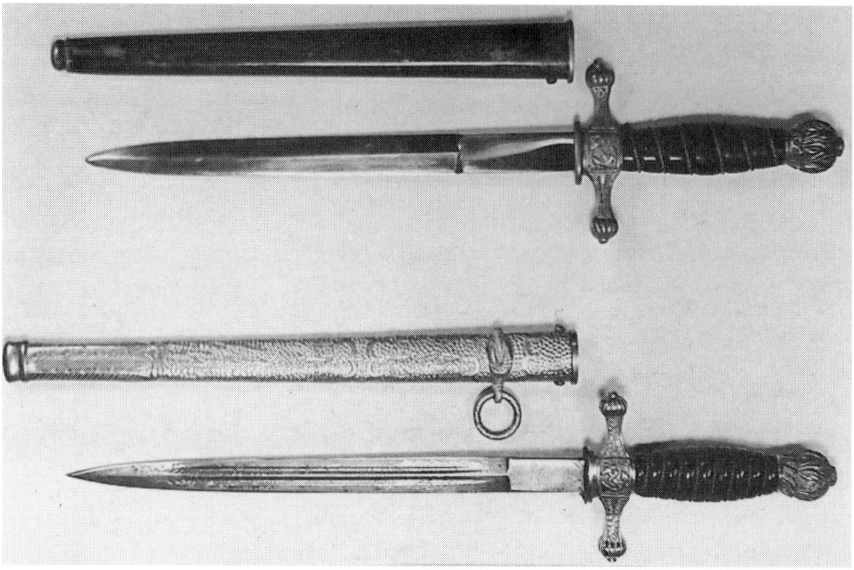

In 1921, a new modification to the Model 1919 dirk came into accepted usage – the restoration of the gilded brass scabbard. The two examples shown are (upper) the basic Model 1919 and (lower) the Model 1919/21. Note that the brass scabbard still utilizes single ring suspension. (Private collection, Denmark. Photo courtesy J. P. Puype).

instituted for the Naval dirk. This was the adoption, once again, of a white grip to replace the black pattern of 1919, and the re-introduction of the brass scabbard with twin suspension bands. This was the pattern that was to remain in service until well into the Third Reich, when it was modified yet again, under the new regulations of 1938.

1938 REGULATIONS

On April 20th 1938 (Adolf Hitler's birthday) the German Admiralty announced the regulations governing the new style of Naval dirk. The basic pattern was more or less identical to that of the 1929 pattern, but with one major difference, the flame pommel form of the Model 1919 was now to be replaced with a new style more representative of the National Socialist State, the eagle and swastika pommel.

Wear of the new pattern was not compulsory, serving members of the Third Reich Navy (now known as the *Kriegsmarine* — literally 'War Navy') who had formerly served with distinction in the old Imperial Navy were allowed to retain and wear their old-style Imperial dirks, which had hitherto been prohibited. Some manufacturers indeed started to produce the dirk in the old Model 1890 style. Many officers, however, who had served in the Imperial Navy, as well as in the post-war Weimar Navy, simply opted for the opportunity to continue wearing their old daggers, but with the new style pommel added.

At the time of introduction of the new style pommel, a special new dagger was also instituted. This was the Honour Dagger of the German Navy, a beautiful, de-luxe quality weapon that was to be awarded by the Commander-in-Chief of the German Navy, for meritorious deeds on behalf of the Navy. The dagger was similar to the regulation pattern, but notably distinct in that it possessed a damascus steel blade with dedication, solid ivory grip bound with a band of gold oakleaves, a decorated scabbard with an oakleaf design, and the swastika of the pommel was inset with 17 diamonds. The dagger pattern is virtually unique, only about 12 cases of the award have been identified so far, and as far as can be checked, about eight examples of the dagger are known to have survived the Second World War.

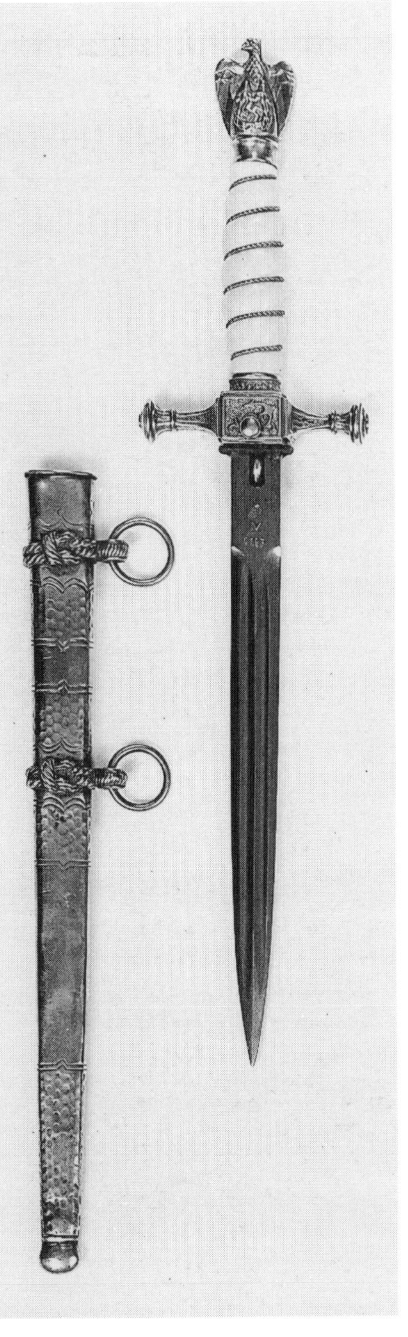

A Model 1890 Naval dirk, with the Model 1938 modification pommel. This dirk presents an interesting combination of fittings. The crossguard is clearly of the Model 1890 pattern, and the scabbard appears to be a de-luxe variation of pre-WWI vintage. The blade, however, is stamped with the Reichsmarine mark that was in use from 1919 to about 1932, and the pommel is the 1938 pattern eagle and swastika type. It is possible that the former owner could have served continually in the Navy through three periods of administration; salvaging his crossguard and scabbard from the 1890 pattern, adding a new blade and grip in the 1919/1929 period, and finally adopting the new pommel in 1938. (Weller & Dufty, Birmingham).

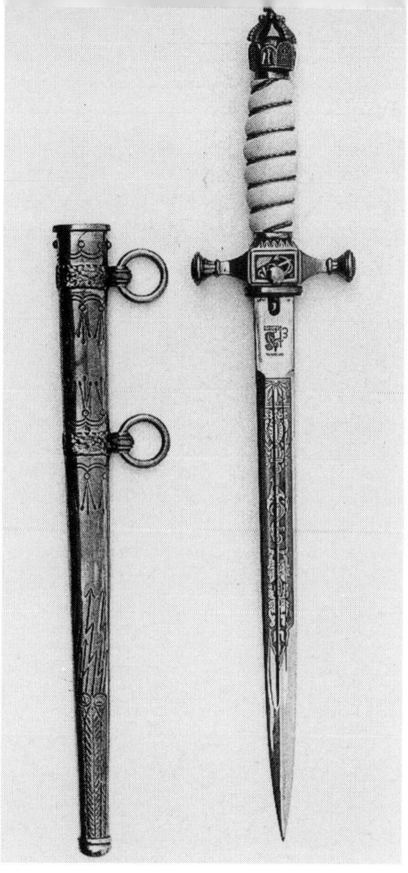

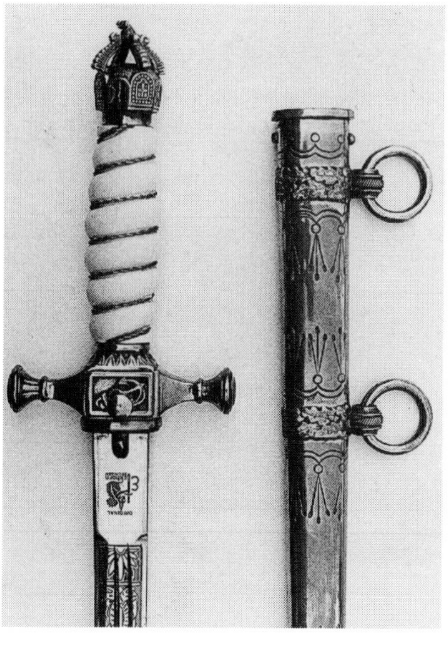

A Naval dirk of the Model 1890 pattern, but produced by Eickhorn of Solingen in the 1936–41 period. The dirk conforms in all proportions to that of the regulation 1938 pattern, and the trademark shown on the blade is that used by the company in the 1936–41 period. The crossguard and pommel are precisely in the style of the Model 1890. Officers who had served in the First World War with distinction, and who had lost their original dirks, could, under the 1938 regulations, obtain and wear a dirk in the old style if they so wished. This is one such example.

Regulation Model 1938 Naval dirk, with the 'lightning bolt' scabbard design. Manufacturer E. ü F. Hörster, Solingen.

The Regulation Model 1938 dirk previously described, shown complete with its portepee knot attached, and the original paper sack in which it was issued from the factory. The trademark on the paper sack, and also on the blade, indicate that it was produced after 1941.

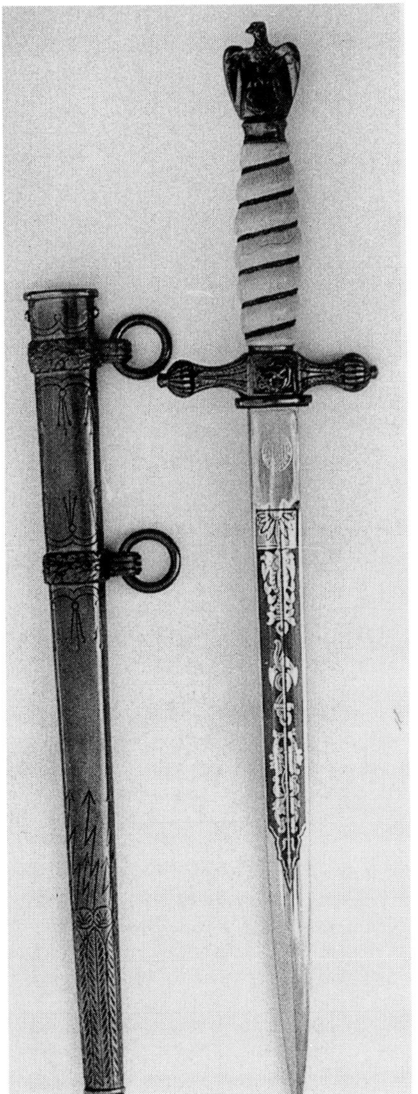

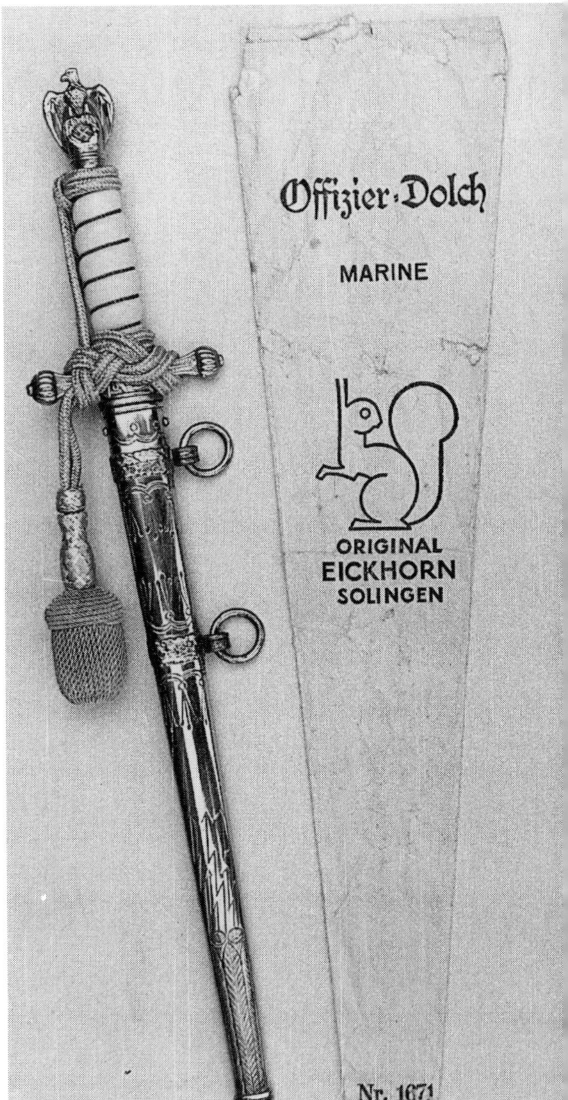

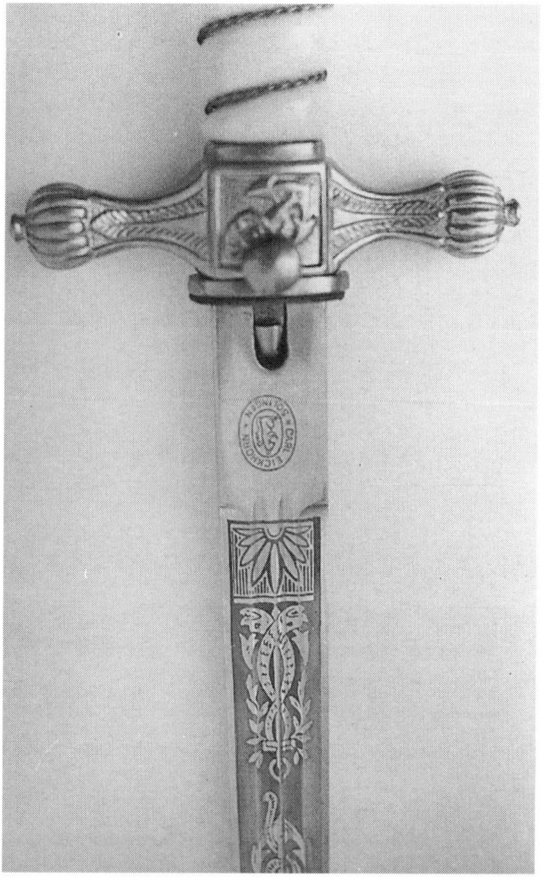

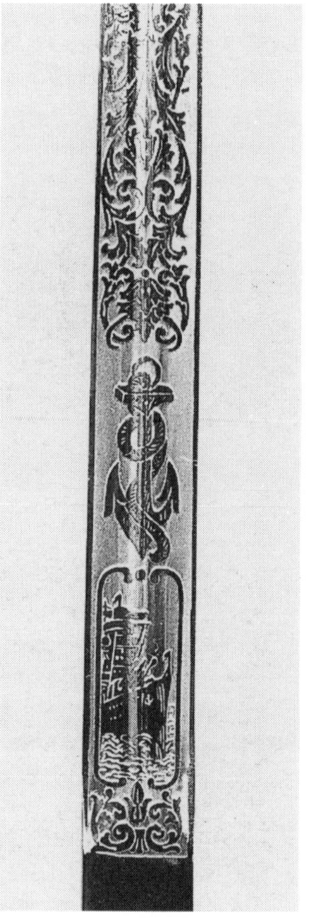

Above *Distinctions in some blade etchings: on the left is shown a detail view of a Naval dirk blade manufactured by Eickhorn, bearing the trademark pattern that was in use from 1934–36. The fine detail of the etching, showing sea-serpents entwined around an anchor, is a common design to many of the Naval dirks. Right: detail view of another dirk, where part of the design on the blade features a warship.*

Top right *A de-luxe quality Naval dirk having a solid ivory grip, plain damascus steel blade, and a hammered pattern scabbard which additionally has the lightning bolt design lightly engraved on the scabbard surface. The dagger is shown complete with its original felt carrying sack.* (John Burden collection).

Middle right *The de-luxe quality Naval dirk previously described, shown compared to a regulation Model 1938 Naval dirk. This particular de-luxe example is approximately 1 in longer, and the scabbard is about 1½ in longer than normal. The overall effect was of a strikingly long dirk.* (John Burden collection).

Right *Model 1938 Naval dirk with de-luxe fittings. The hammered scabbard finish of this dirk has been further enhanced with embossed designs of oak leaf panels.*

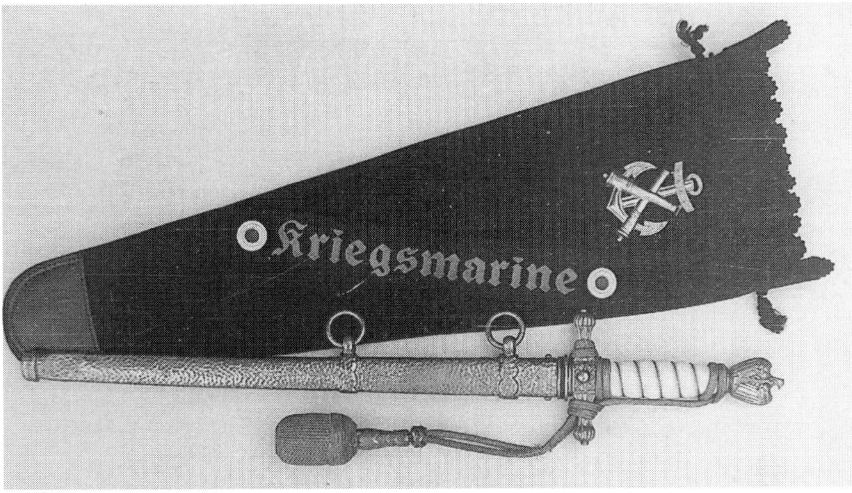
Kriegsmarine

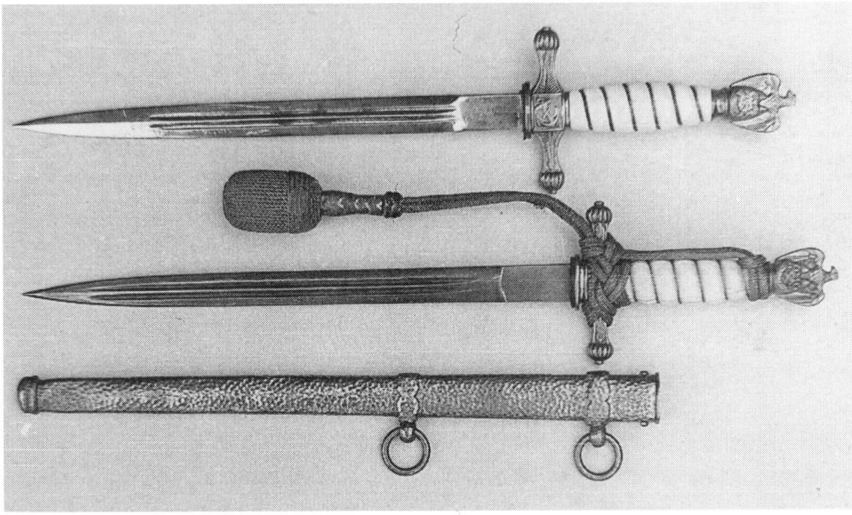

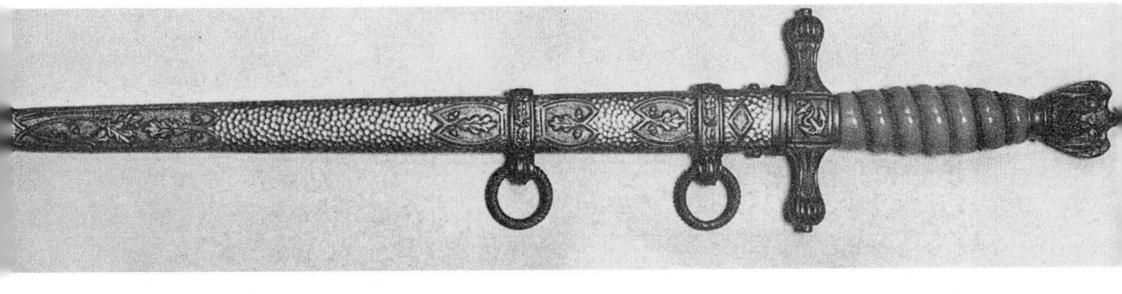

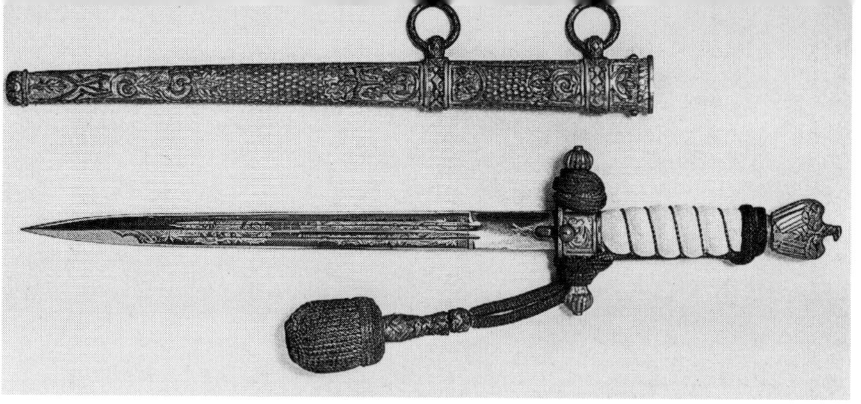

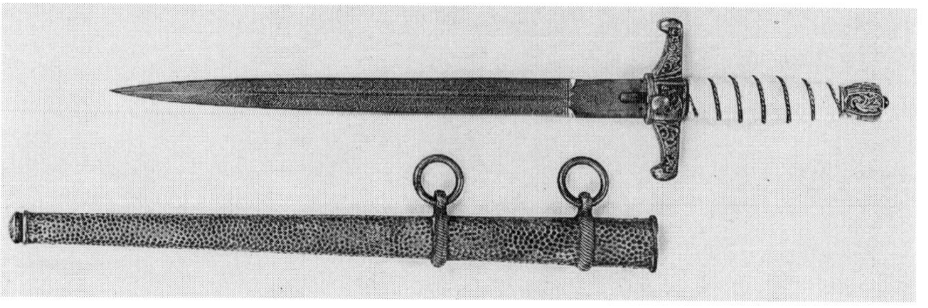

Top *A very attractive de-luxe quality Model 1938 Naval dirk. The scabbard decoration is in the form of scales with scrolled panels bearing the oak leaf motif.* (Lt.-Col. (retd.) J. R. Angolia).

Above *A variation Naval dirk. An unusual pattern of dirk which came into production in 1938, and is known to have been manufactured by at least three Solingen companies. The dirk style did not use the eagle and swastika pommel, but instead featured a dome with the oak leaf emblem, and the crossguard featured the eagle and swastika on one side, and the rope and fouled anchor emblem on the other. As far as can be established, this dirk pattern was simply an alternative design and had no specific application to any élite naval formation.*

Below *A group of senior SA and Party Officials observing a marksman. On the right, Admiral Raeder is wearing his Naval dirk.* (Library of Congress Collection).

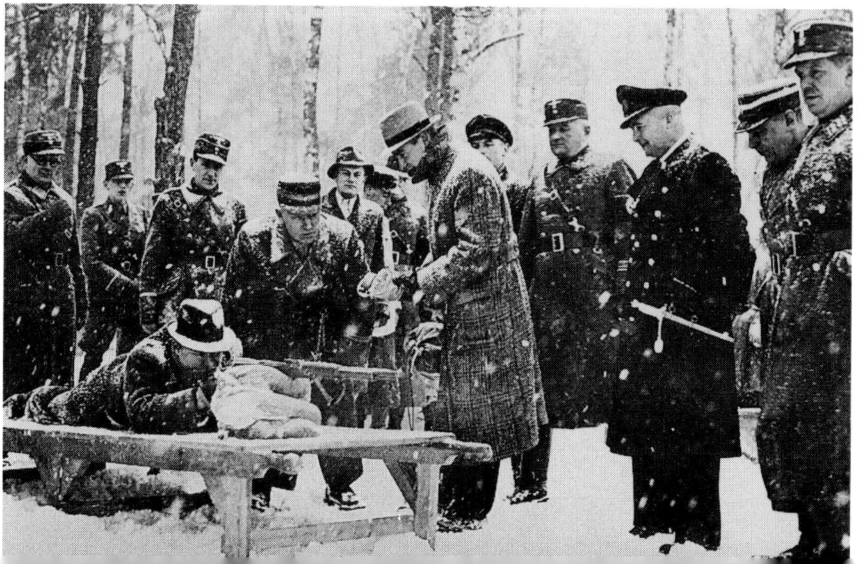

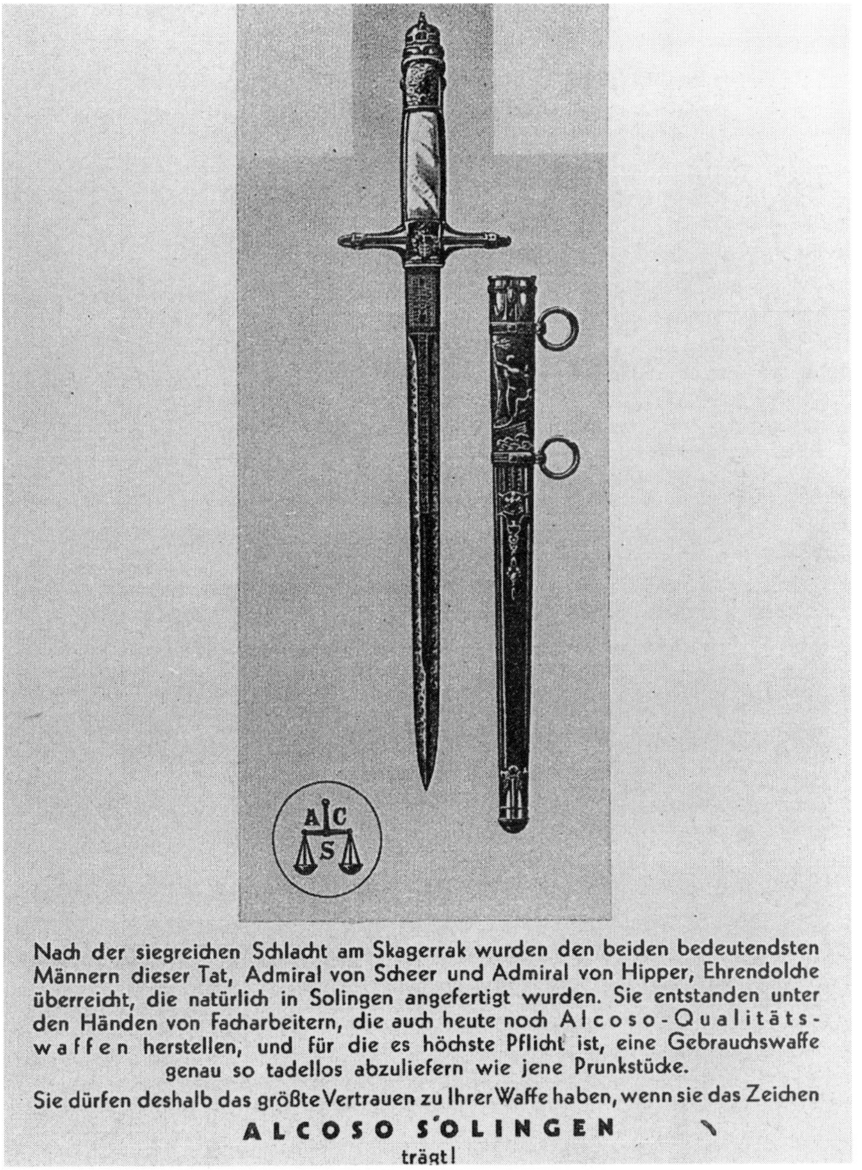

Publicity advertisement published by the Alcoso company, 1938, announcing the creation and presentation of two Honour Dirks to the respected war heroes Admiral von Scheer and Admiral von Hipper. The sole surviving record concerning these daggers appears to be in the form of photographs. Their present location, if indeed they survived the war, is currently unknown.

Luftwaffe daggers and swords

The Luftwaffe, which had its origins in the DLV organization, officially came into existence in 1935. The DLV at that time had been authorized to wear a dress dagger, and the pattern of the dagger was carried over into the new Luftwaffe. This was the Model 1934 Fliegerdolch (the 'Flier's Dagger'), a long, stylistic weapon that bore a striking similarity to a medieval sword. The hilt fittings were usually made of silver plated brass. The pommel was inset with a gold or copper coloured swastika. The crossguards were in the form of stylized wings, with the swastika featured in the central quillon block.

The scabbard was made of steel, and covered with a dark blue leather wrap—the same colour of leather which was wrapped over the wood-based grip. Suspension of the dagger was by two long rows of chains, usually of silver plated brass, which connected to the upper and central scabbard mounts, and then conjoined at the belt catch.

After about 1938, aluminium

A model 1934 Luftwaffe dagger, with the close-up view of the blade showing the trademark (in this case that of the SMF company of Solingen), as well as a small proof mark indicating that the blade had been inspected and tested by the Luftwaffe ordnance authority.

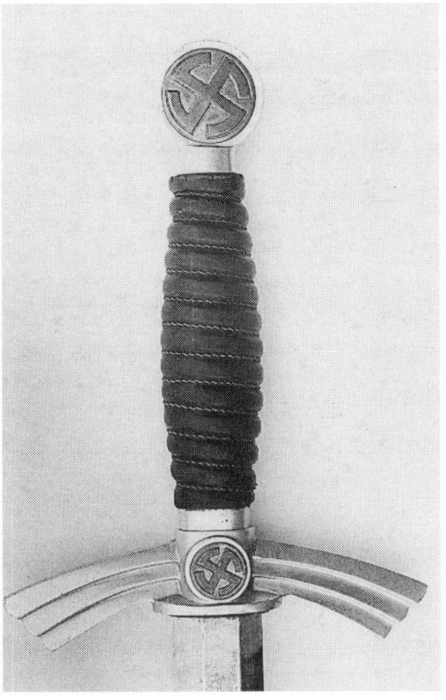

fittings, predominated—the lightweight metal being in some respects symbolic of an aircraft itself.

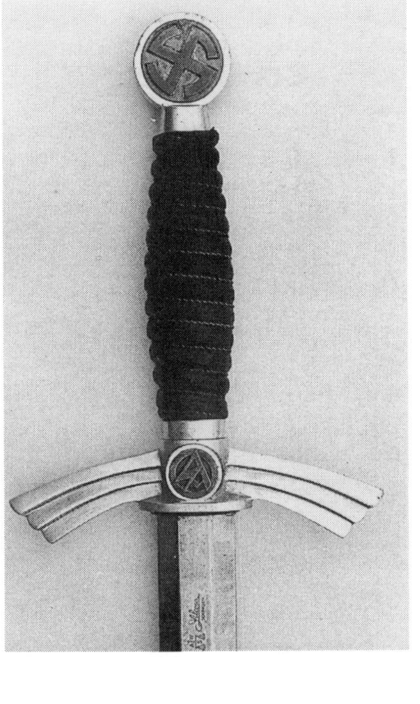

Detail views of an unusual Luftwaffe Model 1934 Flier's Dagger, this example being remarkable in that the reverse of the crossguard bears an SA insignia in the place of the swastika (the obverse side bears the swastika as normal). Although the SA possessed a flying section, it is not believed that the membership carried anything other than the recognized SA dagger. This anomaly on a Luftwaffe dagger appears to have been a private modification, although it is very professionally executed. Possibly a former member of the SA being transferred to the Luftwaffe might have arranged to have this modification carried out by the factory for his own personal dagger. The construction and finish of this item are typical of pieces produced in the 1938–40 period. (Harvey Riley).

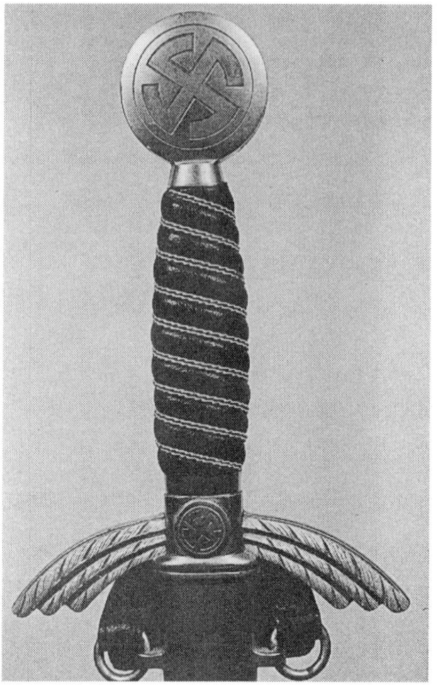

Above left *Hermann Goering, Reichs Minister of Aviation, addressing a meeting, circa 1935. Goering is wearing his DLV uniform, complete with sword. The sword pattern is that which has since become synonymous with the most distinctive of the Luftwaffe weapons, although as this photograph clearly shows, the Luftwaffe sword had its origins in a DLV pattern sword.*

Above *Hermann Goering, on the occasion of his marriage in May, 1935. Now dressed in Luftwaffe uniform, Goering wears what must be one of the first true Luftwaffe swords, although it has the distinction of being different in the grip wrapping to the regulation patterns.*

Left *Hilt detail of the regulation pattern Luftwaffe sword.* (Lt.-Col. (retd.) J. R. Angolia).

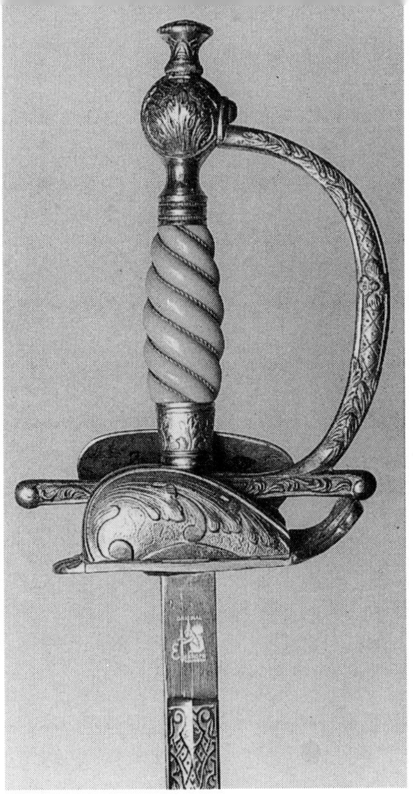

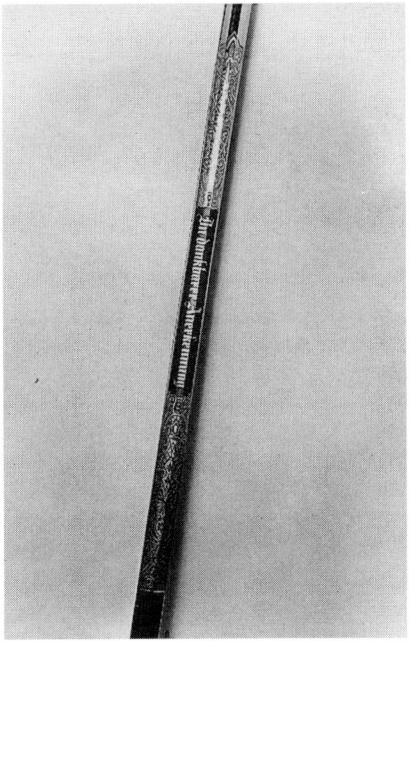

At the time of the adoption of the new dress weapons for the Luftwaffe, the Air Ministry also decreed the institution of a dress sword for General officers of the new Luftwaffe. The sword pattern was that of a Gala Degen ('Court sword'). The first examples of the General's sword had a wire-bound grip, but the design was subsequently altered to produce a version with a white ivorine grip, with the Luftwaffe eagle and swastika emblem mounted on the clamshell guard.

Subsequent to the establishment of the Luftwaffe General's sword, Goering decreed the status of an 'Honour Sword', which meant that certain General staff officers could additionally feature a presentation inscription on the blade of the sword. The wording of the inscription was, on one side: 'In grateful recognition', and on the other side 'The Command in Chief of the Luftwaffe, Hermann Goering'. (Chris Farlow Collection).

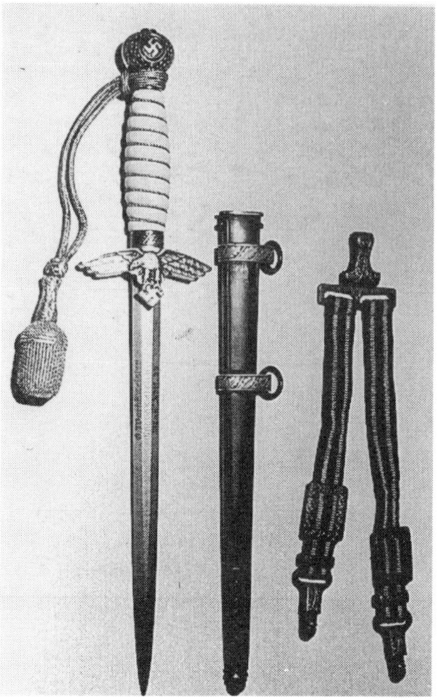

Above left *Hermann Goering, with the 1st pattern General's Sword shown in wear.*

Above *The 2nd pattern Luftwaffe General's Sword shown in wear.*

Left *In 1937, the Air Ministry announced the adoption of a new pattern of dagger for Luftwaffe Officers, and unteroffizier mit portepee (senior NCOs). The original Model 1934 dagger was retained for service, but new officers entering the Luftwaffe could elect to adopt the new pattern dagger.*

The overall size and construction of the Model 1937 dagger was very similar to that of the Model 1935 Army dagger, differing in the shape of the grip, the pommel bearing the swastika, and the crossguard, which was formed in the style of a flighted eagle. The stipple-finished scabbard featured a panel of oak leaves in the lower section close to the tip. The overall finish to the metal hilt fittings and the scabbard body was intended to be a matt, steel grey, to

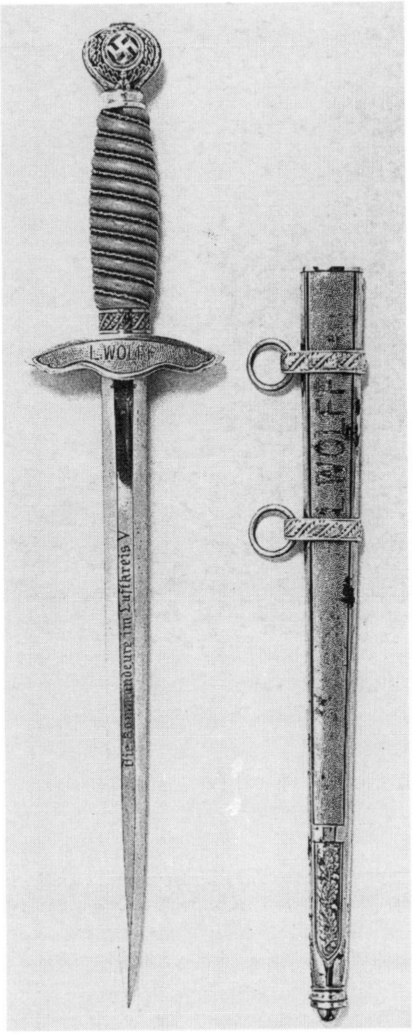

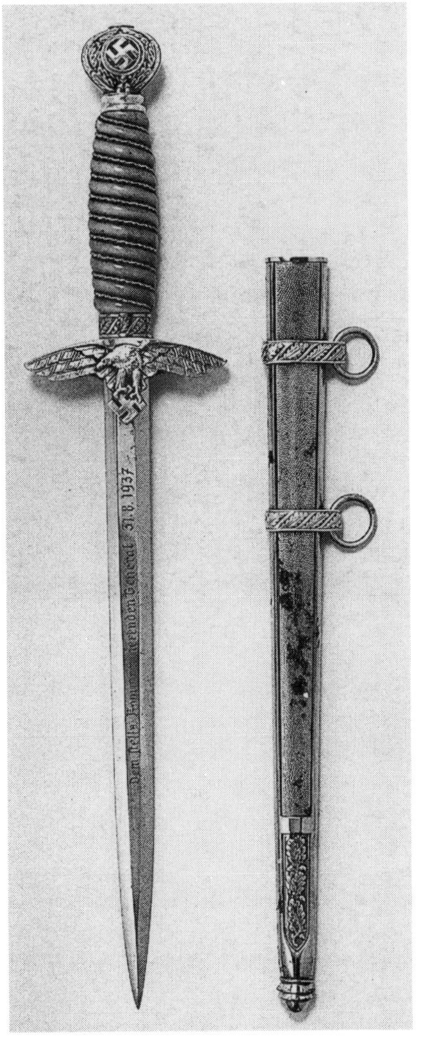

complement the colour of the Luftwaffe uniform. Examination of numerous examples reveals, however, that many were produced with a silver or nickel finish.

This page *Model 1937 Luftwaffe dagger that formerly belonged to General Ludwig Wolff, later commanding general of Luftgau XI. The blade, manufactured by the SMF company of Solingen, bears the etched dedication: 'Dem Stellv. Kommandierenden General 31. 8. 37' on one side, and on the other: 'Die Kommandeure im Luftkreis V'. The dagger was presumably presented to General Wolff on the occasion of promotion from Luftkreis V to take up his command of Luftgau XI.* (Lt.-Col. (retd.) J. R. Angolia).

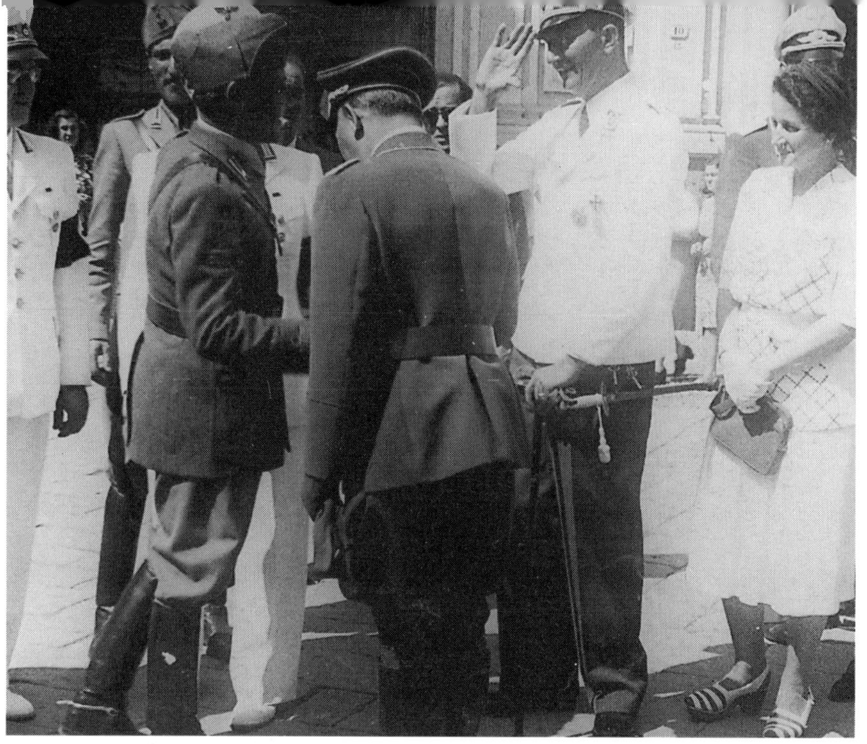

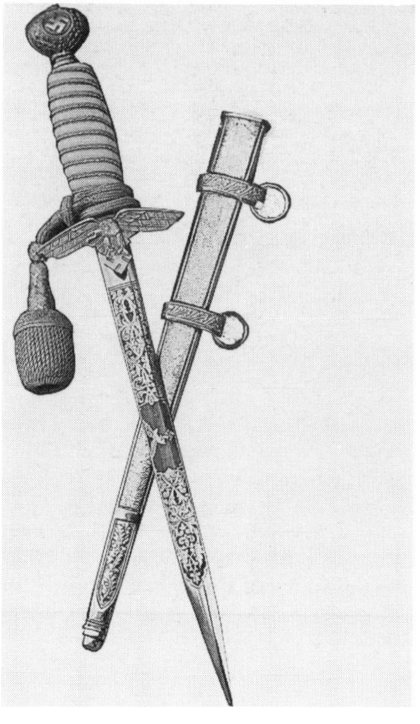

Above *Luftwaffe officer in summer uniform, complete with Model 1937 dagger, greeting a member of the Italian air force.*

Left *Regulation pattern Luftwaffe dagger Model 1937, with de-luxe quality etched blade.* (Gordon White collection).

Above right *The Luftwaffe machette, a service issue tool that was apparently issued as standard equipment to bomber crews. The machette was not carried on the uniform as such, but was apparently stored in the aircraft as part of the inventory equipment. The purpose of the item was to serve as a utility tool/survival weapon, in the event of the crew being grounded in hostile conditions.*

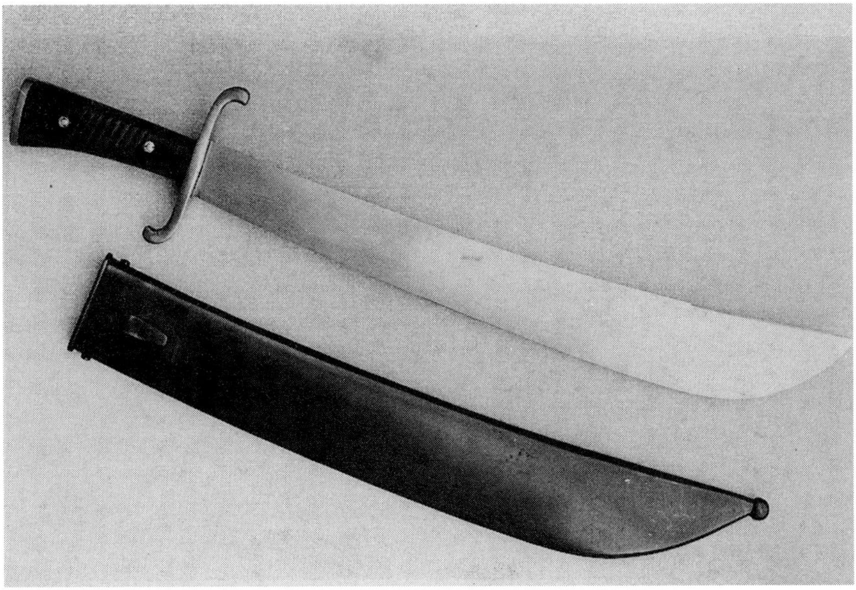

Right *The Paratrooper's gravity knife. This specially designed knife, although popularly referred to as a 'Paratrooper's Knife' was in fact a flight utility knife designed to be carried by all aircrew when on missions. The item is so constructed that the blade is totally enclosed within the hilt when not in use, and release of the blade is effected by pressing a spring clip whilst pointing the knife downwards – the blade drops into position and the same spring clip secures the blade rigidly in position. The intention was to allow the knife to be open and closed in a one-hand operation.*

The design of this item was highly successful, so much so that in 1941 the British started copying the design for production as a special forces weapon. In the post-war years, the knife has also been manufactured for the Bundeswehr Luftwaffe, differing little in style from the original pattern, only in the modern materials used for its construction.

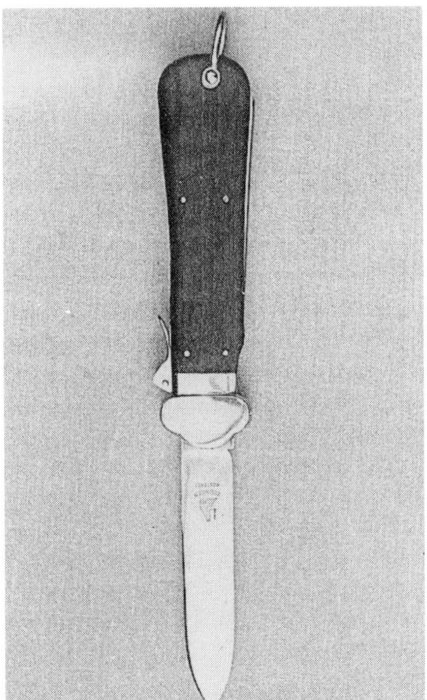

An advertisement page from a 1938 issue of Die Klinge magazine, detailing the extent to which Solingen, and Ludenscheid, catered for the supply of goods to the military formations of the Reich. The ancillary accoutrements of swords and daggers – belts, buckles, chains, clips, etc. were being volume produced, and adverts offering and promoting these fittings were prominently featured alongside the more traditional tailors' offerings of uniforms, badges, and hats etc.

Below left *Luftwaffe Forester's sidearm. Apart from regular flying operations, the Luftwaffe was also put in charge of forestry in areas of Germany, a move no doubt motivated by the fact that the Commander in Chief of the Luftwaffe (Goering) had a strong interest in forests and hunting, so there existed a Luftwaffe Forestry Service. A special dress bayonet/sidearm was designed for the service, being basically a dress bayonet blade and scabbard, to which was fitted a stag horn hilt. All examples studied have been seen to have been produced by the same concern (Waffen—Loesche, of Berlin) and all are issue numbered.*

Below right *In 1941, on the appointment of 12 new Field Marshals, Adolf Hitler bestowed upon Field Marshal Goering a position of new rank, one that had been especially created exclusively for Goering himself–Reichsmarschall, a unique position that elevated Goering to the status of second in command of the Reich. The position naturally required the creation and production of new, unique badges of rank.*

As Goering was known to have a love of daggers and swords, and was seldom seen without one or the other adorning his uniform, the creation of a special dagger was undertaken as a gift for Goering by students of the Berlin Technical Academy, under the guidance of Professor Herbert Zeitner. The dagger was a unique creation, having a pommel encrusted with sapphires and tourmalines, solid ivory grip, and a bejewelled Reichsmarschall pattern eagle, swastika and batons on the crossguard.

Few photographs showing this unique dagger are known, and it was not until 1946, when an exhibition of German war booty was staged in London, that this dagger, and some other choice pieces, was publically exhibited. The photograph below was taken at that time by the press photographer Thomas S. Law. Since that occasion, the subsequent whereabouts of this unique dagger has been a mystery.

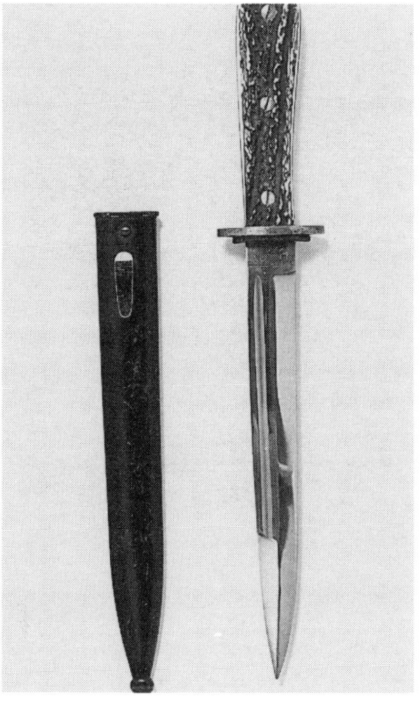

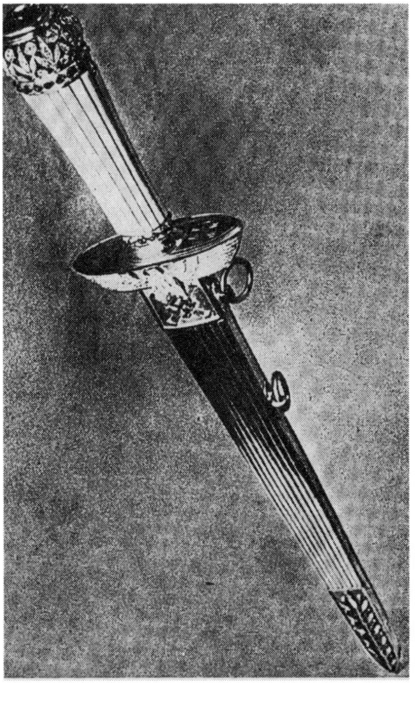

10 The Orderly Society
The Labour Corps, Police and Justice, Fire Service, Railways and Waterways, Customs Unions, The DLV/NSFK, The Technische Nothilfe, The Red Cross, The Reich Air Defence League

We will never approach history impartially, but as Germans
'Die Deutsche Schule'
Educational Paper, September, 1933.

Every government when taking office inherits the institutions and systems of control and power that were maintained by the out-going government. The Third Reich, in adopting the incumbency of the old Weimar Republic was no different; the seat of power, the administration, the ministerial apparatus of the nation was absorbed and emerged as a new generation in place of the old, and was reshaped according to the new ideals.

The essential bodies which ensured the smooth day-to-day running of the nation were, naturally enough, the Police and Judicial systems, together with the Customs and Excise departments, followed by numerous other semi-official or voluntary organizations. They had existed in Imperial times and during the Weimar period, and consequently were carried over into the NSDAP administration.

Other organizations which had formerly been restricted to provincial control, such as the Railways and Communications organizations, were radically shaken up and expanded under the Third Reich. Railways were an indispensable lifeline for industry, bringing in the essential raw materials and enabling the despatch of completed products.

Other organizations were almost new creations, which if not exclusive to the Third Reich were more profitably exploited by it, such as the *Reichsarbeits Dienst* (RAD)—Reich Labour Service.

The Reich Labour Service

During the latter part of the Weimar period, a volunteer organization prepared to undertake manual social services had come into being, the

Freiwilliger Arbeits Dienst (FAD) – Volunteer Labour Service. The FAD was mainly staffed on a part-time basis by unemployed persons, who were paid for their services in performing manual duties of benefit to the community. A full-time cadre of personnel also existed within the FAD, but it was a relatively small portion of the overall membership, and functioned mainly in an administrative capacity.

When the old FAD came under the control of the new Reich government, it was immediately restructured. Under the Reich the FAD would become known as the Reich Labour Service, the RAD, and was organized on a national scale. The full-time professional membership was expanded, and voluntary membership on a part-time basis was encouraged, and—more importantly—mandatory service in the RAD organization was enforced for all persons of suitable age. The RAD became an organization which ensured that school-leavers did not drift off into a wayward life, but instead were re-routed into State service in a manual labour capacity. A short term of service in the RAD was compulsory, and members were put to work on road- and house-building projects, offered as 'free' labour to some industries, or made to perform services that were vital to the agrarian economy of Germany. The RAD motto, *Arbeit adelt*—'Labour ennobles', admirably sums up the objective of instilling the work ethic in groups of young people who had

The RAD Hewer, introduced in 1933; the heavy hewer knife was originally worn only by full-time personnel within the RAD service. The hilt fittings are made of iron, or brass, and heavily silver-plated. The grip scales are made of antler horn, and secured in position by screw-slotted bolts and nuts.

The broad blade is single edged, and bears the etched inscription on the obverse face 'Arbeit adelt' – Labour ennobles.

The heavy scabbard is made of steel, stove enamelled black, and with silver plated fittings – the upper fitting bearing a recurring scroll design, the lower one decorated with the swastika and spade emblem of the RAD service.

The RAD Hewer was normally issue numbered – with the numbers appearing on the reverse face of the grip ferrule, and on the upper area of the scabbard throat.

The two examples illustrated are, on the left, the First Pattern Model 1933, with the full stag horn grips. The Second Pattern Model 1933, on the right, is basically identical, but the stag horn grips are cut back from the 'beak' of the pommel. This pattern of hewer was standard issue for all full-time RAD officers and men.

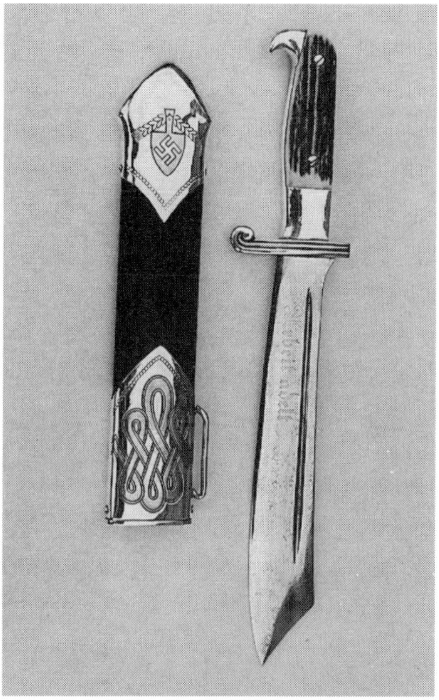

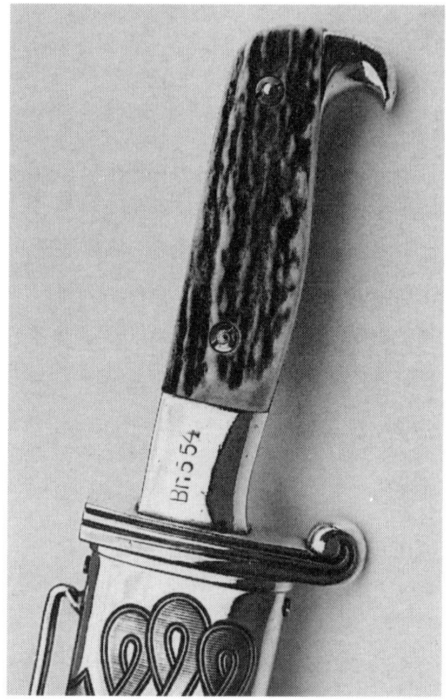

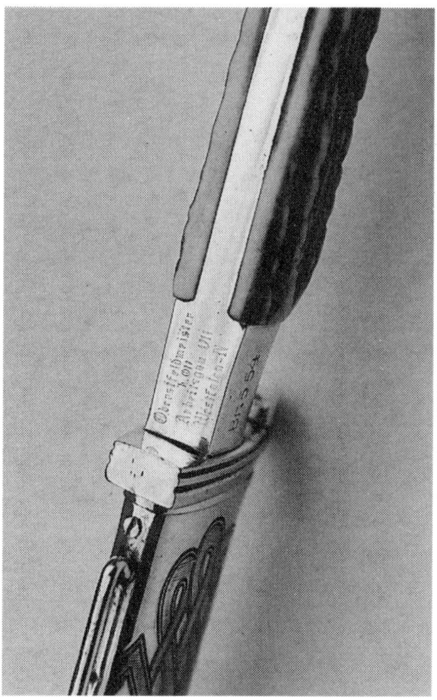

An issue pattern RAD Hewer, which has been personalized by a former owner. These detail views show the location of the issue pattern numbers on the reverse ferrule and scabbard throat, and on the back face of the ferrule/backstrap, the engraved inscription: 'Oberstfeldmeister (Captain) K. Ott, Labour District VII, Westfalen-North.' (Graham Boddy collection).

is suspected, however, that the dagger was probably awarded between April 1938 and September 1939, as all other daggers after this period are known to bear the inscription on the blade ricasso. (Harvey Riley.)

Above *Obverse and reverse of a unique pattern of dagger – the RAD Hewer that was carried by Konstantin Hierl as Reichs Leader of the German Labour Corps. The hewer is basically a Model 1934 pattern, but is distinctive in that the blade is artificial damascus steel, all the fittings on the hilt and scabbard are gold plated, and the suspension system required a double-strap hanger, instead of the single-strap pattern more usual for this hewer. Hierl continued to wear this unique pattern long after the Model 1937 Hewer was devised for the RAD Leaders.* (Dr. R. Distelhorst collection.)

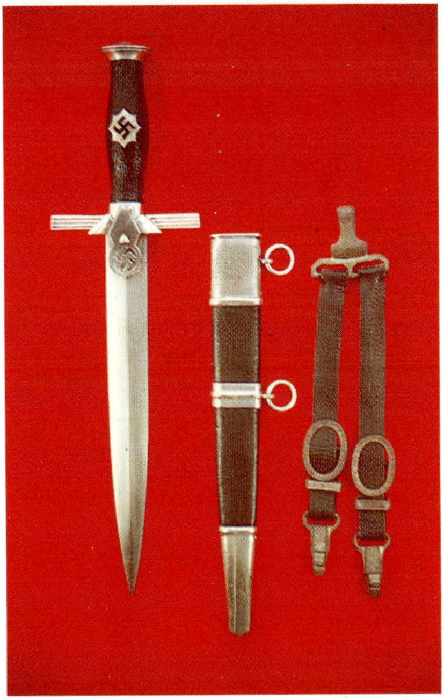

Right *The Second Pattern RLB Leader's Dagger, complete with straps.* (Lt.-Col. (retd.) J. R. Angolia collection.)

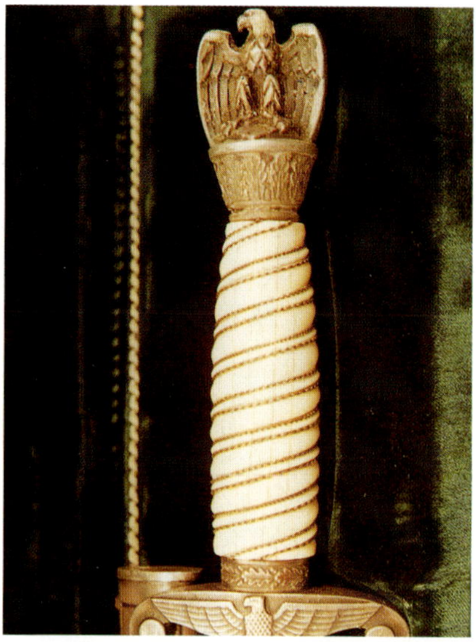

A second known example of the Army Honour Dagger, this specimen was presented to NSKK Reichskorpsführer Hühnlein. The dagger has a damascus blade by Alcoso, with small rose pattern decoration, and a presentation inscription. The presentation case in which the dagger is shown is an authentic case for the Army Honour Dagger, but was discovered separately, and a current owner of the dagger succeeded in obtaining the case for housing the dagger. According to all the available research, only four such daggers were awarded, and due to the unique proportions of the item, and the knowledge governing the pattern of presentation cases used for the other examples, it is highly probable that this case shown is indeed the original case for this dagger – re-united after almost 45 years apart. (Steven Wolfe and N. Neil Hardin Collection: Photos by N. Neil Hardin.)

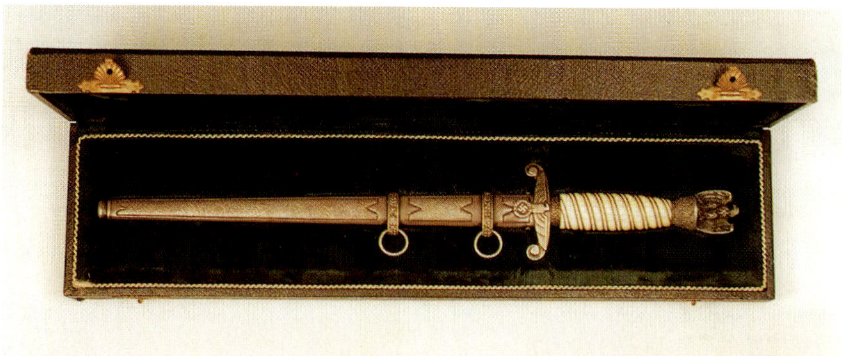

no previous experience of work or labour. The supply of an industrious labour force was viewed as an essential prerequisite to the further stabilization of the Reich economy and industries.

The services of the RAD extended considerably further than the basic concept of a supply of manpower to perform industrial and agricultural duties as a social obligation; the RAD had departments which specialized in welfare and medical matters, and worked hand-in-hand with the ministerial departments concerned with such matters as social welfare, health and safety, etc. Voluntary membership of the RAD was open to males and females, and compulsory conscription for an 18 month period between leaving full-time education and service in the armed forces was, after 1936, mandatory for all males.

In keeping with Hitler's promises of regenerating the national economy, the Nazi government had passed, in July, 1933, the Act for the Formation of Compulsory Cartels. This law was designed to ensure that German businessess and industries would receive German orders. The importation of foreign goods was to be restricted, Germany would henceforth be a predominantly exporting nation bolstered by a demanding home economy. To make this system work, compulsory labour in one of the State

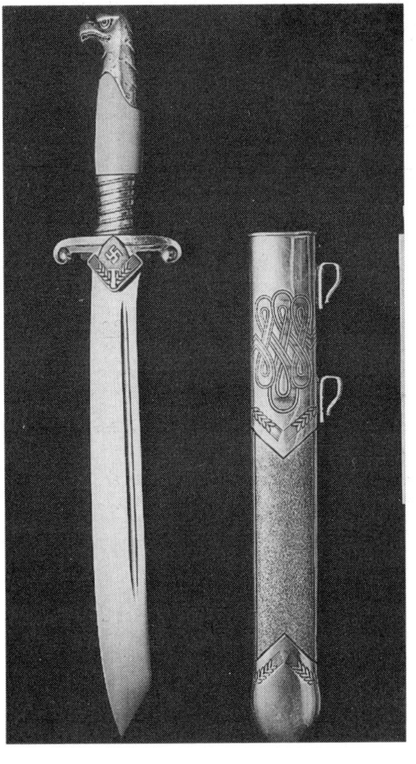

In 1937 the RAD authority decreed the institution of a new pattern of hewer to be worn by all leader ranks within the organization. The new pattern hewer was based along the same lines as its predecessor, but was much more elegant and stylish in construction. All metal portions of the hilt were, usually, made of aluminium or a zinc/aluminium alloy, and the total pommel was cast in the form of a stylized eagle head, with the RAD spade and swastika emblem incorporated in the crossguard design. The grip scales were made of a white ivorine substance, and secured in position by a single screw which fitted through from the reverse side.

The blade was formed in much the same manner as the Model 1933 hewer, with the RAD motto etched on the obverse, but was more slender, in keeping with the style of this new pattern. The flat scabbard was silver plated, and featured a stipple-finished panel in the centre section – originally finished in a blue metallic coating – with a scroll design on the upper (locket) area. The dagger was normally worn suspended from two plain leather straps, although a parade version of the straps, finished in silver bullion, is known to exist. (Melvyn Godfrey collection).

Konstantin Hierl, Reich Leader of the RAD organization, together with Führer Adolf Hitler, review the RAD formation marchpast at the Nuremburg Rally, 1938. Hierl wears his own special version of the Model 1934 Hewer, which was suspended from double straps—see colour section for a study of this unique Hewer. Immediately behind Hierl stands one of the RAD Arbeitsgau Leaders wearing the newly introduced Model 1937 Leader pattern hewers. (Library of Congress collection).

organizations was essential to feed the demand for workers, to operate the system, to produce the goods that would make the Reich both a seller and a consumer on a massive scale.

In 1932, during the recurring turmoil between the Nazis and the Social Democrats and Communists, numerous processions of unemployed workers were to be seen in every major town, chanting slogans and carrying their banners with the words *Arbeit und Brot*—'work and bread'. It is debatable whether or not the Social Democrats or the Communists would have made much headway in meeting these demands that they proclaimed for their members, had they ever achieved power. The need for work and bread for the working man and his family was a strongly emotive issue. The Nazis had already determined that this too would not only be one of their policies, but would be one of their initial, prime objectives: work and bread for the unemployed, and it would be force-fed to them whether they wanted it or not.

In January, 1933, the unemployed figure for the whole of Germany was in excess of 6,000,000. By July, 1935, it was less than 2,000,000. By 1939, Germany actually had a shortage of labour—more jobs were available than hands to work them. The voids were to be filled by *Gastarbeiter*—'guest workers', brought in from neighbouring, less effective states, which had not yet cracked the problem of the unemployed. It was an orderly society in which everything had its place, and every member had a role to play. The socialist ideal of work for everyone, combined with the capitalist idea of making money in order to enjoy it all. The pitifulness of the great Depression was old history in the Germany of the Third Reich.

The Police State

An effective Police service represents the most important and accessible level of civil authority to all members of any community, and the Third Reich was no different to other nations in this respect. From Imperial times the effectiveness, and far-reaching power of the Prussian police system, had rendered outsiders to consider the system as, effectively, one of being a Police State. The power of the Police authority under Prussia was formidable; under Hitler it was almost totalitarian, for the Police service of the Third Reich was virtually an extension of the SS.

Before 1933 the Police power had been in the hands of the individual German states. However, with the assumption of Nazi power in 1933 Hermann Goering—as Minister-President and Prussian Minister of the Interior—immediately took control of the Police service within Prussian territory, a geographical domain of about three-fifths of the whole of the Reich. This situation was more than simply a revision of the Police authorities within a territorial area, it was a conversion into an instrument of personal power for Goering. One of the first activities in reshaping the Police system was the enactment of the law for 'restoration of the civil service' (7 April 1933), and the immediate dismissal of any Police personnel who were suspected of being politically unreliable. The political branch of the Prussian Police, which had hitherto kept observation on political agitators during the Weimar period, was subsequently converted into the State Secret Police (*Geheime Staatspolizei*—Gestapo), which reported directly to Goering himself. In May 1933 the SS chief of Berlin and North Germany, Daluege, was appointed as chief of the Prussian State Police.

During the period in which Goering was restructuring the Prussian Police Service, Heinrich Himmler (later to become the supreme chief of all the SS) was doing exactly the same throughout all the other German states, and becoming in all of them the leader of the political section of the Police. In April, 1934, Himmler was appointed as head of the Prussian Gestapo. Within a year the Prussian administrative court decided that the Gestapo's activities were not subject to judicial control. On 17 June 1936 Himmler (by this time firmly established as *Reichsführer-SS*—Reich Leader of the SS) was additionally appointed Chief of Police in the Reich Ministry of the Interior. The outcome of this was that the Police services of all the German States became progressively more autonomous and free of State administration and influence; and that the connection between the Police and SS became more firmly interlinked, with the SS being the dominant force controlling all aspects of police work.

Generally speaking, the Police organization was divided into two basic groups—the *Ordnungspolizei* (Order Police) with the appointed leader of SS Chief Daluege; and the *Sicherheitspolizei*—the Security Police, headed by Reinhardt Heydrich. The spheres of police-type activity encompassed by these two basic sub-divisions of the Police system were as follows:

Ordnungspolizei
All uniformed police concerning public order
Schutzpolizei (Protection Police)
Gendarmerie (Metropolitan Police)
Gemeindepolizei (Rural Police)
Police Fire Service
Water Protection Police
Technische Nothilfe (Technical Emergency Service)

Sicherheitspolizei
The Gestapo

Other organizations also existed in the Reich which functioned in a police-type protection capacity. Initially these organizations, which worked in close co-operation with the regular Police where necessary, were independent of the national system. However, following the outbreak of hostilities in 1939, many of these organizations were suddenly absorbed into the national police system, in the interests of state security. Amongst these newer members of the Police fold were: the *Reichs Luftschutzbund*—Reich Air Defence League; the *Bahnschutz* and *Reichsbahnwassershutz-polizei*—Railway Protection Service and Railways and Waterways Protection Police; and the *Postschutz*—the Postal Protection Service.

Many of these organizations already possessed their own distinctive dress weapon patterns, and they continued to bear them whilst under the auspices of the expanding Police administration of the Reich.

Police sidearms

In 1933, when the Nazis came to power, the police systems of the Reich were divided between the various German states. As such, Prussia (the largest of the states) had its own police system with its own distinctive uniform and trappings; and other smaller states had, likewise, their own distinctive insignia. One of the first objectives of the new administration was to arrange for the dissolution of the individual state police services, and their replacement by a national police system. There also existed at that time various political police groups, whose role was not diminished but was more effectively incorporated into a new political police system that would function nationally throughout the Reich. This new department, responsible for the political direction of the internal states and the inherent security associated with that objective, was to become known as the Gestapo—*Geheime Staats Polizei*, 'State Secret Police'. Thus the relationship between the Police as a national authority and the SS, as a political policing authority, became firmly established.

The style and wearing of police sidearms in the period following January 1933, was rapidly standardized, and the relationship between the regular/criminal police departments and that of the Judiciary was more clearly defined.

Above *Policeman on point duty, circa 1933–4. The distinctive Police pattern sidearm, the clamshell bayonet, is clearly visible in this photograph.* (The late A. S. Walker photo collection).

Above *A de luxe quality bayonet of the Prussian State Police. In the period following the amalgamation of the German states, more and more police services became amalgamated, and obliged to adopt the emblems of the new National Socialist State. This particular example features the sunburst and eagle emblem which had been the standard emblem on the grips of all police bayonets in Prussia from the mid-1920s through to 1936.* (Dr Julian Milestone collection).

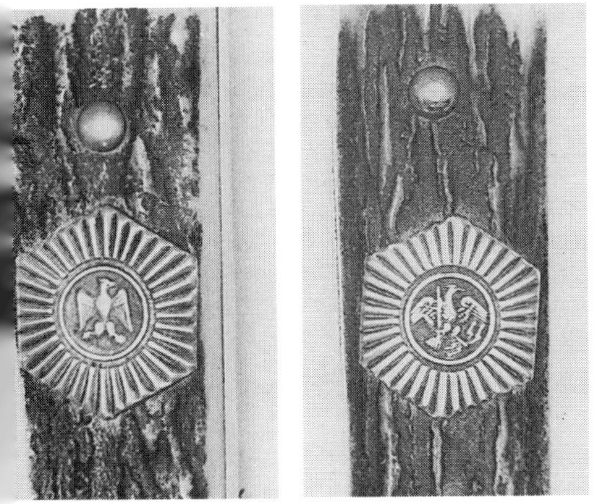

Left *A political police unit, the SA Feldjägerkorps, had existed in Prussia from early 1933. Like the regular police units of the state, the SA Feldjägerkorps carried the regular police pattern bayonets, but with a minute difference in the form of the sunburst emblem on the grip – this bearing the eagle with sword in one talon and lightning bolts in the other, and the swastika apparent on the breast. This detail illustration shows the comparison between the two types of grip emblem.*

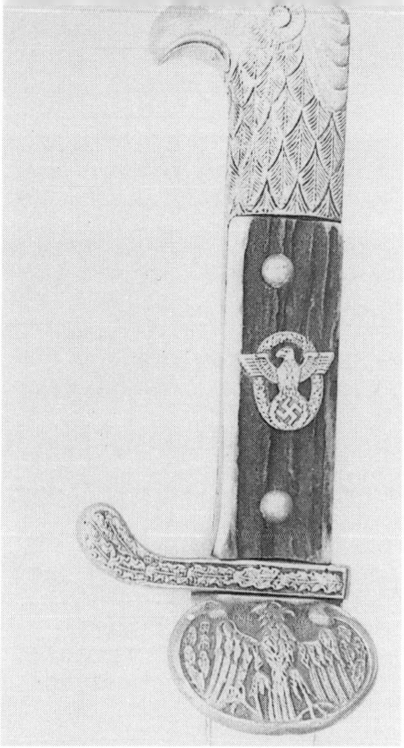

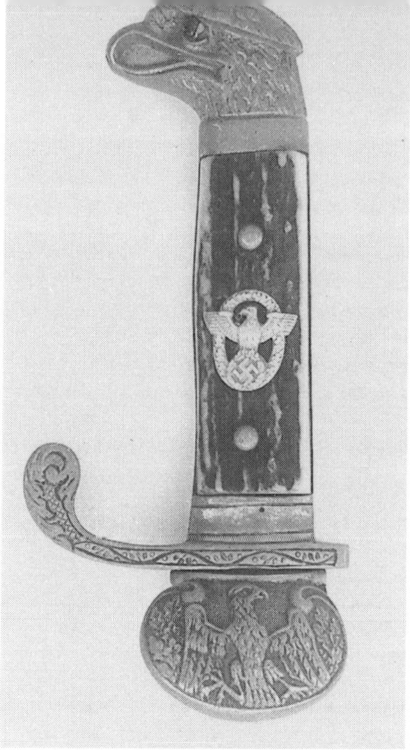

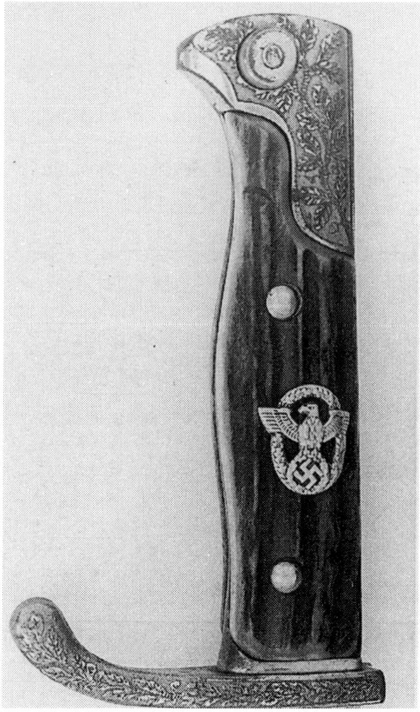

Above left *An example of the Weimarian pattern clamshell Police bayonet, with the newly introduced (1934–6) pattern Police emblem, as used by all of the national police services.* (Dr Julian Milestone collection).

Above *An example of the de luxe pattern Police bayonet, with the national pattern Police eagle and swastika emblem, which gradually replaced the sunburst emblem of the Weimar period.* (Dr Julian Milestone collection).

Left *An extremely rare pattern bayonet for the political police organization of the SA Stabswache. This unit was primarily used to to form police and security groups to protect visiting heads of state and some selected members of the NSDAP. The role of this organization was subsequently taken over by the SA Feldherrnhalle in 1936. The bayonet pattern is that of a service issue Gew. 98/08 bayonet, which has been extensively modified by having the metal portions of the hilt etched and decorated with an oak leaf design, wood grips replaced with stag horn, and the national police emblem added to the grip.* (Dr Julian Milestone collection).

In 1936 a modified version of the Police service bayonet started to appear, and was subsequently adopted on a national scale. This new pattern was based primarily on the old Weimarian style bayonet with the new pattern eagle and swastika emblem, but with the additional refinement of having the clamshell guard removed. Initially the majority of these Police bayonets were in fact regular clamshell bayonets with the clamshell cut away. Subsequent production items were manufactured without the inclusion of the clamshell. The detail illustration shows the hilt of a dress bayonet which originally started out life with a clamshell; then was subsequently modified by total removal of the clamshell (the grip being removed and a new hilt fitted to the blade, with the original stag horn grip being shortened, and the new eagle emblem fitted).

This bayonet originally had a long blade of some 17 in length, which was shortened to 13⅞ in (identifiable by the fact that the blade fuller runs to the end of the blade tip). Manufacturer: Clemen & Jung, Solingen.

Shown below are three regulation pattern Police bayonets, as commonly found in service in the Third Reich. On the left: service and dress bayonet – a long pattern bayonet converted from a 17 in blade Weimar type (note the fuller extending through the tip). The hilt is in the form of a silhouetted eagle's head, with a fletched design on the surface. The bayonet is complete with mortice slot and press stud, even though the bayonet was not intended to actually fit on a rifle.

In the centre, the Seitengewehr – sidearm. A bayonet style, but not produced with the mortise slot and press stud. The most common variation of all the Police bayonet/sidearm series.

On the right: extra-dienstseitengewehr – the 'extra' walking-out service sidearm. A shorter, and more lightweight pattern sidearm, which conforms to the basic bayonet style. The hilt fittings are made of aluminium. This particular example bore the trademark of a Viennese distributor.

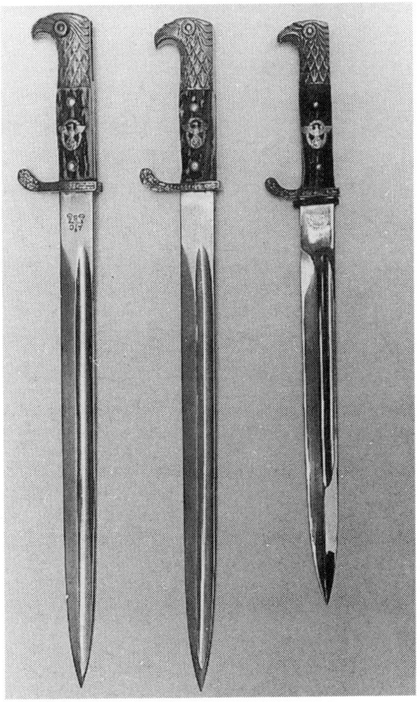

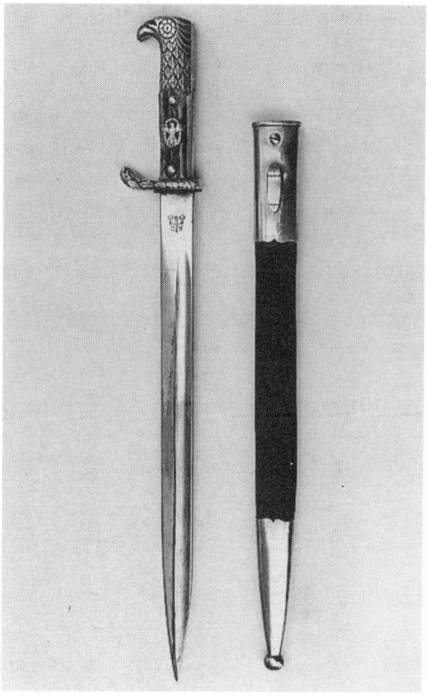

Left *Police bayonet/sidearm shown with its correct pattern leather scabbard. All patterns of Police bayonet/sidearm were carried in a leather scabbard, with white metal or nickel finish fittings. Regular Police units carried the bayonet in a black leather scabbard, and Metropolitan Police were issued with a brown leather scabbard. The long pattern bayonets were most usually issue numbered – on the back of the crossguard and the throat of the scabbard; the short pattern bayonet was a private purchase item, and therefore is not encountered with issue numbers.*

Below *Police official, wearing service issue sidearm, inspecting the personal effects of Polish wood carriers, circa 1940.* (Brian L. Davis).

Prison and Judicial Service

Below *A sword pattern produced by the Eickhorn company, and marketed as the Prison Administration Sword. An identical pattern was produced and marketed as the Justice Administration Service sword. The distinction between the two patterns was that the Prison Service sword was finished in a matt gold plate, and that of the Judicial service was finished in silver plate.* (Source: Eickhorn Kundendienst).

Right *Two examples of a highly unusual production pattern dagger that was manufactured by the Eickhorn company in the 1934–6 period, and which is also known to have been in production with the Hörster company during the same period. The two illustrated examples are basically identical to each other, differing only in the execution of the engraving on the scabbard fittings – the left hand example is finished in silver plate, and that on the right is finished in gold. No positive identification of this dagger pattern has yet been confirmed, but it is believed that they are most probably sidearms intended for the Prison and Judicial Service. The striking feature about the design is the form of the crossguard eagle and swastika emblem – this is distinctly in the form used by State authorities – and the Judicial Service was part of the State apparatus. It is considered likely that these daggers are in fact the precursor of the sword pattern.* (Collection: John E. Pepera).

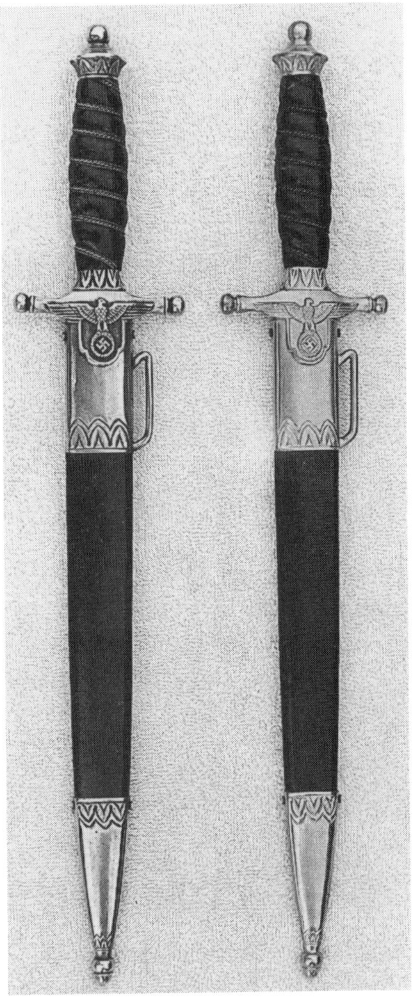

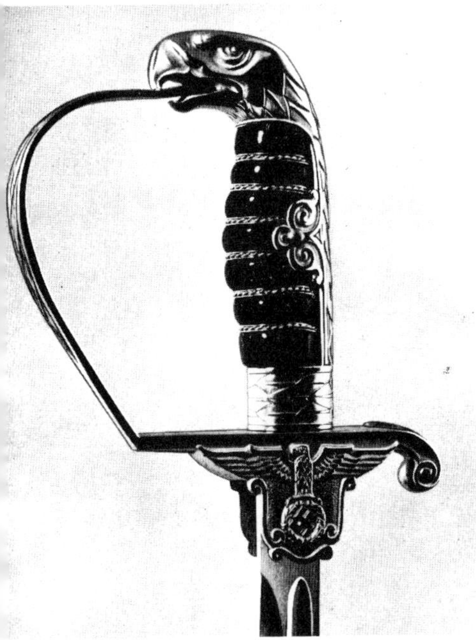

Fire Service

The fire brigade services, which had existed as separate state services in pre-Nazi times, were amalgamated under the jurisdiction of a single, national Fire Service after 1933. They were also put under the overall command of the Police (and therefore the SS). In 1871 the Prussian State Fire Services had adopted the wear of a dress dagger for occasions of ceremony, and this tradition was continued into the period of the Third Reich in the new national Fire Service. As a private purchase item, there was no restriction on the de luxe quality variations of the Fire Department dagger, although most of them appear to follow the original Prussian style fairly closely. (Lt. Col. (retd.) J. R. Angolia).

Opposite *A plain hilted sabre in silver finish, modified by the addition of a Police Fire Service eagle and swastika emblem.* (Lt. Col. (retd.) J. R. Angolia).

Below opposite *Fire department sidearms. A dress bayonet style sidearm, distinct from the military pattern in that it has a plain hilt (in eagle's head silhouette), and a recurved crossguard. No mortise slot, press stud, or barrel ring is incorporated in the design. The grips are made of black chequered plastic, secured by two rivets. The two examples shown are the short blade version (7⅞ in blade) available with either the saw-tooth blade (on left) or the regular pattern blade (right). A longer pattern sidearm, with a 9⅞ in blade, was also manufactured in both the plain and saw-tooth versions.*

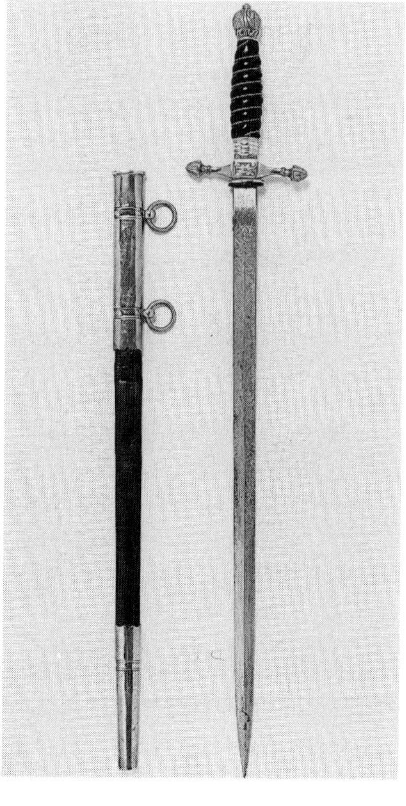

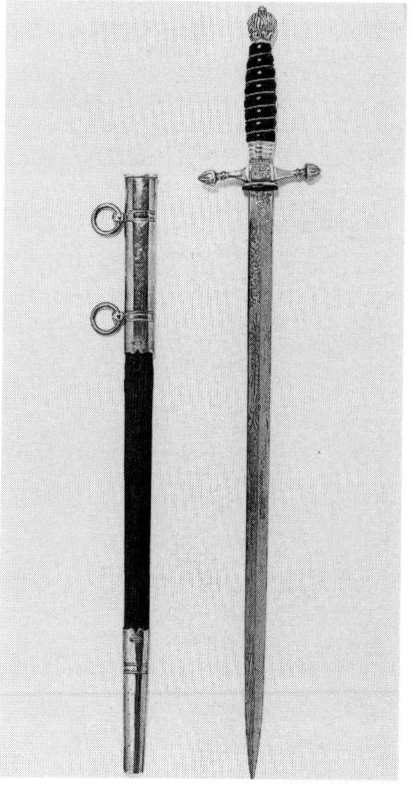

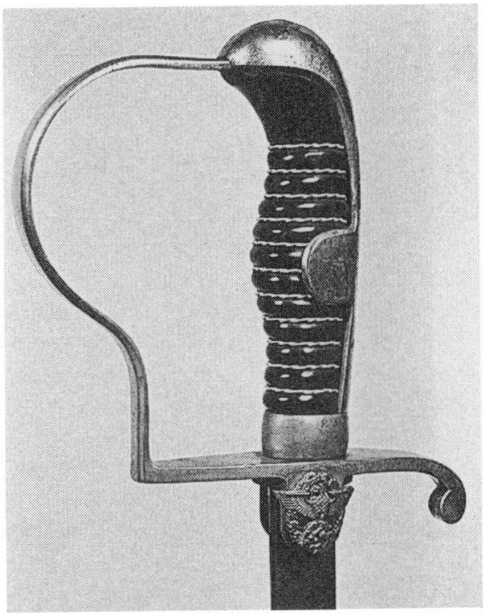

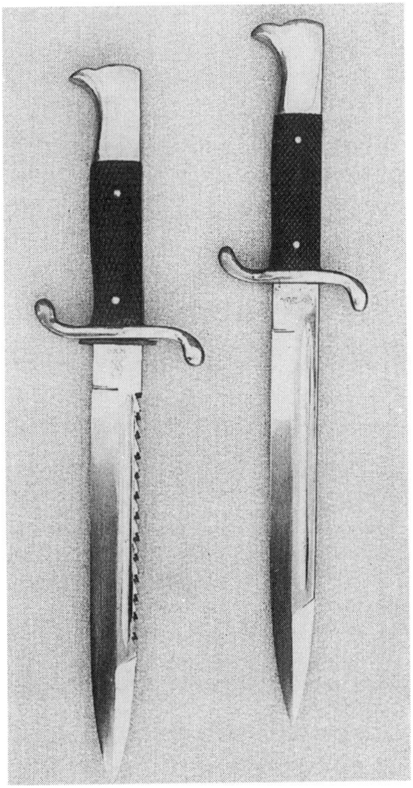

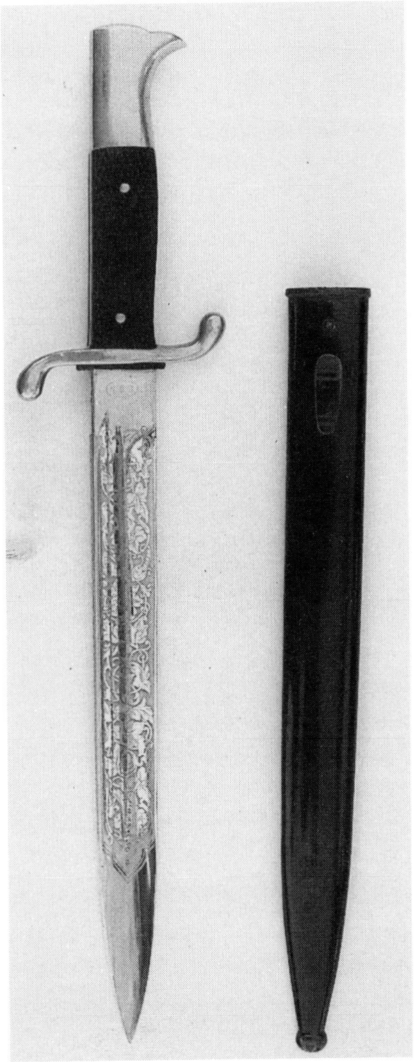

Above *A long pattern Fire Department sidearm with a de luxe quality etched blade. Etched bladed versions of the Fire Department sidearm are rather rare. This example features a foliage design on the reverse side, and had a presentation inscription on the obverse.* (Dr Julian Milestone collection).

Railways and Waterways

Towards the end of the nineteenth century, the strategic and military importance of railway systems became increasingly evident to the European powers. Communication, both in the form of the transmission of physical products as well as intelligence, started to play an expanding role in the success of the individual states. Correspondingly, the need to physically protect these systems of contact became an increasing requirement of the emerging European powers.

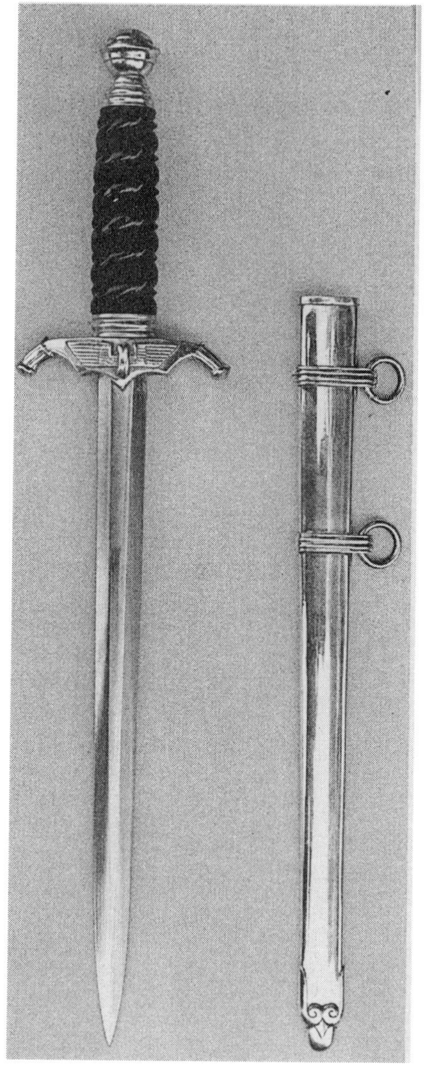

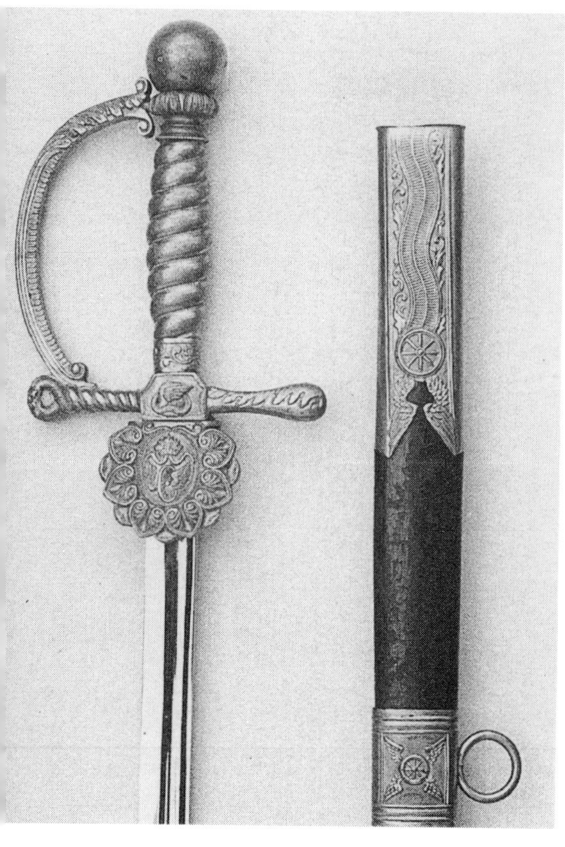

Left *A German manufactured sword for a Railway Protection Service, circa 1900. Produced by Eickhorn, in Solingen, this sword is considered to be one of a series produced for the old Austro-Hungarian empire. The winged railway wheel subsequently became one of the standard emblems of the German Railway Protection Service during the Third Reich.*

Left *The 1937 Model Reichsbahnschutz (Railway Protection Service) dagger. This stylistic dagger was originally produced in aluminium, with a silver plate finish. The top of the spherical pommel was ornated with a curved arm swastika, and the crossguard bore the winged wheel emblem of the service. The grip was made of a dark purple/black phenol resin. The scabbard was plain in finish, bearing two scabbard bands having a fluted design, and a Prussian-style terminal to the scabbard tip.*

Below *Detail view of the hilt of the Reichsbahnschutz dagger Model 1937.*

Below *In 1938, a special protection unit for the Reich Railways and Waterways was established. In reality a sub-formation of the Bahnschutz, it was principally concerned with the protection of rolling stock within the confines of waterways environments – railway marshalling yards at harbours, and along canals where transportable goods were moved from ferries on to rolling stock. A special dagger was introduced for wear by its leaders. Basically that of a Railway Protection Service dagger, it differed in that the scabbard was of a pebbled finish, and the national eagle and swastika emblem appeared on the crossguard in place of the winged wheel emblem.* (R. McCarthy collection).

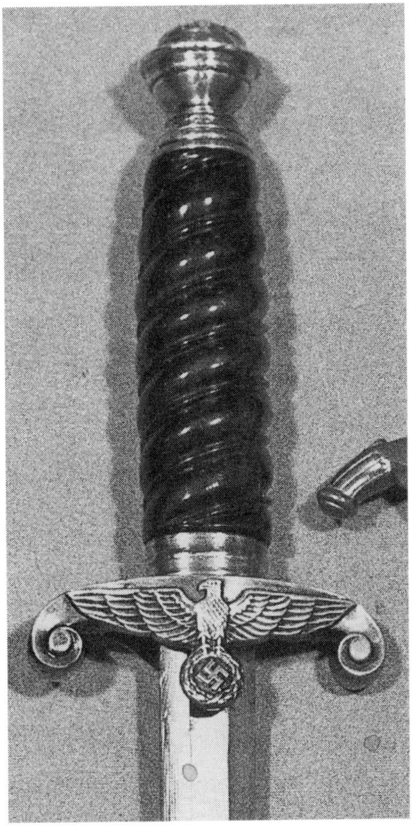

Below *A dagger of the Water Protection Police – a water-borne service which functioned from speedboats which serviced the canals and navigable rivers of the Reich. The function of the service was to act as police units in liaison with regular shore-based police, or with harbour authorities. The dagger pattern authorized for the service was basically that of a Model 1929 Naval dirk, distinguished by having a blue leather wrap to the grip. The evidence suggested by examination of early Water Police daggers is that they were in fact originally part of the Navy, as some daggers bear marine issue stamps and numbers. Sometime after 1933 the Water Police were apparently put directly under the jurisdiction of the regular police services. The illustration shows a Water Police Dagger, with a trademark indicating the 1934–6 period of manufacture. Note the presence of the marine issue stamp and numbers on the blade ricasso and the scabbard throat.*

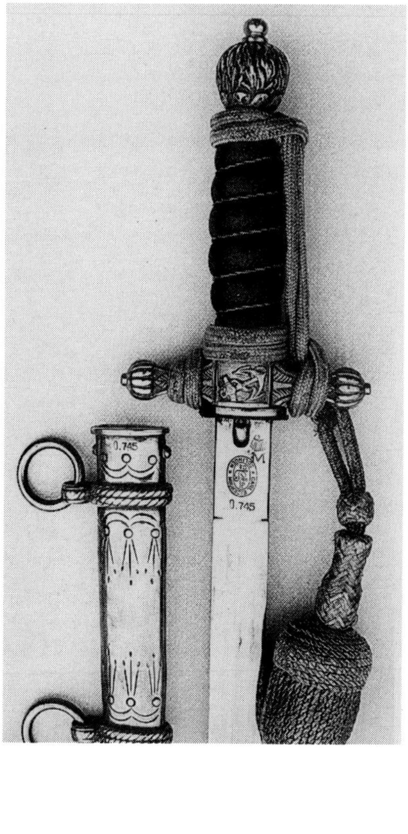

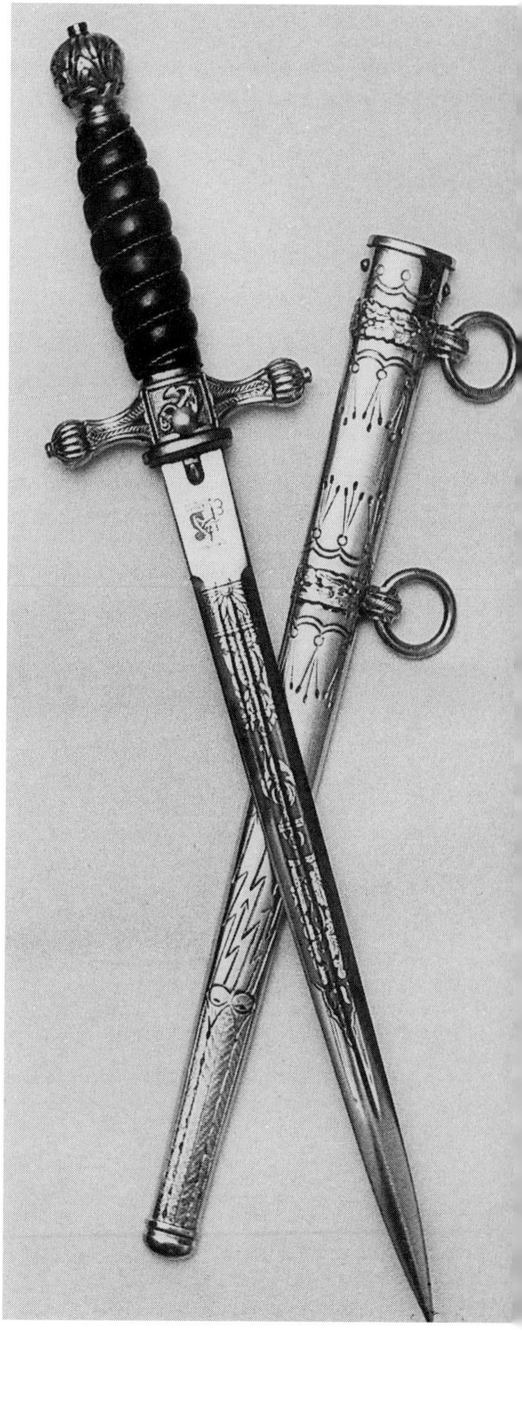

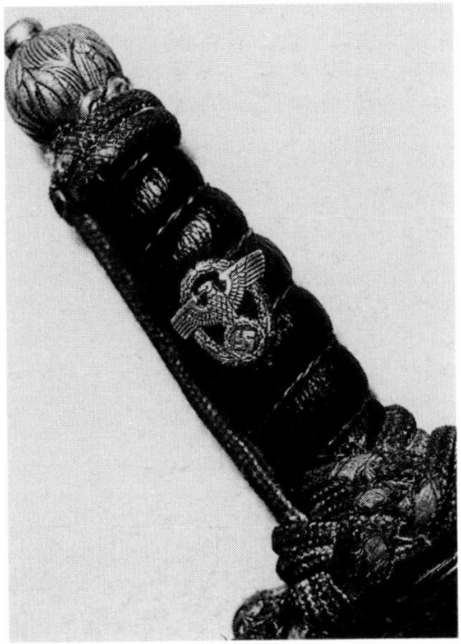

Left *Water Police dagger, a full view of a later period Water Police dagger. The trademark indicates a period of manufacture between 1936 and 1941.* (Gordon White collection).

Right *Detail view of a Water Police dagger, with the Police emblem affixed to the leather grip. The attachment of such emblems appears to have been a manufacturer's endeavour to make the dagger pattern more appealing to the purchaser, as the feature was not standard on all manufacturers' products.* (Gailen David collection).

The Red Cross

The German Red Cross Organization (*Deutsches Rotes Kreuz*—DRK) was an off-shoot of the international organization, having its origins in the Geneva Convention of 1864. The fundamental objective of the organization was to provide aid and assistance to the sick, injured, and casualties of war, with a particular emphasis on the lot of the Prisoner of War. As a non-political and non-military organization, Red Cross societies have generally functioned free of any major governmental interference wherever they have formed. Within the new order of the Third Reich, however, the role of the Red Cross organization was slightly different. The Party and State apparatus automatically embraced the Red Cross within its overall structure.

The requirements of industrial and public health were high on the priorities marked for attention when Hitler came to power. The general wellbeing of the population, which in 1933 still carried a high proportion of disabled ex-servicemen, widowed and orphaned families, deprived communities both in the inner cities and the rural areas, was destined for special attention. The circumstances of these sections of the community were not a condition unique to Germany. Similar communities of equally under-privileged status existed throughout all the European nations, but National Socialist Germany had a most positive

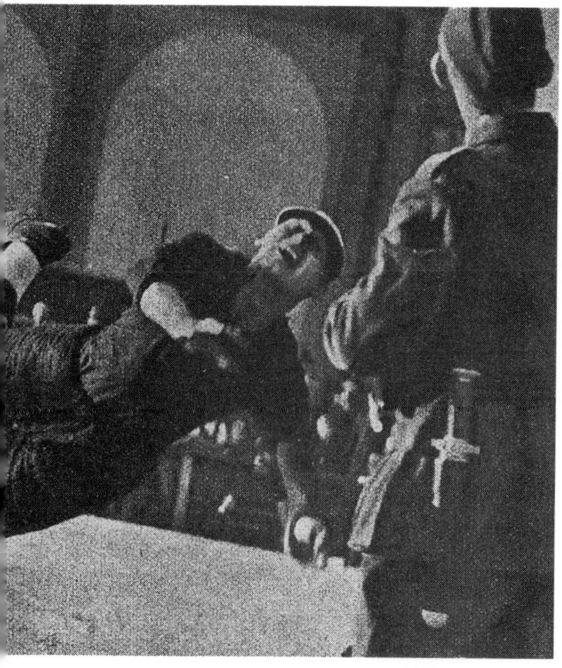

Left *A German Red Cross official in attendance at a sports match. Note the Red Cross hewer seen in wear.*

Below *The Red Cross hewer. Hilt detail and full-length view of the Red Cross hewer, introduced in 1938. The hilt portions are made of a heavy zinc-based alloy, finished with nickel plate, and decorated on the langet with the German Red Cross organization eagle and swastika. The grip scales are made of a black plastic, chequered on the obverse face, and smooth on the reverse.*

The blade of the hewer is highly distinctive in being a sawtooth pattern, but with a 'square' or 'chiselled' tip. The saw back is intended to signify the facility of being able to cut wood and the square tip to the blade denotes that the weapon is not for offensive purposes.

The scabbard is made of steel, stove enamelled black, and with nickel finished fittings. This example is shown complete with its black leather frog and Red Cross issue silver and blue braid knot. (The Old Brigade, Northampton).

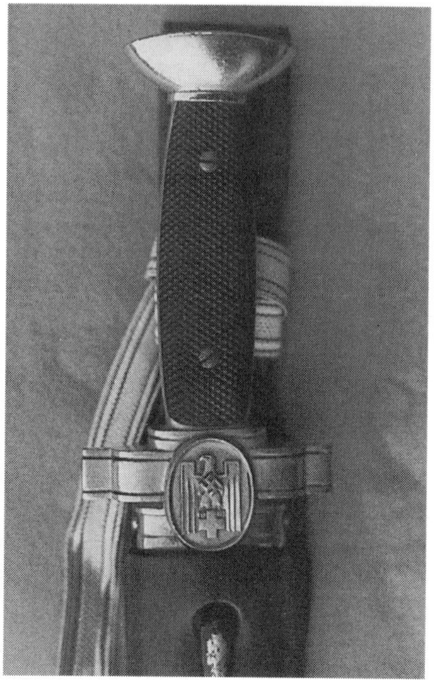

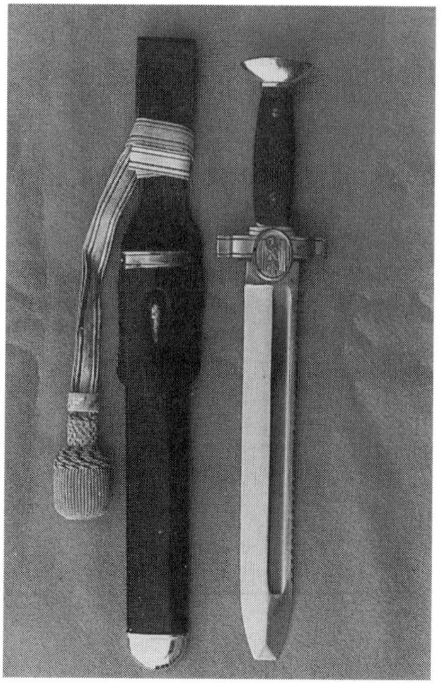

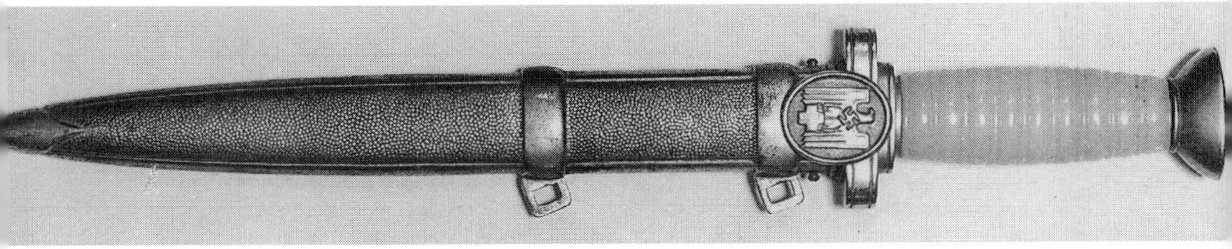

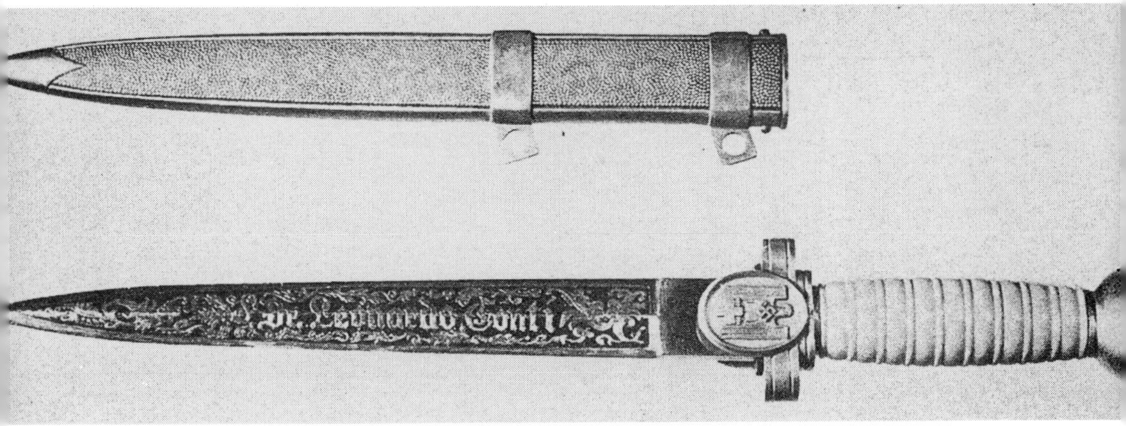

Top *The Red Cross Officer's dagger, Model 1938. A handsome dagger, constructed of a heavy, zinc based alloy, and finished with a nickel plate. The grip was originally white in colour, but is most usually found to have discoloured to a yellow/orange hue. The emblem of the German Red Cross organization was featured on a cartouche in the centre of the crossguard. The dagger pattern was carried by members of both the Red Cross organization, and also the Social Welfare organization, which was a part of the State health administration. The daggers carried were identical, but differed in the form of the hanging straps from which they were suspended.*

Above *A presentation example of the Red Cross Leader's Dagger Model 1938. The blade is etched on the obverse with the recipient's name – Dr Leonardo Conti, and the reverse of the blade bears the inscription 'In grateful recognition'. The reverse langet of the crossguard is reputedly engraved with the signature of Adolf Hitler.* (N. C. Heilman collection, via Raidl and Leslie).

plan in mind to resolve the situation as far as the Reich was concerned.

Within the structure of the Reich Ministry of the Interior existed several health departments, which were concerned with numerous aspects governing the health and wellbeing of the population. Amongst these departments were some which concerned themselves with control of infectious diseases, legislation governing the manufacture of serums and vaccines, hospitals, public baths, mental diseases, social problems (such as alcoholism), nutrition, maternal and child welfare, etc. One department specifically dealt with matters concerning the Red Cross.

To promote the integration of the activities of these departments, and to foster a central structural policy for the application of all necessary areas of overlap, a Party-promoted organization was established, the *Nationalsozialistische Volkswohlfahrt*—NSV, the National Socialist Public Welfare Department. The NSV was governed from above by the Ministry of the Interior bureau, the *Hauptamt für Volkswohlfahrt*—Head Office for Public Welfare under the direct control of Dr Leonardo Conti, *Reichsgesundheitsführer*—Reich Minister of Health. It is interesting to note that some of Dr Conti's involvement with Public Welfare and the treatment of Prisoners of War during the Second World War was questioned during the Nuremburg Trials, and he was executed as a war criminal. During the 1930s, however, it is evident from the available records that the application of Welfare and Health Acts was established and implemented with a thoroughness that was commendable. The general wellbeing and health of the average German was equal to that in any other society in Europe, and a good deal better than most of them.

The Red Cross, although principally functioning along the lines prescribed by the international council in Switzerland, was subject to interference by the National Socialist State. And in keeping with the policies being implemented to promote the products of Solingen, the Red Cross was authorized to wear dagger and sidearm patterns to complete the overall uniform appearance of the NSDAP society. Two aspects of this use of bladed dress weapons—an unlikely addition to the uniform of an essentially medically-orientated organization—are worthy of mention. Enlisted and lower-ranking volunteers carried a sidearm which had the distinctive feature of a saw-tooth blade, with a flat, or chisel-ended tip. It was not a weapon intended for assault—this unique design was intended to symbolize the need for a tool which could be used to fabricate splints (the saw-tooth on the blade), whilst the absence of a pointed tip indicated the noncombative status of the bearer. Officers and senior ranks within the German Red Cross (DRK) carried a dagger which conformed more closely to the conventional form, having a long, double-edged pointed blade. It was, however, purely a dress weapon intended to indicate a leader rank. The suspension straps by which the dagger was borne are worthy of mention, for they denoted a particular aspect of the bearer's role. Both sets of straps were identical in form and colouring, but the buckles of the straps were different. Round buckles denoted members who were concerned with primary Red Cross activities, and square buckles were worn by those members whose role of duty dealt with Social Welfare (i.e. relief work).

The Customs Unions

The departments of Customs and Excise had, like many other organizations within Germany, come about from the amalgamation of the

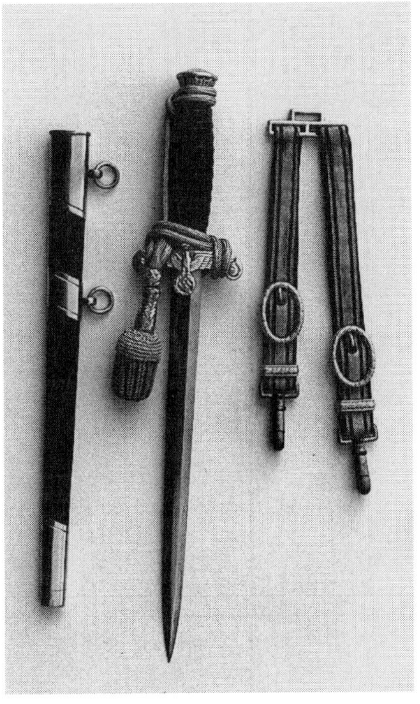

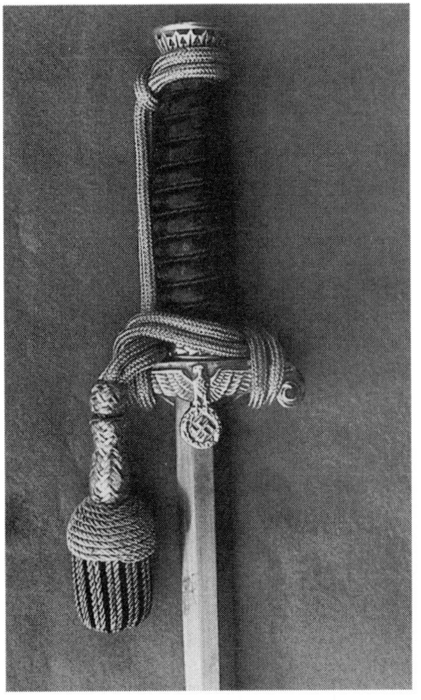

Officials of the Customs Service, which was part of the Reichsfinanze Verwaltug (i.e. Treasury and Taxation) had been permitted to wear a sword from the earliest times; indeed the nature of their work in former times had been such that the bearing of a weapon at all times was mandatory. The practical necessity of carrying a sword had—by the early twentieth century—virtually disappeared, but the traditional entitlement to continue so doing was carried on in the Third Reich.

The old style swords were retained in service, modified only by the addition of the eagle and swastika emblem. In 1936 astute manufacturers, recognizing that the dress weapon was an optional portion of uniform wear, to be paid for by the customer, gained approval to produce a new pattern of dagger, designed exclusively for wear by members of the Customs Service.

This new dagger was designed in two basic finishes: an example finished in green leather, with white or silver fittings, which was to be carried by the Land Customs; and an identical pattern dagger but finished in blue leather with gilded fittings, to be carried by the Water Customs.

The basic form of the dagger was based, more or less, on the Model 1935 Army dagger, but with some refinements. The oak leaf decoration of the pommel was not so clearly defined, and the crossguard eagle was in the distinctive Customs pattern, in that the ends of the wing tips were slightly upturned. The grip was covered with leather, and featured a wire grip wrap in the grooves. The scabbard body was made of steel, with a leather wrap, and smooth finish fittings were slid over the leather wrap to complete the pattern. The example illustrated is that of a Land Customs dagger, and is shown complete with its original green and silver portepee knot, and green and silver braid suspension straps. (An example of the Water Customs dagger is shown in the colour section.) (The Old Brigade, Northampton).

A dress bayonet of the Customs Service. Sidearms for officials of the Customs and Financial Administration Services (i.e. Excise and Tax authorities) were optional purchases at the whim of the bearer. As such, a number of design alternatives were offered by competing manufacturers, including Army-style swords, and Police-type dress bayonets. The police-style bayonets were more or less identical to the regular police patterns, but did not bear any insignia on the stag horn grip. Examples are found both with and without the clamshell guard. (Private collection).

numerous State Customs departments which had formerly existed. Under the Third Reich, the independent State Customs Unions (the *Zollverein*) were reformed under a national Government Ministry, the *Reichsfinanzeverwaltung*—Reich Ministry of Finance. The role of the Customs and Excise was similar to that of the Customs organizations of other nations, mainly to apply and collect taxation and levies, at both direct, and indirect levels. Daggers, swords, and bayonets were worn by the Customs departments on various occasions, and the two principal departments which were most predominantly seen in this capacity were the Land Customs (*Landzoll*) whose officers were present at all frontier posts and air terminals; and the Water Customs (*Wasserzoll*) whose sphere of activity centred on ports, harbours, and waterways where traffic from a foreign domicile might enter the domain of the Third Reich.

German Air Sports League

The DLV (*Deutsche Luftsports Verein*) has already received some mention in this work, inasmuch as it was the organization which had clandestinely trained pilots and ground crew for the fledgling *Luftwaffe* before the emergence of the Air Force in 1935. Ostensibly the DLV had existed as a peaceful organization devoted to fostering the recreational aspects of air sport activities. Following the creation of the *Luftwaffe*, and the almost total absorption of the DLV membership into the ranks of the new air power, the DLV underwent a change. The primary role of training crew was abandoned, as the Air Ministry took over this requirement, and the legitimate sporting and recreational activities of the organization were given greater exposure. The organization also changed its name to the *Nationalsozialistische Fliegerkorps*—NSFK (National Socialist Flying Corps). The overall appearance of the organization's membership, however, was relatively unchanged; they still wore the same uniforms, and carried a similar dress dagger as that formerly worn by the DLV. The recreational pursuits of gliding, model aircraft building, parachuting, etc., were still promoted by the new organization. The Hitler Youth organization, which maintained a Marine Division as well as an Aeronautical section, maintained close co-operative links with the NSFK in the air sports area. Recreational activities, wherever possible, were always organized in such a manner as to be of beneficial use to the State if a national emergency so required.

Members of the Deutsche Luftsports Verband (DLV – later the NSFK, 'National Socialist Flying Corps'), shown wearing the two patterns of dagger attributed to the organization. On the left, the long pattern DLV dagger, from which the Luftwaffe Model 1934 dagger took its pedigree, and on the right the short pattern DLV knife. (The late Col. C. M. Dodkins photographic collection).

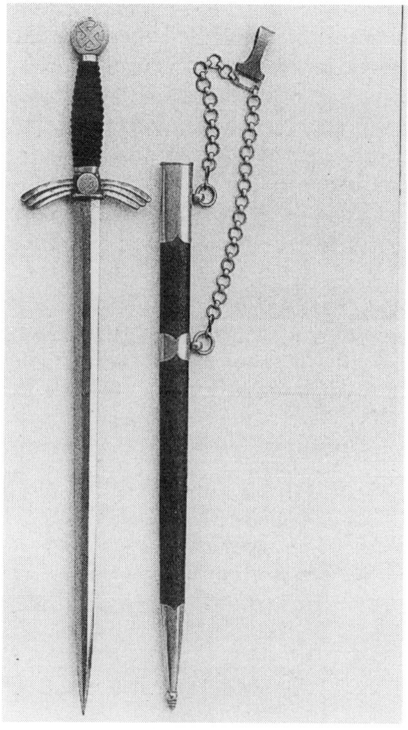

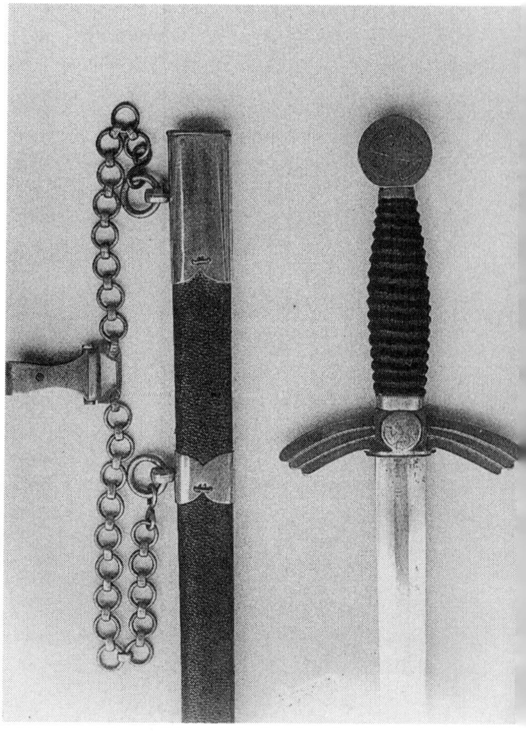

Above *Full length and hilt detail of the DLV long pattern dagger. The grip is made of wood, with a dark blue leather wrap, but no grip wiring. The scabbard body is solid leather, and the fittings are secured to the body by means of staples featured on the reverse side. The assembly of the dagger is such that once the pommel had been fitted over the tang, which projected through the pommel, it was peened over and secured. Thus the dagger was not designed to be disassembled.*

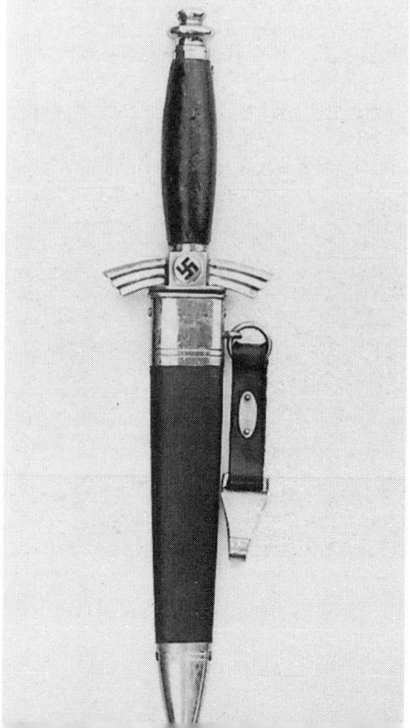

Left *The DLV/NSFK Fliers' Knife. A short pattern dagger that was simplistically designed. The pommel and crossguard are made of brass, with a nickel plate finish. The centre section of the crossguard features a black enamel swastika. The grip and the scabbard body are covered in a blue leather wrap. The throat of the scabbard is marked with the DLV emblem.*

Following the creation of the Luftwaffe, and

the wholesale transfer of trained personnel from the DLV, the DLV was replaced by a new formation, the NSFK (Nationalsozialistische Fliegerkorps) which promoted the recreational aspects of flying and gliding. The uniforms of the old DLV were continued, in slightly modified form, and the dress knife was kept in service under a new, modified style – the leather finish of the grip and scabbard gave way to a crackle finish paint, and the metal fittings of the hilt were made of aluminium.

Few people could have lived through the Third Reich without, at some point in their lives, either willingly or otherwise, becoming involved in some recreation or voluntary work that was being manipulated by the National Socialists. Such was the determination to create an Orderly Society, within which every member of the nation would have a part to fulfil.

Technische Nothilfe

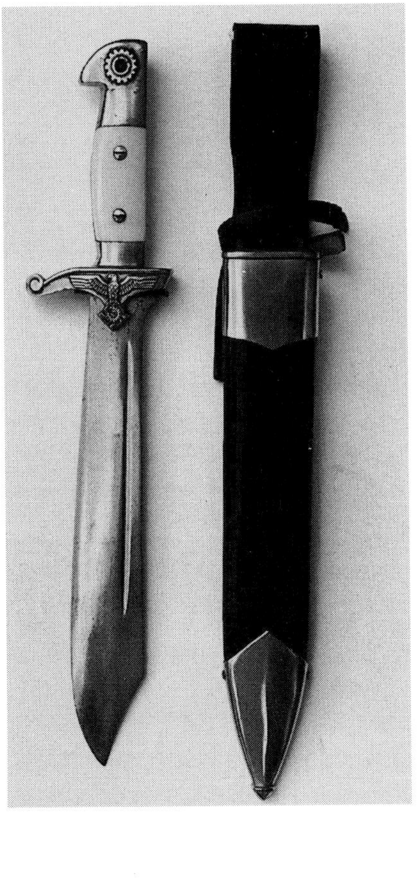

Left and overleaf *Detail view of the hilt, and full length view of the TeNo hewer, believed to have been first introduced in 1938. The Technische Nothilfe was a voluntary organization, which had a small full-time staff of Leaders and Senior Personnel, and provided manpower and expertise for a variety of industrial and building projects.*

The hewer, designed for the lower ranking officials, was rather similar to that of the RAD hewer, but differed in that the hilt was made of a heavy alloy, and decorated in the form of a stylized eagle head pommel, with a cog wheel emblem, and the crossguard featured the TeNo eagle emblem, with the cogwheel superimposed over the swastika and encompassing the letters TN. The grip scales were made of an ivorine material, and secured to the hilt by two bolts.

The falchion shaped blade was plain, and marked only with the TeNo eagle emblem and the Eickhorn trademark. The obverse of the blade, under the langet, was marked with the TeNo issue number. (The Old Brigade, Northampton).

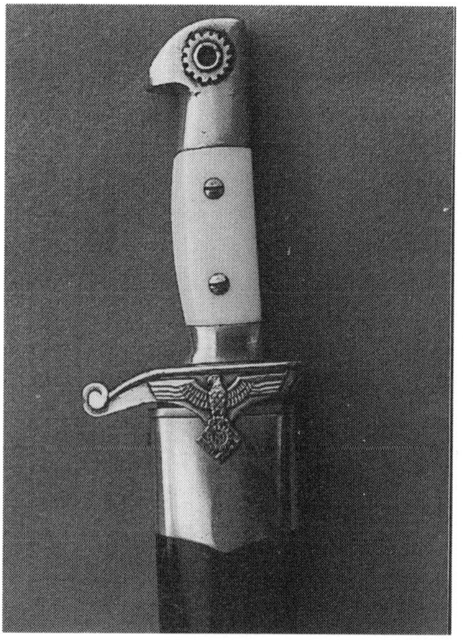

Below *Technical Corps Officer's dagger, Model 1938. As far as can be established, all the officer pattern daggers of the TeNo, like the hewers, were apparently manufactured exclusively by the Eickhorn concern. The metal portions of the hilt were manufactured out of a zinc based alloy, which was silver plated, and then chemically blackened. The pommel design featured the emblem of a cogwheel, and the crossguard featured the TeNo eagle and swastika with a cogwheel and the TN emblem. The steel scabbard had a stippled design, and was silver plated and finished with a black coating. The grip was made of a white phenol resin, although most examples examined to date show that portion to have discoloured to a deep orange hue. The upper lip of the scabbard throat, and the blade beneath the crossguard langet, were stamped with an issue number.*

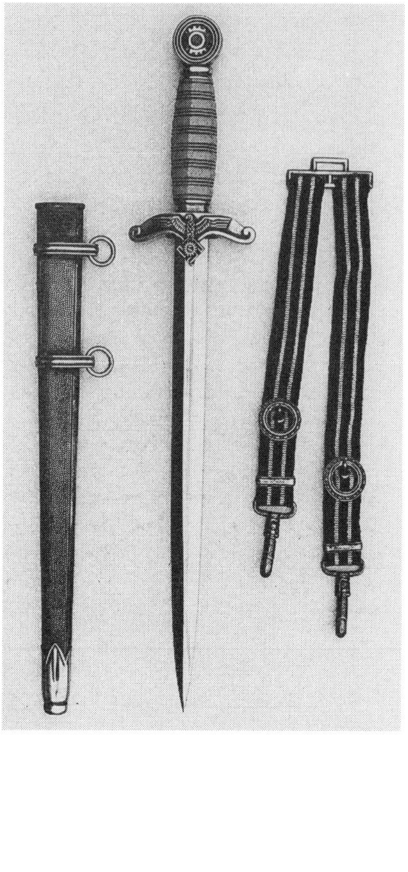

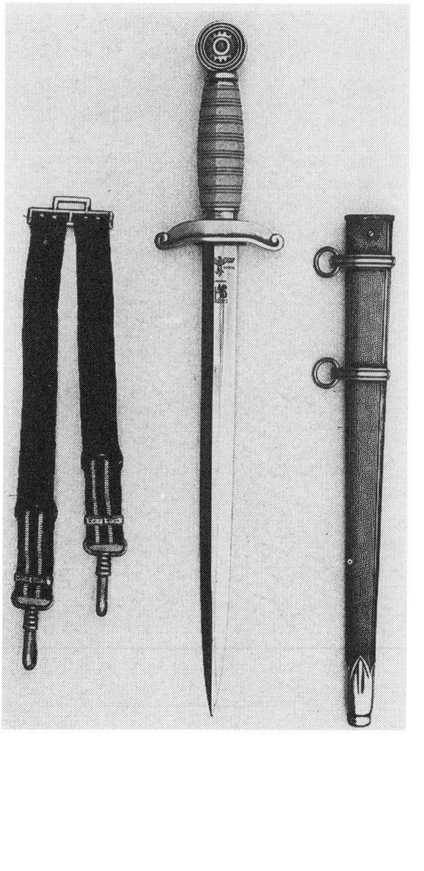

Reichs Luftschutzbund

Below *Junior Leader's Dagger of the RLB – Reichs Luftschutzbund (Reich Air Defence League), an organization which primarily fulfilled the same capacity as that of the Air Raid Precautions units in England during World War Two. The dagger has silver-plated brass fittings, bearing a stylistic eagle and swastika emblem on the crossguard. The grip is made of a black hardwood, and bears the emblem of a sunburst with a deep blue enamel swastika. The scabbard is black stove enamelled steel, with a nickel or silver plated end fitting. The dagger was suspended from a single leather strap which was permanently affixed to the suspension loop.*

Bottom *Leader pattern dagger of the RLB. Based in similar style to that of the Junior pattern, the Leader's dagger had a flat/mushroom shaped pommel, and a blue leather wrap to the grip and the scabbard. The scabbard body was segmented into two sections by a central band, which served to accommodate the twin leather strap suspension.*

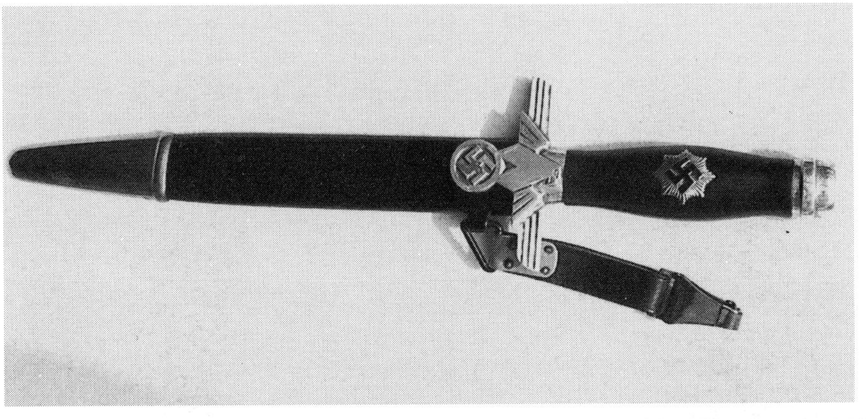

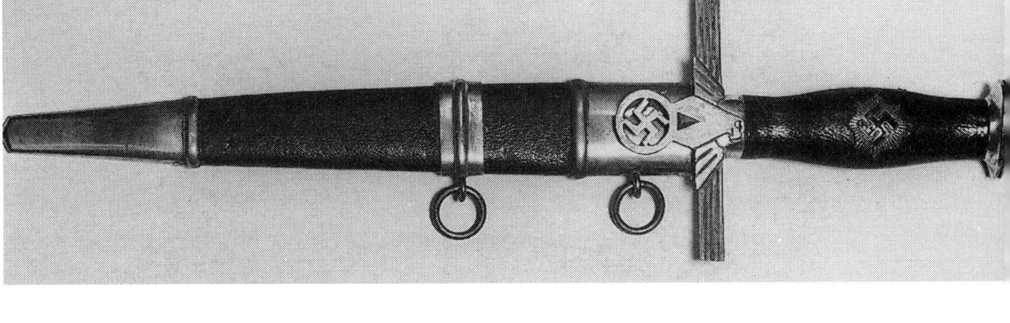

BURGSMÜLLER

Left *Collecting donations for the Winter Relief Fund, 1939. The RLB Leader pattern dagger seen in wear.* (Library of Congress photo collection).

Below left *An alternative series of daggers for the RLB is known to exist, differing only slightly in that the sunburst emblem on the grip bears the letters RLB as well as the swastika, and the Leader pattern dagger was carried by a single strap suspension. The reason for these differences is unclear; one school of thought suggests that those with the RLB letters on the grip emblem are the earlier pattern; an alternative theory is that the RLB emblem versions are for those members who were part-time rather than full-time. One point which is certain, both patterns were recorded as being available in the Eickhorn sales catalogues of 1938 and 1942. The photograph shows the hilt of a Junior Leader pattern, with a close up of the trademark seen on the blade, in this case that of Karl Burgsmüller of Berlin, not a manufacturer but a distributor.* (The Old Brigade, Northampton).

Postschutz

Obverse and reverse views of the dress dagger of the Postschutz – Postal Protection Service. The dagger conforms to the same basic proportions and size as that of the RLB Leader dagger, but has a distinctly different crossguard, being a stylistic eagle head, with an enamelled swastika inset in the central quillon block. The grip is made of hard, black wood, and carries the Postschutz emblem of an eagle and swastika with lightning bolts. The scabbard is made of steel, with a black stove enamelled finish and nickel plated brass mounts. The suspension chains are made of brass, with a nickel plate finish.

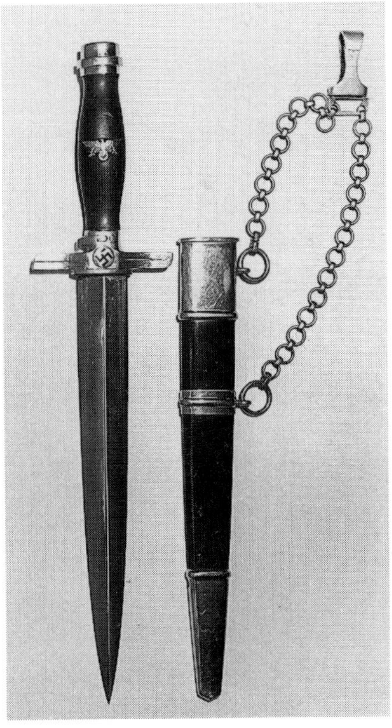

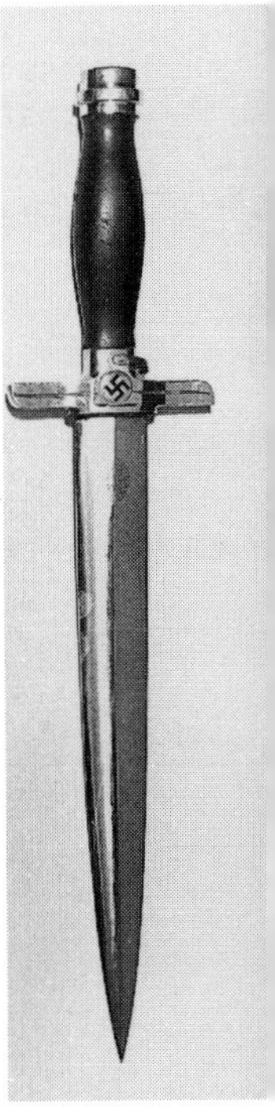

Obverse and reverse, and hilt detail views of an extremely rare dagger. The Honour Dagger of the Postschutz. To date only one example of this dagger pattern has been identified. Manufactured by the Paul Weyersberg company, the dagger is basically a standard Postschutz dagger, but with all hilt and scabbard fittings ornately decorated, and silver plated. The chains shown attached to the dagger were added some time after its 'liberation' by a British soldier, and it is considered that the original suspension system was most probably by means of ornate, bullion straps. The blade is made of artificial (acid etch) damascus, and bears an inscription denoting that the piece was awarded by the Postschutz authority of the district of Erfurt.

11 Fraternity of Knights
Hunting Organizations, Forestry Organizations, Shooting and Markmanship

Our spiritual and internal political German future depends on whether and to what extent we succeed in merging the German spirit with the Prussian Monarchy

Ernst von Bülow, 1916.

From the shores of the Baltic Sea, down to the mountain regions of the Alps and the Tyrol, Germany is a rich and fertile land. Great forests are spread over the green landscape, clear rivers bisect valleys, and lush vineyards pepper the steep slopes of the hills. High in the Bavarian mountains, Hitler and other notaries of the Third Reich built for themselves grand retreats where they could escape from the stresses of political life and gaze out upon the mountains and valleys. The views around Hitler's private retreat, the 'Eagle's Nest' at the Berghof, are astounding. This splendid structure, which once had an immense window which could be mechanically lowered from the wall to allow an unimpaired view across the mountain, is no more. All that remains are the foundations and rubble upon the hillside. Even so—scarcely mentioned in any of the tourist handbooks of this day and age—its reputation survives as a tourist site to see; where the historically-minded, or the casually curious, can visit to observe the breath-taking beauty. Some visitors have been known to dig up a few of the original bricks, unique in style with a hole formed through them, and take them back as mementos of a bygone age.

Hermann Goering, aside from his capacity as Minister of Aviation, not only maintained a fine home at the Berghof, but also owned several choice hunting lodges in the thickly wooded forests of Prussia. There, the flamboyant Goering could indulge himself with another of his great passions of life—the hunt. Goering was also bestowed with the capacity of *Reichsjägermeister*—Reichs Hunting Master. Hunting and shooting, the sport of kings and princes, was also very much evident as one of the affordable sports of the less wealthy members of the Third Reich.

One of the recurring themes of life in the National Socialist state was the preoccupation with tradition. Being part of an old tradition, or in the creation of new ones for future generations, endows the holder of the tradition with an elevated social status. More importantly, the presence of tradition manifests itself in a physical form that can be observed—perhaps even envied—by outsiders. Within the Hitler regime, to be part of some form of tradition was to become part of the legally ordained, accepted, and respected Order of Life. The image of tradition gave legitimate purpose to the new Germans of this new Germany, conjoining as it did the colourful pageantry of old Prussia with the drumbeat of the National Socialist cause.

Hunting fraternities

The professional hunter, at one time an indispensible part of German rural life, survived through the years of the Depression to experience a new role in the Third Reich. The fauna which abounded in the great forests had always been a valuable source of food to country folk, but with the growing population in the 1930s came an increasing demand for national legislation to govern the culling of wild livestock. The result entailed the numerous hunting fraternities being amalgamated into a national hunting body (*Deutsche Jägerschaft*—German Hunting Association), whose role was to govern the limitations of hunting during the season; protection of wild livestock during the breeding season; enforcement of law relating to unauthorized hunting and poaching; and to generally oversee the consistency of the livestock population. In keeping with the traditions of the hunters, the elaborate, functional hunting weapons of past years were retained for wear on the uniforms of the Third Reich hunters, differing only slightly in that they became primarily dress weapons rather than the working tools of the trade.

Forestry officials

The preservation of the wild livestock of Germany, although the responsibility of the German Hunting Association, also received the attentions of the National Forestry Association. The successful preservation and breeding programmes for wild livestock were only truly effective where adequate space and habitat were maintained; and the maintenance of suitable habitats, including protection against their erosion or destruction, became the responsibility of the *Forstbeamte*—Forestry Administrator.

The whole of the German agrarian economy, as well as several other associated industries, were governed through the National Food Estate Organization, a governmental body which took its guidance from the National Economic Chamber. The National Food Estate was just one of the contributory organizations that created the Reich gross national product, and its organizational divisions and sub-divisions concerned themselves with matters which were as diverse as they were related. This covered such areas as the fishing industry, animal feedstuffs, the sugar industry, farmers and collectives, land tenancy and labour force, etc. Not least amongst these areas of business were the wood, garden, and forest industry.

The forests, and the industries they supported, were one of the great natural sources of wealth of the Third Reich. Numerous other national commercial enterprises relied upon the forests for their basic raw material—the printing industry, for wood pulp and paper; textiles and dye makers; wood products manufacturers—the chain of connected interests was seemingly endless. As such, the correct and efficient administration of forests was vital to the survival of the economy. Long-term plans were devised and implemented to ensure that this natural source of raw stock, by-products and usable commodities, was not decimated to the point of no return. The Forestry Administrators were there to keep the balance in favour of future growth. Uniforms and dress weapons reinforced the official status of the guardians of the Forestry Service.

Shooting and markmanship

Familiarity and involvement with firearms was, from the outset of the Nazi regime, an instrumental foundation stone upon which the militaristic traits of all young Germans could be developed. In the publication *Hitler Jugend im Dienst* ('Hitler Youth in Service'), pub. Bernard & Graefe, Berlin (1935) the following explanation is proffered:

> The National Socialist people's youth affirms battle, and submits to the carrying of arms as the obvious foundations of all people's labour. They hope for the day in which the weapons will be placed in their hands which are associated with the full consciousness of manhood.*

This need to familiarize young persons with weapons was all part of the plan to prepare the younger generation for its role as future soldiers; protectors of the nation and the people. Such

* Quoted in Brady, R.A., *The Spirit and Structure of German Fascism*, p. 177, pub. Gollancz, London, 1937.

Below *Two examples of hunting cutlass. Both of these specimens date from Imperial times, and are typical of the traditional type of weapon that was carried forward after the First World War and through into the Third Reich period.*

The example on the left is a particularly handsome piece, and was probably carried by a senior official of a Hunting Lodge. The example on the right is distinctive in that it features on the quillon block the emblem of a lion. The lion was the national emblem of Bavaria, and this probably indicates a Hunting Lodge based in Bavaria. (Thomas J. Gorman jr. Collection).

Below right *A fine quality hunting cutlass, manufactured by the J. A. Henckels Company of Solingen,* circa *1930. The hilt fittings are made of brass, with a very heavy silver plate. The crossguard is formed in the style of a branch enveloped in oak leaves.* (Malcolm Bowers).

involvement with shooting sport '. . . develops inner and outer calm and coldbloodedness, awakens and promotes decision and self-confidence in the shooters.'** In the short-term, it is easy to see how involvement and interests developed in shooting skills became recreational pursuits amongst those groups who enjoyed the challenge and skills of marksmanship. To cater for the recreational interests of shooting, numerous shooting sports clubs had already existed in Germany before the advent of the Third Reich. In 1936, however, all these organizations were obliged to amalgamate themselves into a nationally recognized federation, the *Deutsche*

** ibid.

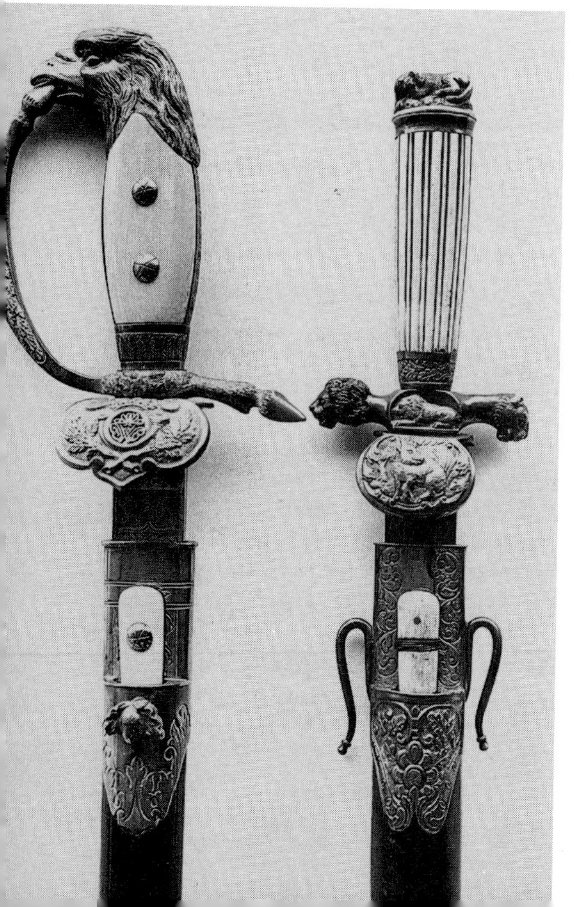

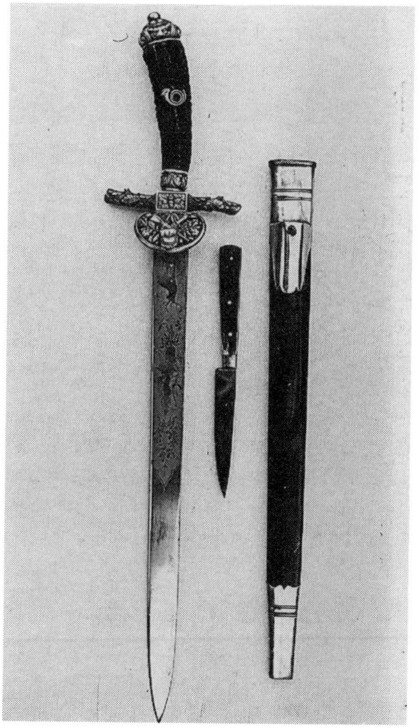

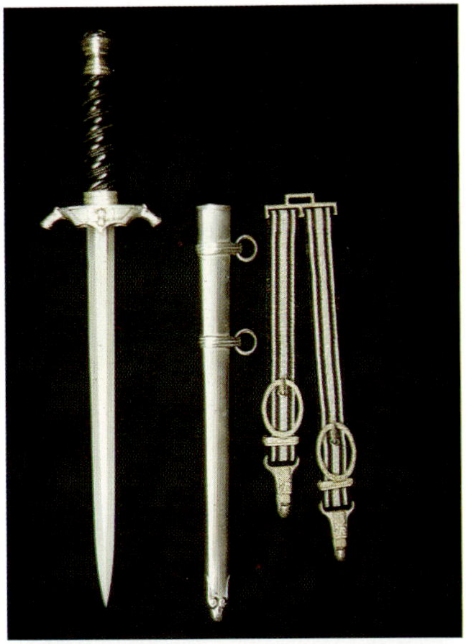

Right *The Model 1938 Railway Protection Service Leader's Dagger, complete with straps.* (Lt.-Col. (retd.) J. R. Angolia.)

Below *Obverse and reverse of a unique prototype dagger. Designed by Paul Casberg, this dagger is the precursor to the Army dagger Model 1935. Manufactured by the Eickhorn company, to a design produced by Casberg, the prototype example follows the original Casberg design very closely, but differs primarily in the decoration of the scabbard. The dagger is rather large—about 18 inches overall length, and is more in the form of a short sword than a dagger. The pattern was not adopted, and as far as can be traced, this is the sole surviving example of the prototype series.* (Dr. R. Distelhorst collection.)

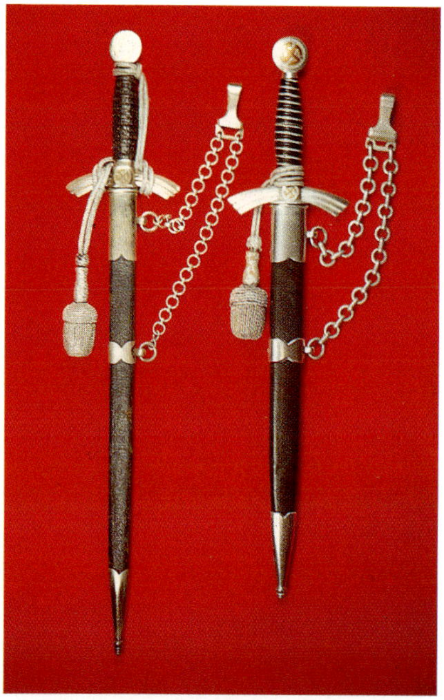

Left *Comparative views of the DLV Flier's Dagger (on left) and the Model 1934 Luftwaffe dagger which superseded it.* (Lt.-Col. (retd.) J. R. Angolia.)

Below *Obverse and reverse views of a cased, presentation Fire Department sidearm. The workmanship on this item is absolutely superb, with engraved hilt fittings heavily silver plated, and a blue and gilded inscription on the blade denoting that the item was presented for 50 years service with the Solingen area Fire Service.*

This illustration was taken when the dagger was in the collection of Dr. J. Milestone, Los Angeles. Subsequently this sidearm, and many others, were stolen in a robbery, and it has not been seen since.

Right *A fine quality, de-luxe example of the Bergbau – Mining Association Official's sword.* (Dr. J. Milestone collection.)

Below *Two examples of the gilt finish Water Customs Dagger. The example on the left shows the dagger with its regular, dark blue service hangers, and on the right the example is complete with its highly rare blue and silver-gilt fabric hangers.* (Courtesy John Watts and Barry Brown.)

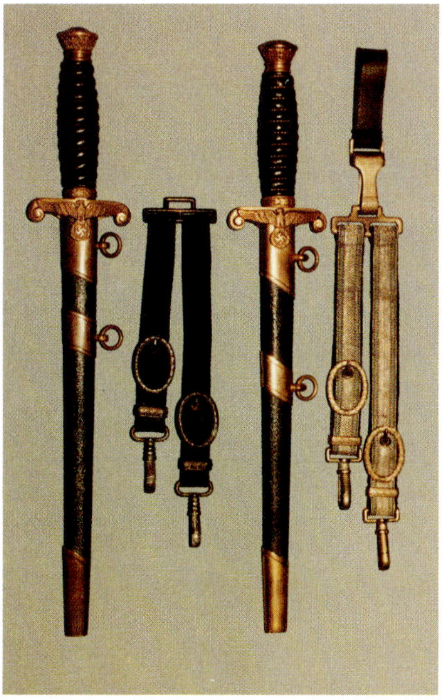

Below right *A rare example of the pre-1936 German Marksmanship Presentation Sword. The sword is Court Sword pattern (Galadegen) and bears the emblem of crossed rifles, hat, and swastika emblem on the guard. The blade is etched with a presentation inscription.* (Stewart Wilson, The Old Brigade.)

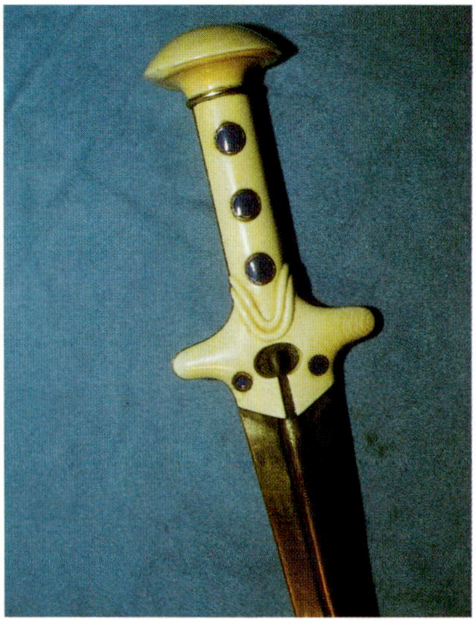

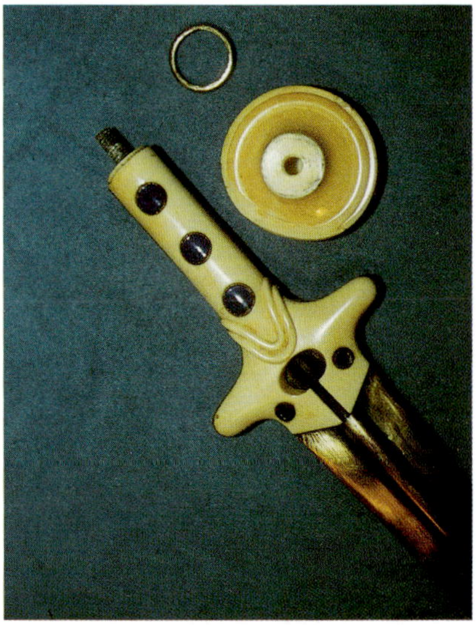

A Hunting Dagger which belonged to Hermann Goering – the same example as shown in the period photograph in Chapter 11. The blade of the dagger is made of bronze, cast in one piece, with the grip scales, made of ivory, secured to the tang by copper rivets. The heads of the rivets are decorated with blue enamel. The pommel is secured to the tang by fitting directly on to a screw thread, and is separated from the main body of the hilt by an aluminium ring. (Barry Brown.)

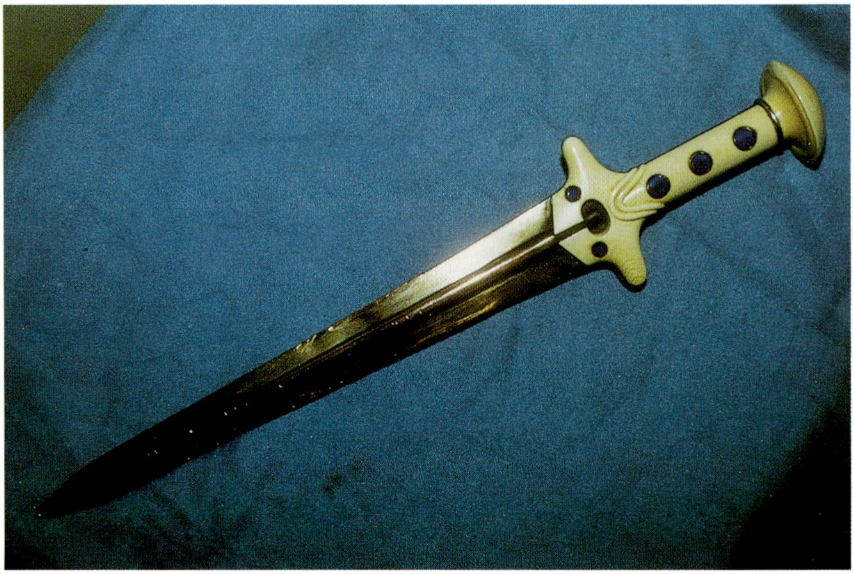

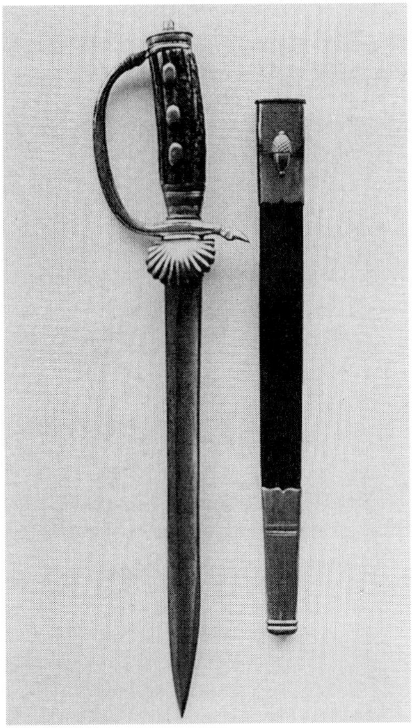

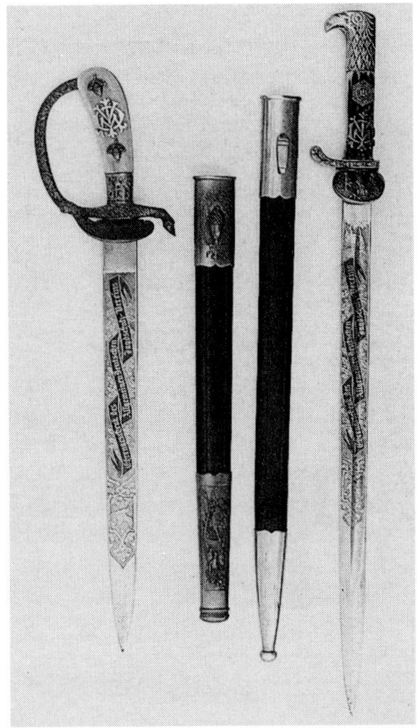

Above *A hunting cutlass, circa 1920. Although designed as a dress weapon, with its shell guard and lightly decorated fittings, this piece is still substantial enough to have been intended for physical use in the hunt. The blade is strong and sharp. The grip is made of horn, and decorated with three plain brass studs. All hilt fittings are made of brass, as are the fittings to the black leather scabbard.* (Thomas J. Gorman jr. Collection).

Above right *A matching presentation pair of hunting cutlass and sidearm/bayonet, produced as honour gifts given by the National German Hunting Protection Association (Allgemeinen Deutschen Jagdschütz Verein–ADJV). This organization was devoted to controlling the shooting of game and livestock so as to conserve the balance in favour of a reliable future supply of game for the hunter. The cutlass, on the left, has gilded brass fittings with ivory grips and bears a silver emblem of the entwined initials of the organization. The blade is etched, blued and gilded with the inscription 'Ehrengeschenk des Algemeinenen Jagdschütz-Vereins'. The bayonet/sidearm, on the right, has the long pattern (17 in) blade similarly decorated.* (Thomas J. Gorman jr. Collection).

Schützenverband (D.Sch.V.—'German Marksmanship Association'). Smallbore rifle and pistol shooting was taught, competitions were organized, and international matches undertaken. The advent of the Olympics in Berlin in 1936 presented the opportunity for the keenest marksmen to be enlisted in the national team, to compete against other world class sharpshooters. Although rifles and

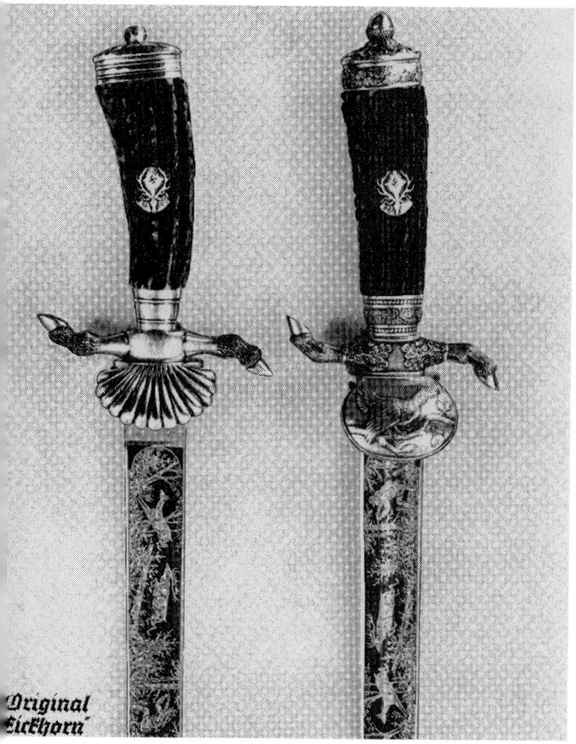

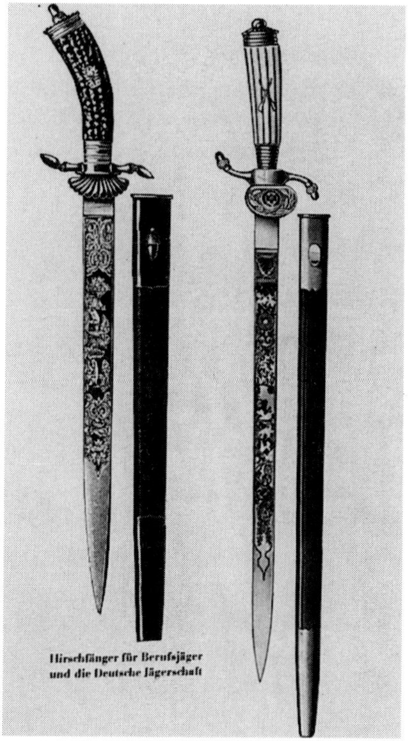

In about 1936, all hunting organizations in Germany were obliged to incorporate themselves into one, nationally recognized hunting association. This was the Deutsche Jagerschäft. Uniform patterns, which had hitherto been devised at the personal whim of individual members and clubs, were required to conform to a defined standard, and the hunting cutlass which each member carried was reintroduced in a prescribed pattern. This pattern continued the general theme of the hunting cutlass as previously worn, but restricted the style now prescribed by the National Hunting Association. This was a style of Hirschfänger which did not have a knuckle bow. The fittings were white or silver plated, and the grip was of horn. In the centre of the horn grip a small badge was affixed, being in the form of an antler head with swastika, and the letters 'D J'. the Deutsche Jagerschäft emblem. The blade was usually fully etched, and bore a similar style etching to that on the Foresters' cutlass. The scabbard was covered in a dark green leather, with silver finish to the fittings. The photograph shows two such examples, as featured in the Eickhorn sales catalogue of 1938.

Above *Detail from a page of the WKC catalogue, circa 1938. The illustration shows the Hirschfänger for the Hunting Association and the Marksmanship Association. The caption beneath the hunting cutlass clearly states that it is the dress weapon of the Berufsjäger – the professional hunter, as opposed to the part-time or weekend enthusiast.*

Above right *Foresters, those who administered and attended to the preservation of the national forests of Germany, also had their own specific dress sidearm. Their cutlass*

was distinct from the hunting pattern, in that it was finished in gilt, and featured a knuckle bow. The blade decoration was more or less similar to the hunting pattern, depending on manufacturer. Junior officers in the Forstbeamte carried their sidearm with a stag-horn grip, whereas the senior officials were permitted to utilize a white bone, or ivory grip to distinguish their status. Synthetic materials, such as ivorine, were also used. The scabbard was made of black leather, with gilded brass fittings. This illustration is taken from the Eickhorn kundendienst, the Eickhorn sales catalogue of 1938.

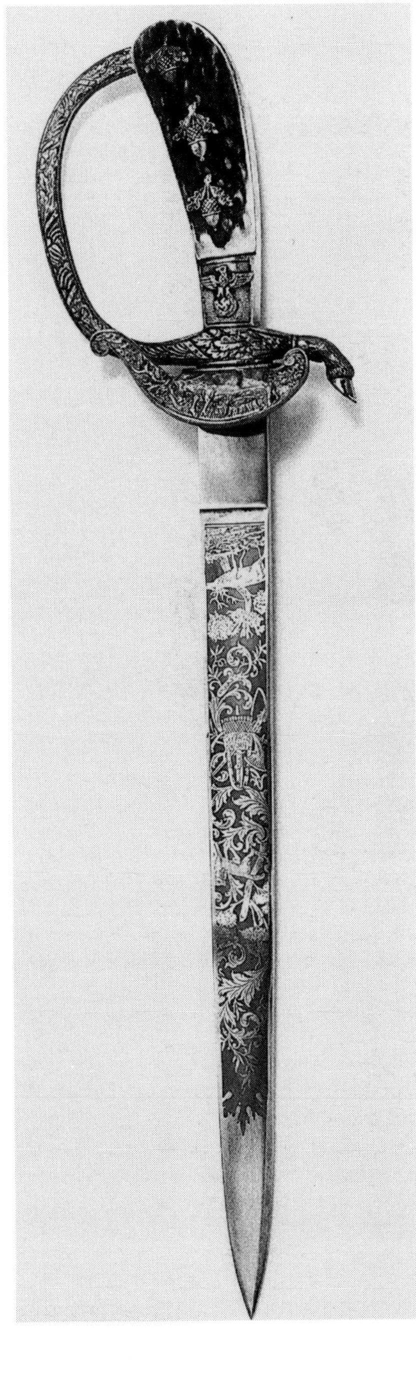

Right *Full length view of a junior Forester's cutlass, showing the fine detail etching on the blade. This example, manufactured by the concern of F. W. Höller, Solingen, features the national eagle and swastika emblem on the grip ferrule.* (Lt. Col. (retd.) J. R. Angolia).

Right *Publicity advertisement for the Alcoso company, showing the details of a Forester/Hunting cutlass which the company had exhibited at the Paris Exhibition of 1937. The cutlass pattern is highly ornate, with a wolf's head pommel, and a delicately carved ivory grip displaying the scene of a huntsman blowing the hunting horn.* (The late A. S. Walker photo collection).

Below *One of the many hunting knives owned by Hermann Goering. This illustration is taken from a contemporary publication about Goering, and shows one of his favourite hunting knives, together with his elaborate signet ring. Little was known about this particular dagger, other than the reference photograph record, until the late 1960s when the dagger turned up at an English auction. See colour section for further details.*

Far right *Goering in the presence of other dignitaries of the Third Reich: a still from a captured movie film held by the United States Army. The dagger seen worn by Goering is one which is known to have been given to him by his brother-in-law, Eric von Rosen. This actual dagger was returned to the United States after the Second World War, and is held as an exhibit at the West Point Military Museum, USA.*

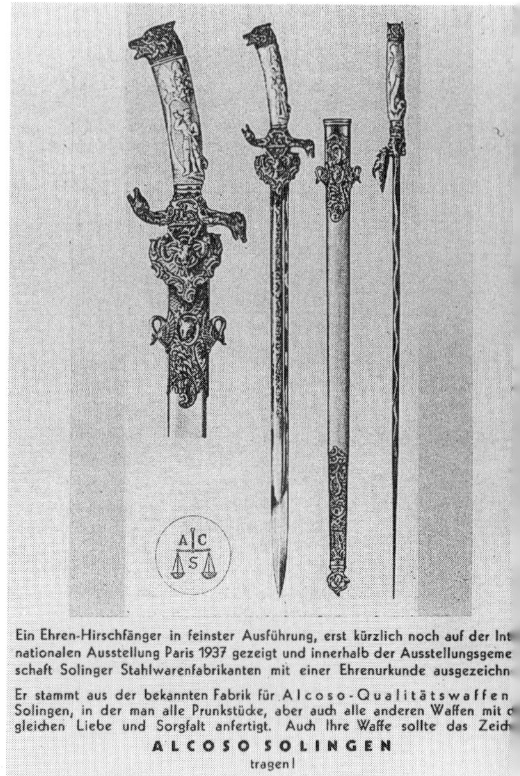

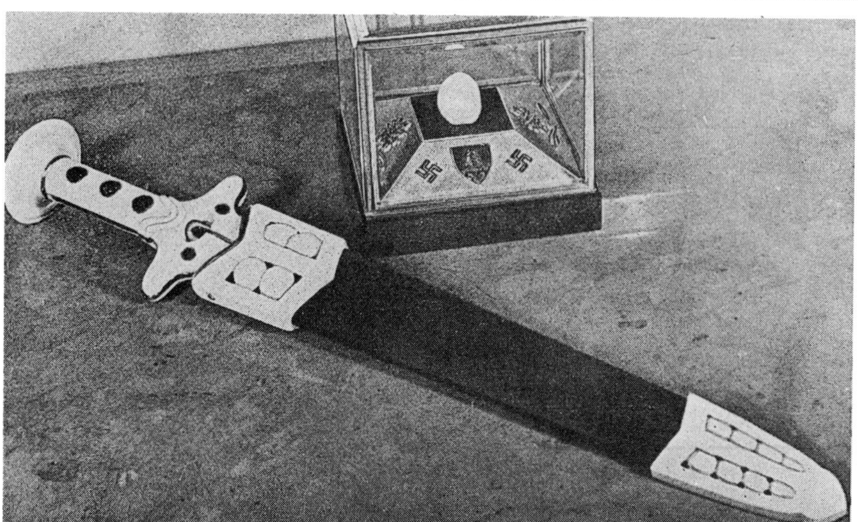

Below *The Goering hunting knife, on exhibit at the West Point Military Museum. The dagger is shown together with the Reichsmarschall baton awarded to Goering in 1941, when 12 Field Marshals were appointed to the German High Command, and Field Marshal Goering was elevated to a new rank that was created especially for him.* (West Point Military Museum).

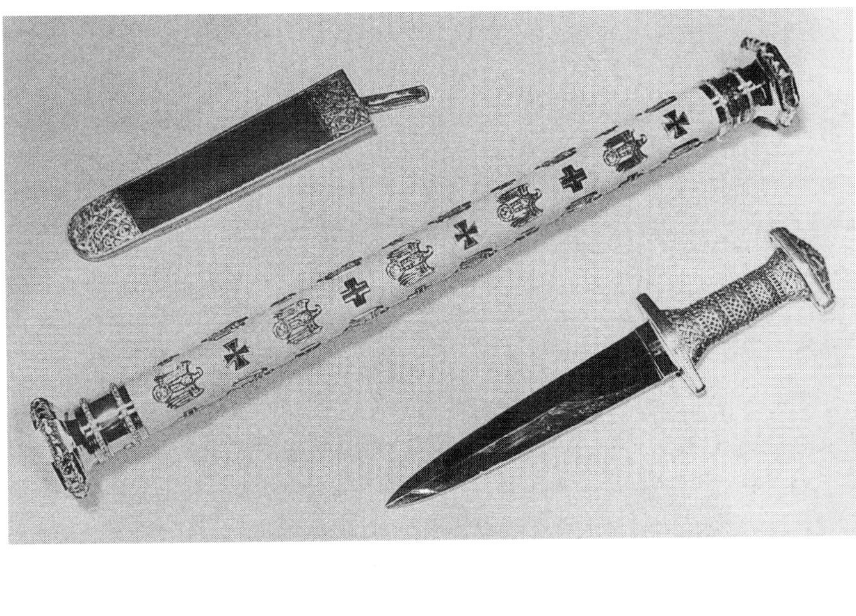

pistols were sometimes awarded as prizes and gifts, for off-duty and ceremonial occasions, full time members of the D.Sch.V. were permitted to wear the dress weapon of a handsome cutlass to complement the official uniform.

In the long-term, as history has recorded, the shooting skills taught to the Hitler Youth membership were—in the closing days of the Second World War—deployed in the defence

Below left *Detail view of the hunting dagger given to Goering by Eric von Rosen. The hilt and scabbard fittings are finely decorated in gilded bronze. The scabbard facing on both sides is inset with red leather. The blade is double edged, with a central spine, and the only marking on the blade is a small swastika etched on the forte beneath the crossguard.*

An inscription, in runic style letters, is engraved on the obverse face of the crossguard, and reads: 'A knife, from Eric to Hermann.' (West Point Military Museum).

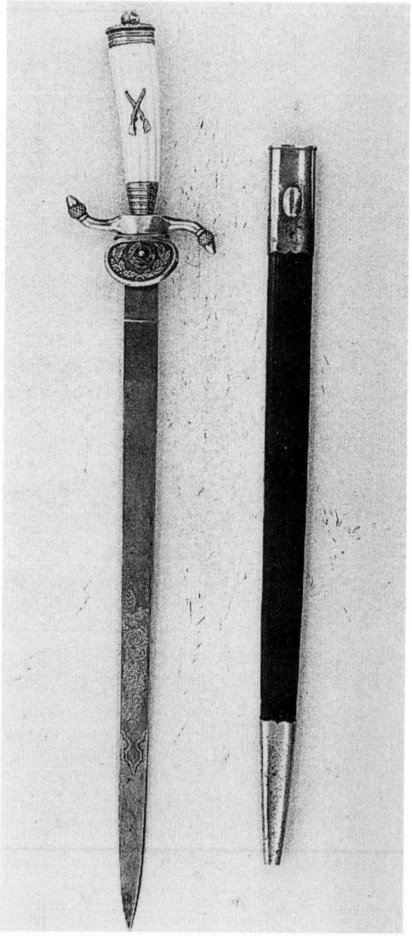

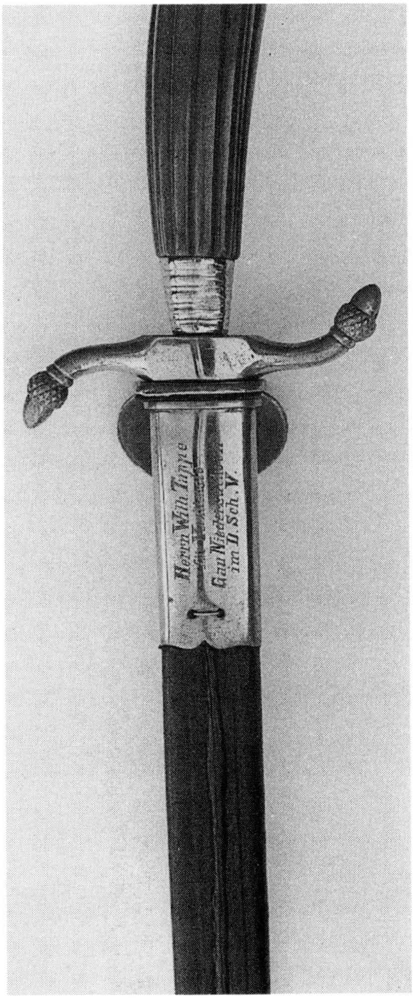

Left *The cutlass of the German Markmanship Association. This example was manufactured by Alcoso, Solingen. A full description of the Marksmanship Cutlass is given in the translation of the article on page 184.*

Above *Detail views of the hilt of a Marksmanship cutlass, and the reverse of the scabbard locket bearing a presentation inscription to the former owner from the D. Sch. V.* (Dr J. Milestone collection).

of Berlin. The battle-hardened Red Army had to conquer the capital city street by street, block by block, against trained snipers from the Hitler Youth, some of whom were as young as twelve years of age. The defeat of the Reich had been made just that little bit harder.

EIN NEUER HIRSCHFÄNGER FÜR SCHÜTZEN
('A NEW HUNTING KNIFE FOR MARKSMEN')

by Heinz Auelmann, Solingen

(English translation of an article which appeared in a 1937 issue of Die Klinge *magazine.)*

Text translation by Fiona Petrou. Edited by F. J. Stephens.

'In the course of re-equipping the German Marksman, it was to be expected that the Leader of the German Marksmanship Association[1] would consider a reorganization of the sidearm patterns of its members.

'Until now it had been the responsibility of each unit of Marksmen, indeed in most cases of the individual Marksman himself, to select suitable sidearms from the large number on the market—always presuming that the Marksman wished to carry a hunting knife or dagger[2]. If the desire for such a weapon was there, then aesthetic considerations ultimately determined its choice. Since everyone's taste is different, weapons factories undertook to produce a variety of designs, with something to suit all tastes[3].

'These self-contained bands of Marksmen, with their varied styles of equipment, often presented a strange spectacle when they appeared in public. To call a halt to the prevailing confusion, the German Marksmanship Association had by this time developed a standard Marksman's hunting knife to be carried by all German Marksmen as part of their new uniform[4].

'Although extensive manufacture of these weapons could not yet take place—mass production would first entail the establishment of a whole series of costly workshops—specialist workers had already begun to prepare the model specified by the Führer[5], to be ready for future production by authorized firms[6]

After preparation the smooth—or to use the technical term, 'blunt'[7] blade was drawn out between the segments of a heavy, purpose-built machine to a length of 39 centimetres and a breadth of 22 millimetres overall, including the blade facing which would be bevelled later. The tang was formed in a drop-forge. After being ground[8], tempered and marked, the blade was finely honed and finished[9] The tang end of the blade, having reached its correct length, was equipped with a screw-thread to facilitate attachment of the hilt.

'The grip itself was fashioned out of wood and carved with a series of fluted grooves along its length, covered in a protective sheet of white celluloid, decorated on its obverse side with two crossed rifles in a light metal of oxidized gold[10]. The guard, or shell guard[11], and the pommel cap are cast from a light metal alloy, of the same composition of white metal already used, then embossed, nickel plated and polished. The 'mussel'[12] with its chase-work[13] was furnished with the emblem of the German Association of Marksmen; the gleaming crossguard likewise decorated with an acorn. The nickel-plated tang nut was passed through the cap on to the curved tang within the grip[14].

'The scabbard construction comprises a body made of black leather to which two fittings made of sheet metal are attached. The 6 cm long mouthpiece[15] has an oval carrying clasp[16]. The 8 cm long scabbard chape, with its flattened drag, is similarly positioned on the leather and, like the mouthpiece, clamped in place[17]. Before the expert sword-finisher could assemble all the parts, the blade still had to be decorated with etching, in the style of the Marksman's organization. One final, thorough inspection, and the finished knife could leave the workshop and make its way, via the distributors, to its future bearer, the German Marksman.'

Editor's footnotes to the Heinz Auelmann article:

1 The official title was *Deutsche Schützen Verband*, or D.Sch.V. for short.

2 In the context of the original text, the suggestion is that wearing the weapons was purely a personal option, and the reference to a *Stichdegen* is made in this context. This is specifically a pointed 'thrusting' weapon, and would be deployed by hunters who, having shot down their prey, would finish the beast off with *a coup de grâce* to the animal's heart.

3 Auelmann confirms that a variety of dress forms were adopted by Marksmen, and similarly that a diversity of blade patterns were also carried by them.

4 A prescribed pattern of uniform, insignia, and sidearm was definitively established in 1936.

5 In the original text the term *Führer* is used, confirming that the approval for the D.Sch.V. dagger had been authorized by Hitler in person.

6 There was apparently some restriction on the manufacturing of the D.Sch.V. sidearm, and only approved companies were permitted to manufacture the weapon.

7 In the original text the word used is *derb* which means 'rough' or 'blunt'. In the context of the article, the probable English word would be 'unfinished'.

8 The actual word in the text is *eingräten*, which means 'to remove the bones' as in 'to bone a fish'. It most probably means, in this context, to remove (by grinding) excess swarfs of metal on the unfinished blade.

9 Final grinding and polishing, with soft mops rather than a hard grindstone.

10 The appearance is described as *goldfarbe eloxierten*, probably more accurately described as 'gold colour plating'.

11,12 In the original text the word *Muschel* (meaning mussel, as in the family of moluscs of the same name) appears in the context of *Stichblatt oder auch Muschel*. The *Stichblatt* is taken to mean the 'guard' area, generally with the *Muschel* being the extension immediately below the quillon block area of the crossguard. Guards in this area, of an oval style form, are referred to as 'shell-guards', or alternatively as 'clamshells' in the American definition. The shell of the clam, or scallop, is known in German as the *Schale der Venusmuschel* or 'Shell of the venus-mussel'.

13 Chase work refers to decoration (cast or pressed) which is further enhanced and finished by handwork.

14 The definition in the original text translates as 'forward bending'; this might seem difficult to comprehend, unless the reader is familiar with the concept that the normal (lower) cutting edge of a blade is known as the 'fore-edge'; therefore the definition described a handle which bends in the direction of the forward cutting edge of the blade.

15 The textual definition of 'mouthpiece' (*mundstück* is not totally explanatory. Strictly speaking, as far as the English (or American) researcher is concerned, the mouthpiece is the specific opening at the top of the scabbard, and it is also known as the 'throat of the scabbard'. In the case of a metal sleeve fulfilling this purpose, the whole sleeve is referred to as the locket, with the mouthpiece being simply the open-ended portion. An alternative exists in

another German word—*mundblech*, which as far as can be established more properly refers to the whole fitment which we refer to as the locket of the scabbard.

[16] The carry clasp is described as being on the mouthpiece. In reality, after examining numerous examples the definition to the English reader would be of a 'frog stud', a simple stud device which mates with a recess in a leather sleeve, and thus secures the whole item in a suspended position. In actuality, the D.Sch.V 'carry clasp' is an oval stud decorated in the form of an acorn, and mounted on the obverse face of the locket.

[17] Auelmann uses the word *verklammert* to describe this manner of fixing the metal portions to the scabbard. The literal translation of 'clamping'—or to secure with 'clamp-irons—appears to be an archaic usage describing a technique whereby metal fitments are affixed to leather with heavy wire stitches. Heavy duty 'staples' would be the nearest modern equivalent.

12 The Culture of the Blade

Miniature edged weapons and miscellaneous items

All the paraphernalia of war, including tin hats, toy guns, sabres, miniature canteens, and the like were to be had for children from the ages of three to fourteen in the greatest profusion

Quoted in *The Spirit and Structure of German Fascism* by Robert A. Brady (1937).

The militaristic trait engineered by the Third Reich was instilled into young minds at as early an age as possible. The production of child-sized uniforms, and weapons to match—small bayonets and swords (*Kindersabel*, 'Child's Sabre') did much to create an appreciation of the edged weapon, for some of these small sized weapons were rather better than toys. They were professionally made, they had the feel of the real weapon, they encouraged the stance and the gait of the bearer in the military mould. The culture of the blade is as psychologically deep, as it is ancient.

Of all the implements which have advanced the development of mankind, few can have had such a profound effect as that of the knife. It is such a simple and basic item that its usefulness is taken for granted. Yet had early man not comprehended the advantages to be attained with a sharp piece of flint, then human civilization might have taken aeons longer to develop, if at all. That the knife exists today—still invaluable in its simplicity as a tool—is a tribute to its contribution as a foundation stone in the development of civilizations. Historians frequently point to technological miracles such as the wheel, or the steam engine, as the instruments which changed the world, yet none of these would have been possible had the knife not existed to fashion essential portions. It is no wonder that the skilled hands which have produced the finest of blades, have revered some of their products as art forms of the highest order. Good blades demonstrate some of the developments of leading cultures.

In the years following the First World War, the German cutlery industry experienced very lean times. The whole of the steelware industry was sinking into a depression, not only in Germany, but elsewhere throughout the rest of Europe. The demand for blades for military purposes was virtually non-existent; only in the area of agricultural and industrial tools was there any real market for the products of Solingen, and that too was a somewhat reduced market—there was not enough money circulating for high investment in bladed tools. To salvage something by which to make a living, the cutlers of Solingen looked towards foreign nations in the hope of being able to supply blade and cutlery requirements; or indeed anything else that would deploy steelware products.

One of the spin-off developments that had received impetus during the volume production period of the First World War was the need to mass-produce goods to a continuous, uniformly high standard, and as a result, consumer appreciation of what constituted an acceptable standard became the norm. Conversely, however, in the post-WWI period, the consumer's ability to pay for high quality goods manufacture was severely restricted. With mass unemployment eroding the whole spectrum of society, even basic commodities such as razors became costly items for families where the working man was unemployed. The combination of these two circumstances: the good serviceable product at the attainable price; had created a potential market just waiting to be discovered. It was to become the disposable product market.

For many men, the morning ritual of shaving becomes a habit they are unwilling to break. The implement by which the act was performed was the cut-throat razor. A good razor, of surgical quality, was not a cheap item. For those who could afford it, a daily trip to the barber shop completed this aspect of the morning ritual; for others the purchase of their own razor (costing as much as a whole day's wages for the poorer working man) was not an investment they could make with any frequency. To fill the void in this unexpected market came a new development that was relatively cheap to produce, simple to manufacture, and adequate for its purpose. It was the short-time use, throwaway, safety razor blade. Manufactured from wafer-thin steel, it could be pressed out from sheets and extruded through a sharpening die in an almost continuous operation. It did not require the skills of temperers, grinders, and polishers to laboriously finish the product. It was a mechanical product that could be machined out by the thousand. As a commercial product, to rich and poor consumer alike, it was an instantaneous success. Reference to the Solingen trades magazines of the early 1930s records just how successful this innovation was—literally hundreds of brands of safety razor blades were registered. A vibrant mini-industry had come into being to cater for a budget-conscious market. The consumer could afford this new product; more importantly it generated some employment for Solingen. The manufacturers had a product for which there was a continuous demand, enough to keep their businesses ticking over. It left open the opportunity, and some finance, to try and generate other market purchases.

The two single advantages which the craftsmen of Solingen retained, despite the Depression, were their skills, which had been developed over centuries; and their cheap labour costs, caused by the fall of the *Reichsmark*.

Regardless of the state of the national economy, the cutlers of Solingen could at least function at competitive levels, and there were other countries where the collapse of currency had been less devastating. In the period from 1930 to about 1936, the Carl Eickhorn concern made a determined effort to capture the edged weapons market of some of these foreign states. They produced a series of about two dozen catalogues printed in foreign languages aimed at precise national markets, and with the swords and daggers offered designed to appeal to those specific markets. At a time when many European businesses were contracting to contain the economic situation, the Eickhorn concern attempted a policy of expansion and export. From Finland in Scandanavia, and Chile in South America, to Siam (Thailand) in the Far East, they contracted agents to represent them, and submitted catalogues to display their products. They even produced one for the English market—the very enemies who had overseen the dismantlement of much of the Eickhorn production capacity in 1920—offering dress swords and Scottish basket hilts for the regiments of the British Army. The Great War might have been past history, but the commercial war and the acumen to undertake it, was still being fought.

English military swords of the 1930s, manufactured by Eickhorn, undoubtedly exist, although examples bearing the company name have not been observed by this author. In all probability they were produced bearing the names and addresses of English merchant distributors, reviving the commercial policies that had been undertaken by some of the better producers during the 1880s. It was good business sense that kept the business going, in preparation for some really substantial orders. That event, as has already been shown, came about in 1933 when the first orders for daggers for the SA and SS arrived in Solingen.

The grinding wheels of the cutlery shops were, once again, to start turning with increasing rapidity, and good fortune.

One of the fascinating by-products of the edged weapons industry, and so appealing because of its attractiveness, is the existence of small-sized, or miniature versions of swords and daggers.

In the 1880s, and for many years afterwards, a popular souvenir item was a miniature replica of a unique sword that had been given to Chancellor Bismarck. The original sword had been donated by the nation to commemorate Bismarck's iron-willed efforts to unite the German states in the formation of the (then) Second Reich. This magnificent sword, with its finely chiselled hilt and lavishly decorated blade was a masterpiece of the swordsmith's art. It was an object of beauty, and before long, miniature copies were being turned out for sale as souvenirs. The German love affair with a handsome blade was an enduring relationship. All Germans were proud of Solingen and the craftsmen who worked there, and the creation of miniature replicas of classical weapons was an acceptable business. The obvious weapons to recreate were the famous swords that had made German history, such as the Landsknecht sword of the Middle

Ages, as well as some of the popular swords and daggers which had started to appear in the pre-First World War period. The appeal of these miniature items is understandable, and there were undoubtedly collectors of them at the time they were produced, as well as the casual purchasers looking for mementos on their visits to famous cities. The production of miniature weapons continued in the post-war period, and through into the Third Reich. They have become, yet again, collectable in their own right, and some very fine quality examples were produced during the 1930s, worthy of a place alongside the full-sized examples. As a general theme, the miniature weapons fall into four basic categories: true miniatures, miniatures/letter openers, sub-miniatures, and special miniatures.

True miniatures

To qualify as a true miniature, the article in question would, of necessity, be a totally accurate, correctly formed, scale-sized, detailed and finished rendition of the full-size version. True miniatures of Third Reich items, accurate to the finest detail, are exceedingly rare. Very few of the arms manufacturing concerns appear to have produced them, and the reason is seemingly the inordinate costs involved. With the exception of the saving of the material used in their production, the labour and tooling required to produce a perfect miniature item is about equal to the costs of producing the full size example. As such, the true miniature was something of a rarity at the time it was originally produced, and the variety of the known examples appears to be limited to a few versions of the most mass-produced patterns, namely the daggers of the Army, Navy, and *Luftwaffe*.

The purpose of the true miniature has never been satisfactorily explained, for these exquisite little knives—on average about half-size to two-thirds the size of the production example, and proportionately correct in detail and construction—are far superior to anything which might fall into the 'souvenir' or 'letter opener' market. One theory is that they are salesmen's samples, carried and given to demonstrate the high quality of the manufacturer concerned. It is a possibility; but a parallel theory suggests a more plausible alternative: the true miniatures were probably given as gifts upon the successful completion of a bulk order. Officer cadets passing out from academies on completion of their military training would seek to obtain their rank insignia and dress weapon. A salesman, astute enough to persuade someone in authority to recommend a particular company as the best supplier of dress weapons, would be in receipt of a very worthwhile order—with perhaps as many as 200–300 graduates suddenly becoming eligible from one single academy in one year alone, and all wanting their dress dagger or sword immediately.

The favour of putting this amount of business in any one direction was surely worthy of some reward. As the recommending officer concerned probably already had his own dress weapon, a true miniature version, which could not be bought over the counter, might well appear as a most pleasing gift, a distinctive ornament which could rest upon the desk. Other purposes for the true miniature could, just as easily, be as display items in military tailors' shops. Whatever the real purpose of the true miniature, it is notable that they reflect aspects of weapons production that were catering for a very large market. The true miniature, with its accuracy of fine detail, and paucity of availability, is a highly desirable acquisition to most collectors.

Miniatures and letter openers

An article published in a 1938 edition of *Die Klinge* makes mention of a new product being launched by the Alcoso (Alex Coppel) concern of Solingen, a miniature version of the RAD Officer's Hewer, pattern 1937. The item is shown complete with its pressed metal scabbard, and blade etched with the *Arbeit adelt* motto of the RAD organization. The article clearly defines this miniature item as a *Brieföffener*—letter opener.

The miniature/letter opener is amongst the most prolific of all the small-scale copies of daggers, swords, and bayonets. They were clearly designed for a mass market, and the production techniques and quality of the items reflects this situation. They range in size from about one-third to one-half the size of the full scale example, but the range in quality is considerable. Most of the examples are well detailed, but proportionally they frequently reveal disparity with the full-sized versions: scabbards are frequently too long, flattened instead of convexed etc. One aspect of the miniature/letter opener series of daggers is certain, they were available for sale in unrestricted quantities, and the manufacturers of the better quality examples of these items appear to have been mostly the arms manufacturing companies who produced the real thing. That the precision of these items is somewhat removed from the full-sized versions or the true miniature in no way reflects upon the reputation of the manufacturer concerned. The miniatures/letter openers were destined for a totally different market with a different economic structure. Many of the better quality versions were used for their advertising potential, not specifically for arms manufacturers, but for other companies whose business interests might encompass the military purchasers, a particular example known being a version of the Model 1937 *Luftwaffe* dagger, which bears an advertisement etched upon the blade for a carpet company—possibly a manufacturer seeking to contract with regimental establishments for the supply of carpeting. A novel form of advertising which, if placed on the right desk, might have secured the right order. Other companies, such as radio stations, are also known to have advertised their businesses this way. The growth of military establishments from 1936 onwards would have meant a lot of business for a whole range of civilian contractors; it was business worth touting for.

The majority of the miniature/letter openers, however, are devoid of etched advertisements on the blades, other than (sometimes) the name of the manufacturing company. They were undoubtedly production items intended for retail sales to those who liked the appearance of a sword or dagger.

Sub-miniatures

At the lower end of the miniature market were the businesses who produced the sub-miniatures—swords and daggers of a recognizable pattern, but scaled down to between one-quarter and one-third the size of the full production version. A high proportion of these pieces appear to be in the form of Naval dirks, both of the 1890 pattern and the 1938 pattern. The quality of production and accuracy of detail and proportion indicates that they were most probably intended for the gift shop market. They were cheaply constructed, and most usually fall into the category of inexpensive souvenirs. Most of them are unmarked as to their source of manufacture, and it is widely believed that most were the products of companies not actively engaged in the edged weapons market. Occasionally, some examples are encountered which have been utilized for their advertising potential as inexpensive give-aways. One particular example is known with the blade etched with an advertisement for a printing company, and—of especial interest—bearing the trademark of Flöcke and Company. The business of Flöcke was not known for its production of edged weapons, but they are known as having been successful producers of razor blades. Sub-miniature swords and daggers might very well have been one of the company's profitable sidelines, as the quality of production of most of these pieces suggests that they were produced in the thousands.

Special miniatures

A highly unusual aspect of the miniature edged weapons theme is that of the special miniatures—extremely rare pieces, of good, but seldom exceptional construction, and depicting scale versions of dagger or sword patterns not found in the more prolific miniature/letter opener series. Amongst some of the distinctive weapons patterns known to fall into this special miniatures category are the SA Dagger Model 1933, SS Dagger Model 1936, NPEA Leader's Dagger Model 1936, the Goering Wedding Sword, and the Feldherrnhalle Dagger—all patterns which are apparently unique to this category, and distinct from some of the known post-war reproduction miniatures which have been produced in Spain, America, Germany, and France. Whether or not such pieces were the product of individual initiatives of workers in the arms factories, or if they were created to special order by enthusiasts at the time, remains a speculation for which a definitive answer remains to be confirmed.

Letter openers

The production of letter openers, produced solely for that purpose, is a well established facet of the production of Solingen. Innumerable variations were churned out, often with city or state crests emblazoned on the hilt, some looking like daggers (Naval dirks were always a popular theme) and others looking like nothing other than a letter opener or paper-knife (*Papiermesser*). Many of the versions styled as known dagger patterns are rather crude in construction, with solid metal hilts, no scabbards, and generally not reflective of the better production of Solingen (if indeed that is where they originated). Nevertheless, they did exist at the time, and numerous examples found their way back after the Second World War as souvenirs looted by soldiers. The occasion of the Olympics in Berlin gave Solingen an opportunity to capitalize on the vast tourist trade which, temporarily, would be thronging through the Reich. Quality paper-knives bearing the Olympic crest of interlinked rings were put into production, and were featured in *Die Klinge* during 1936. Other commodities also subjected to this type of commercialism were penknives, lighters, ashtrays and all manner of souvenir products. They were opportunities not to be lost, and as such, while the impetus to produce such items remained, they were sold to eager visitors from every corner of the globe.

Relics such as these, and all others portrayed in this work, have long outlived their usefulness. Those that remain are now mostly in the hands of interested collectors curious about this, perhaps the most awesome epoch of modern history.

For twelve years Solingen had experienced an unexpected revival of impressive proportions. Until, finally, the dark forces which recreated it collapsed, and pulled the furnaces and reputation of Solingen into the pages of history.

Above *Although the culture of the bladed weapon was spread right across the spectrum of National Socialist life, the supreme architect of it all – Adolf Hitler – was almost never seen to wear a dress dagger.*

Hitler undoubtedly was the recipient of dagger and sword gifts by individuals and organizations, but apparently was never seen to wear them, except on one notable circumstance, on the occasion of his State visit to Italy, when Benito Mussolini awarded the German Chancellor the appointment of Honorary Corporal in the Italian MVSN organization – doubtless a reference to the fact that Hitler had been a corporal in the Bavarian army during the First World War. In offering this honorary rank, Hitler was presented with the special sleeve insignia for his uniform, and also with a special version of the MVSN dagger.

Hitler was photographed adorned with this insignia, and the dagger, throughout his three-day tour – after which both the dagger and insignia disappeared from view, and have never been seen since. (Original photo by Luce, Rome).

Above *Members of the Hitler Youth on parade. A rare photograph showing the presence of a Kindersabel ('Child's sword') being carried. Although the sword was not officially approved for wear by the Hitler Youth, this photographic evidence clearly displays the evidence of such an item, in defiance of the regulations. In all probability the item is a basic Kindersabel – the private property of the carrier – who adopted it for the purposes of enhancing the militaristic appearance of his HJ unit.* (Stewart Wilson, The Old Brigade).

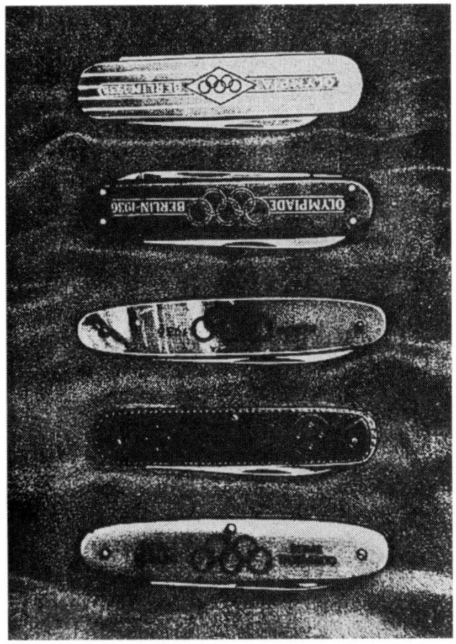

Below left *Pocket knives were widely produced in the 1930s, both for home consumption and export purposes. As inexpensive purchases, pocket knives readily lent themselves to additional marketing in the form of gifts, and every opportunity to exploit this potential was seized. The illustration depicts an example that is embossed with a scene of the old town in Nuremburg.*

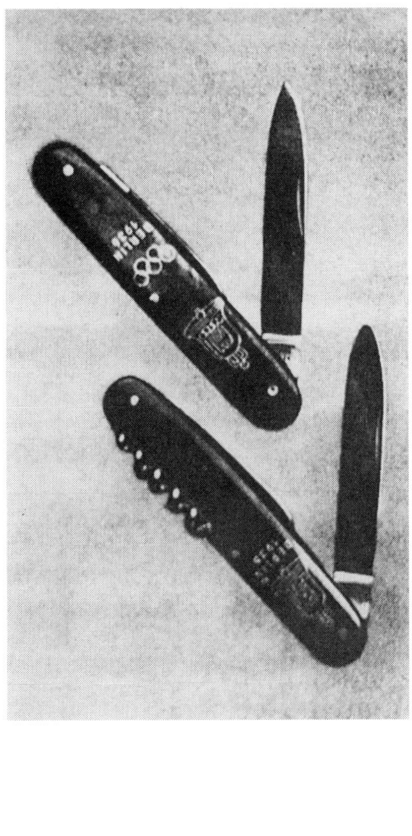

This page *The occasion of the Olympic Games, held in Berlin in 1936, presented an excellent opportunity for cutlers and metalware producers to market commodities commemorating the Games. Pocket knives were seen as an ideal medium to promote this event, and many thousands of the visiting tourists must have purchased examples to take home as keepsakes from their visit. Like all collectable items, these goods, which appeared in vast quantities, are now scarcely seen today, and as such are regarded as highly collectable.* (Die Klinge, 1936).

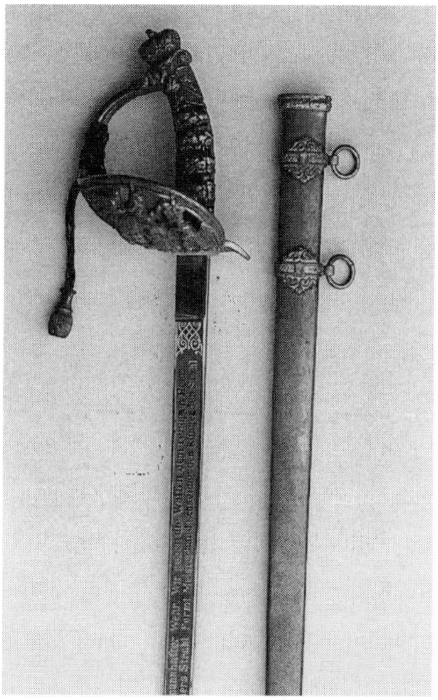

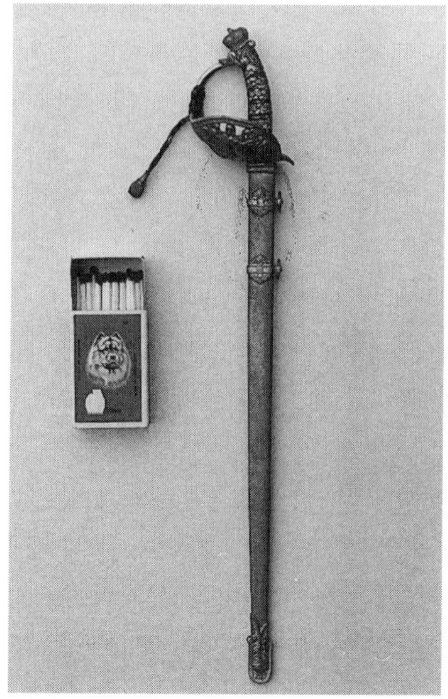

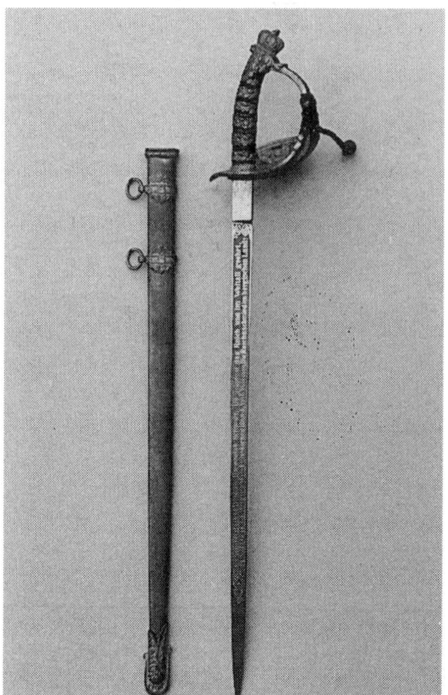

This page *A finely detailed miniature example of the sword that was presented to Bismarck (see reference in main text). Although the sword had originally been presented to Chancellor Bismarck in 1871, miniature copies of the item were still being produced and sold in the 1930s, some 60 years later.*

Right *A selection of swords and a dagger, showing, on the right, a Luftwaffe sword, and next to it a miniature example of the Luftwaffe sword.* (Wallis and Wallis).

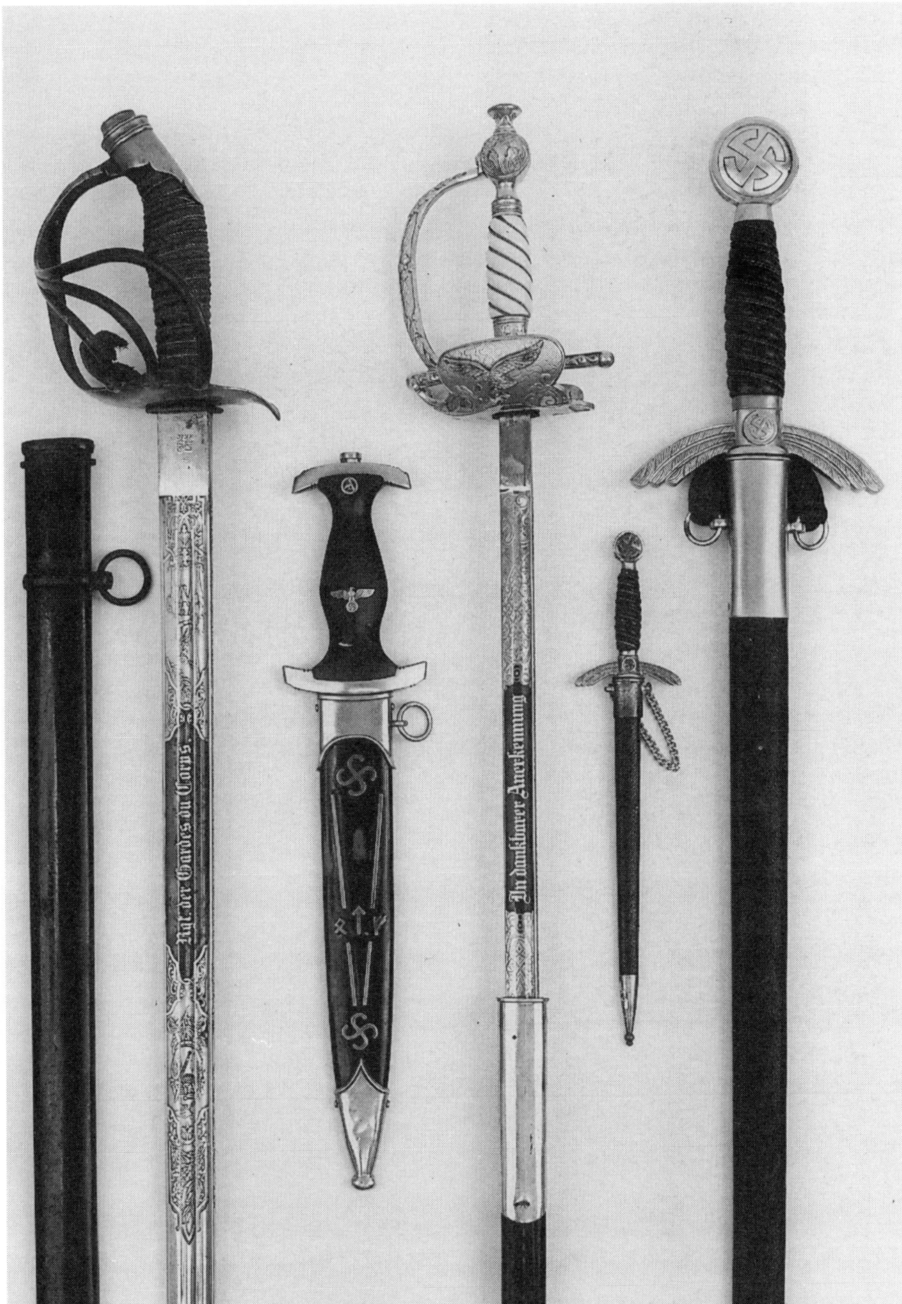
Rgt. der Gardes du Corps
In dankbarer Anerkennung

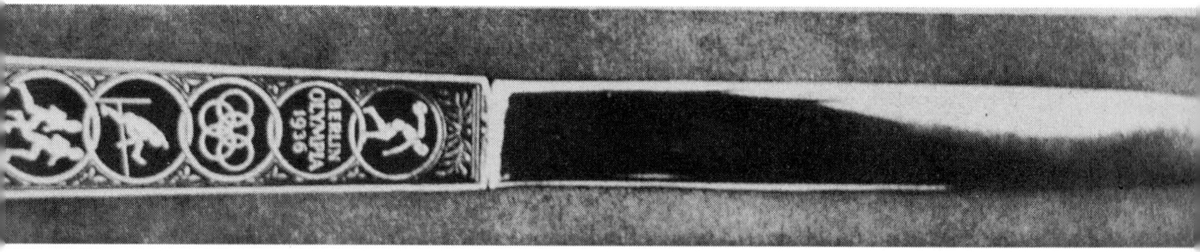

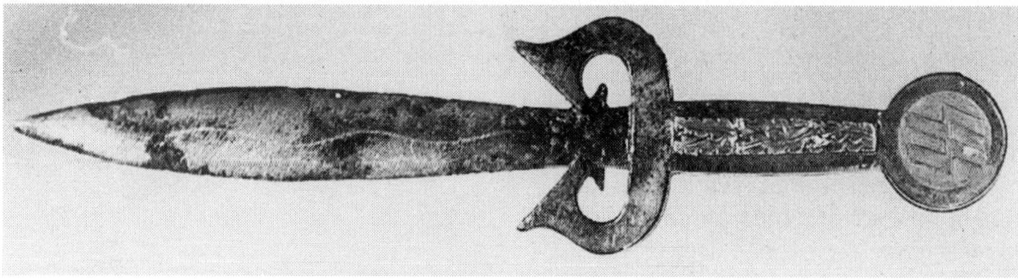

Top *A paper knife, one of many designs which, although widely produced in the 1920s and 1930s, was given an even greater impetus for sale when decorated with Olympic Games insignia.* (Die Klinge, 1936).

Top *An unusual paper knife in the form of a classical sword, bearing the SS runes in the pommel. The item was most probably a privately made item.* (Weller & Dufty).

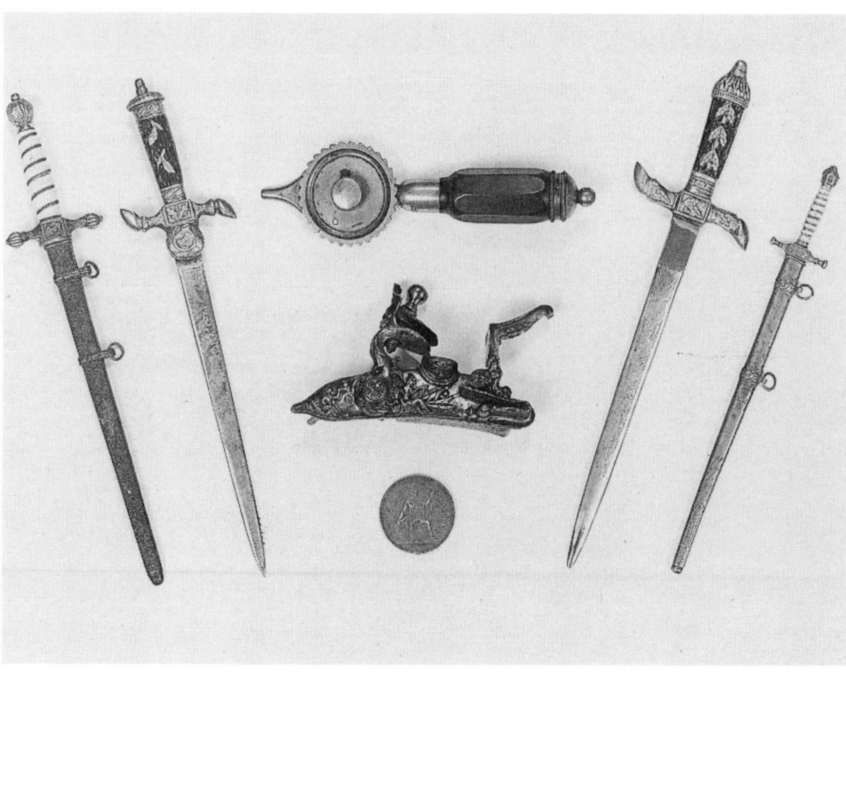

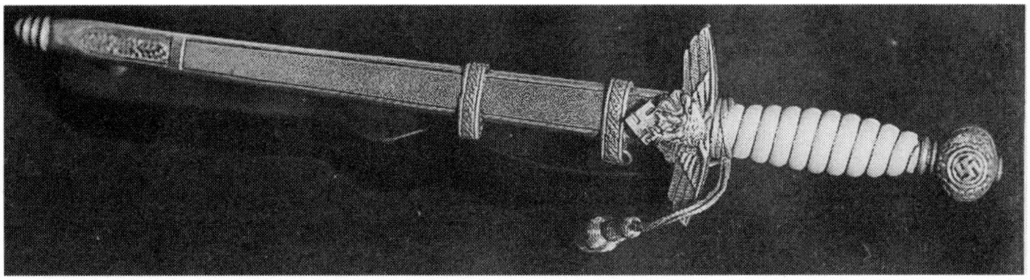

Below left *A selection of miniature daggers, shown together with a gun lock and an old style 1d coin for comparison. Left to right: Model 1929 Naval dirk, but fitted in an Army pattern scabbard. The miniature completely disassembles – the pommel can be unscrewed and the celluloid grips can be removed; a hunting cutlass, of all-metal construction, including the simulated stag horn grip; a variation pattern of the hunting cutlass, similarly all-metal construction; and a sub-miniature example of the Model 1890 Imperial Naval dirk. One of the characteristics of the majority of sub-miniature patterns is that they are frequently out of proportion when compared to the true miniatures.* (Weller & Dufty).

Above *A miniature example of the Luftwaffe dagger Model 1937, on a display mount in the form of a propellor. The item was clearly designed to function as an attractive desk ornament, as well as a paper knife. Note the miniature style portepee knot.* (Chris Farlowe).

Below *A selection of Third Reich miniature daggers, shown with a Naval war badge for size comparison. Left to right: Army dagger model 1935; Naval Dirk model 1938 – note the eagle and swastika pommel; Luftwaffe dagger Model 1937.* (The late Barry Smith).

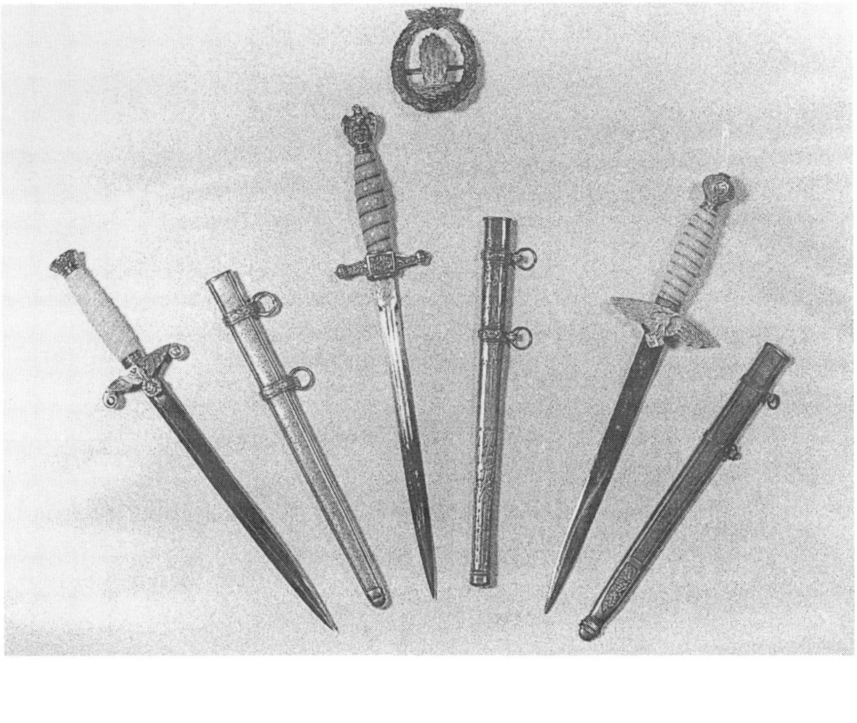

Bibliography

Maj. James P. Atwood (1964), *The Daggers and Edged Weapons of Hitler's Germany*, privately published by the author, South Carolina, USA, 1964.

Reidl R., & Leslie D. (1958), *A Handbook on German Daggers*, R & L Enterprises, Ohio, USA, 1958.

Major J. R. Angolia (1969), *Swords of Hitler's Third Reich*, Stephens, Southend-on-Sea.

Major J. R. Angolia (1974), *Edged Weaponry of the Third Reich*, Bender Publishing, California, 1974.

Eickhorn Kundendienst, Sales Catalogue, Solingen (1938).

Die Klinge, Solingen trade magazine, various issues, February 1934–October 1939, *Die Klinge*.

WKC Sales Catalogue, Solingen 1938.

Paul Weyersberg Sales Catalogue, Solingen (*circa* 1939).

Paul Seilheimer Sales Catalogue, Solingen, 1938.

Lt. Col. T. M. Johnson (1975–86), *Collecting the Edged Weapons of the Third Reich*, Vols 1–5, privately published by the author, South Carolina.

F. J. Stephens (1971), *Edged Weapons of the Third Reich*, Almark Publications, London, 1971.

Leisten und Dienen (1940) 75th Anniversary catalogue of the Eickhorn company, Solingen.

Andrew Mollo (1970), *German Third Reich Daggers*, Historical Research Unit Publications, London, 1970.

F. J. Stephens (1976), *Edged Weapons—Collector's Guide*, Spur Books, Bourne End, Buckinghamshire, 1976.

Mermet and Marault (*circa* 1984), *Les Dagues du III Reich*, Editions du Portrait, La Tour du Pin, France.

Frederick Wilkinson (1967), *Swords and Daggers*, Ward Lock Ltd., London.

Weinand and Walker (1985), *German Clamshells and Other Bayonets*, privately published by the authors, Illinois.

Stephens and Evans (1985), *The Bayonet*, Militaria Publications, Milton Keynes.

Skipper Greenwade (1987), *Me Fecit Solingen*, privately published by the author, Houston, Texas.

Blank Waffen, Solingen Chamber of Commerce, 1940.

Index

Combat Medals of the Third Reich

Compiled by the well-known and respected collector Chris Ailsby, this book begins with an introduction to collecting Third Reich combat decorations, including descriptions of the actions resulting in typical awards. Five main chapters then describe all badges, medals, shields and commemorative cuff titles awarded from the Spanish Civil War to the end of the Second World War, and there are photographs — many in colour — of each, making identification of the real thing as opposed to the reproduction much easier. The Iron Cross, Knights Cross, Grand Cross, U-boat badge, wound badge, campaign badges, Spanish Cross, assault badges and dozens of others are all described, together with details of their makers, the criteria for their award, and all significant details of their construction, materials, presentation boxes or packets and citations, where known.

Its unique cataloguing system, coupled with unparalleled photographs, makes it *the* book all militaria collectors and historians of the Second World War will turn to for reference.

Allied Combat Medals

In this the first of two volumes, Chris Ailsby turns his collector's and enthusiast's eye upon the medals issued by the Allied powers during the Second World War. (The awards of America, the Soviet Union, Poland and Czechoslovakia will be covered in a subsequent volume.)

The book is divided into sections on the awards of Britain, Canada, South Africa, Australia and New Zealand, France, Holland, Norway, Denmark and Belgium, the provenance and criteria for each award are described, as is the physical construction and appearance of each medal and its ribbon (where appropriate). Also included are the various awards for gallantry bestowed on civilians.

Chris Ailsby explains the fascination of collecting such well-known decorations as the Victoria Cross and Legion of Honour, as well as campaign stars and bars, flying wings and other distinctions, many of them extremely rare and fine examples of the jeweller's craft. With quality photographs of individual decorations, several in colour, this superb and authoritative guide is a must for all militaria collectors.